KENNETH NOLAND

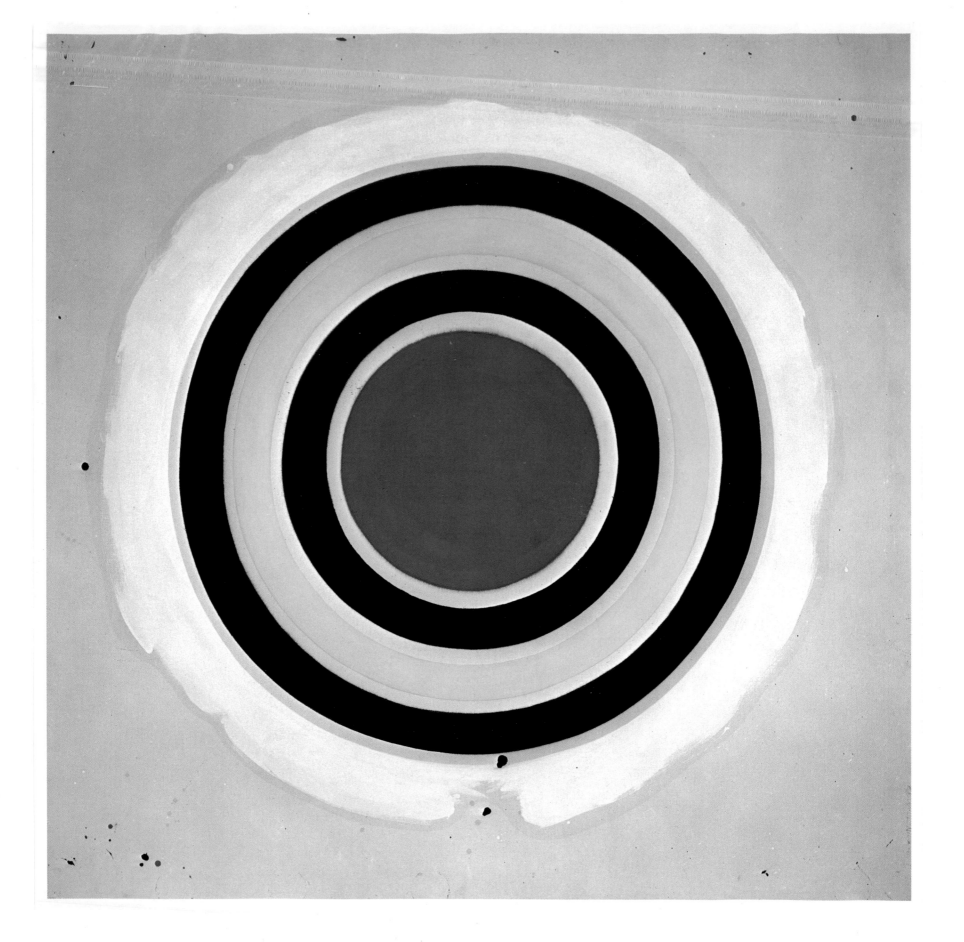

KENNETH NOLAND

KENWORTH MOFFETT

HARRY N ABRAMS, INC., PUBLISHERS, NEW YORK

Frontispiece: 1. *Virginia Site*. 1959. Acrylic on canvas,
70 x 70″. Collection, Mr. and Mrs. Joseph A. Helman, St. Louis, Missouri

FOR MY FATHER

Editor: John P. O'Neill
Designer: Patrick Cunningham

Library of Congress Cataloging in Publication Data
Moffett, Kenworth.
  Kenneth Noland.

  Bibliography: p.
  Includes index.
  1. Noland, Kenneth, 1924-   I. Noland, Kenneth,
1924-
ND237. N594M63   759.13   76-50564
ISBN 0-8109-1351-8

Library of Congress Catalogue Card Number: 76-50564

Published in 1977 by Harry N. Abrams, Incorporated, New York
All rights reserved. No part of the contents of this book may be reproduced
without the written permission of the publishers

Printed and bound in Japan

CONTENTS

List of Plates   7

KENNETH NOLAND by Kenworth Moffett   13

Notes to the Text   94

Plates   105

List of Exhibitions   233

Selected Bibliography   236

Index   238

Photocredits   240

2. Installation view of Noland exhibition at André Emmerich Gallery, New York, New York, 1964

LIST OF PLATES

All colorplates are marked with an * / All unattributed paintings and sculptures are by Kenneth Noland

*1.   Frontispiece: *Virginia Site*. 1959.

2.   Installation view of Noland exhibition at André Emmerich Gallery, New York, New York, 1964.

3.   Kenneth Noland in the grounds outside his studio/house, South Shaftsbury, Vermont, mid-1960s.

4.   Still life in oils painted by Harry Noland, Sr.

5.   Kenneth Noland in 1931.

6.   Kenneth Noland as a glider pilot in World War II.

7.   Kenneth Noland in his studio/house, South Shaftsbury, Vermont, 1965.

8.   Kenneth Noland in the grounds outside his studio/house, South Shaftsbury, Vermont, in March, 1965, with his children.

9.   Kenneth Noland in 1976.

10.   Josef Albers, *Homage to the Square: Apparition*. 1959.

11.   Ilya Bolotowsky, *Arctic Diamond*. 1948.

12.   Untitled. 1947.

13.   Piet Mondrian, *Composition with Red, Yellow, Blue, Black*. 1928.

14.   Paul Klee, *Arab Song*. 1932.

15.   *Inside*. 1950.

16.   Untitled. 1950.

17.   Untitled. 1951–52.

18.   Untitled. 1951–52.

19.   Kenneth Noland in his studio, Washington, D.C., c. 1952.

20.   Helen Frankenthaler, *Mountains and Sea*. 1952.

21.   *In the Garden*. c. 1952.

22.   Untitled. 1952.

23.   Untitled. 1953.

24.   Kenneth Noland and the critic Clement Greenberg in Greenberg's New York apartment, 1976.

25.   Untitled. c. 1956.

26.   Untitled. 1957.

27.   Untitled. c. 1957.

28.   *Catherine*. 1959–60.

*29.   *That*. 1958–59.

*30.   Jackson Pollock, *One*. 1950.

31.   Untitled. 1955.

32.   Untitled. c. 1955.

33.   Untitled. 1956.

*34.   *Globe*. 1956.

35.   *Tip*. 1961.

36.   *Plunge*. 1958.

*37.   *Sunshine*. 1961.

38.   Robert Delaunay, *Disc*. 1912.

*39. *Tondo*. 1958–59.

40. Frank Stella, *Sinjerli II*. 1967.

*41. *Cadmium Radiance*. 1963.

42. Piet Mondrian, *Lozenge in Red, Yellow, and Blue*. c. 1926.

*43. *Tropical Zone*. 1964.

*44. *Shade*. 1965.

45. Barnett Newman, *Onement #3*. 1949.

46. Installation view of Noland exhibition at André Emmerich Gallery, New York, New York, 1967.

*47. Jules Olitski, *Seventh Loosha*. 1970.

48. Morris Louis, *Ksi*. 1960–61.

49. Morris Louis, *Horizontal VII*. 1962.

50. *Nursery*. 1972.

51. Piet Mondrian, *New York City No. 2* (unfinished). 1942.

52. Installation view of Noland exhibition at André Emmerich Gallery, New York, New York, 1973.

53. Ronald Davis, *Two-Thirds Yellow*. 1966.

54. Installation view of Frank Stella exhibition of Irregular Polygons at Leo Castelli Gallery, New York, New York, 1966.

55. Installation view of Noland exhibition at André Emmerich Gallery, New York, New York, 1975. Left: *Inverted Mordent*. 1975. Right: *Beam*. 1975.

56. *Splay*. 1976.

57. Kenneth Noland supervising two assistants in his studio at South Shaftsbury, Vermont, 1976.

58. View of Noland's sculptures in the garden adjoining his studio/house, South Shaftsbury, Vermont.

59. *Around*. 1968.

60. *Jenny*. 1970.

61. Anthony Caro, *Shaftsbury*. 1965.

62. Kenneth Noland and the sculptor Anthony Caro in the grounds outside Noland's studio/house, South Shaftsbury, Vermont, 1975.

63. *Vermont*. 1971–73.

64. Another view of *Vermont*.

65. *Loom*. 1971–74.

66. Another view of *Loom*.

67. *Shadow*. 1973–76.

68. Another view of *Shadow*.

69. *Homage: David Smith*. 1973–76.

70. David Smith, *Voltri V*. 1962.

71. *Ridge*. 1974–76.

*72. *Lunar Episode*. 1959.

*73. *Song*. 1958.

*74. *Rocker*. 1958.

*75. *Blue Painted Blue*. 1959.

*76. *A Warm Sound in a Gray Field*. 1961.

*77. *Round*. 1959.

*78. *Bloom*. 1960.

*79. *Rose*. 1961.

*80. *Ring*. 1964.

*81. *Turnsole*. 1961.

*82. *Spring Cool*. 1962.

83. *Point*. 1959.

84. *Mesh*. 1959.

85. *Alliance*. 1960.

86. *Ember*. 1960.

87. *Spread*. 1958.

88. *Fete*. 1959.

89. *Split*. 1959.

90. *Missus*. 1959.

91. Untitled. 1959–60.

92. *Flutter*. 1960.

93. Untitled. 1958–59.

94. *Breath*. 1959.

95. *Franklin*. 1960.

96. *Blue Circle*. 1960.

97. *Probe*. 1959.

98. Untitled. 1959.

*99. *Fiord*. 1960.

100. *Shallows*. 1961.

101. *Time's Motion*. 1959.

102. Untitled. 1959.

103. Untitled. 1959.

104. *Straight Flush*. 1959.

105. *William*. 1960.

106. *Quadrum*. 1961.

107. *Hub*. 1961.

108. *Harvest*. 1962.

109. *New Green*. 1961.

110. *Egyptian Discovery*. 1961.

111. *Teton Noir*. 1961.

112. *Karen's Gift*. 1961.

113. *Ex Nihilo*. 1958.

114. *Reverberation*. 1961.

115. *Drought*. 1962.

116. Installation view of Noland exhibition at Kasmin Limited, London, England, 1963.

*117. *Noon Afloat*. 1962.

118. *Shield*. 1962.

119. *Red and Purple Octuple*. 1962.

120. *Lebron*. 1962.

121. *Inner Warmth*. 1961.

122. *Horizontal Focus*. 1963.

*123. *Fugle*. 1962.

124. *Tinge*. 1963.

125. *Advert*. 1963.

*126. *Rite*. 1963.

127. *Tripex*. 1963.

128. *Solar Thrust*. 1963.

129. *Dusk*. 1963.

*130. *Blue Veil*. 1963.

*131. *Blue-Green Confluence*. 1963.

*132. *Magenta Haze*. 1964.

*133. *Sarah's Reach*. 1964.

*134. *Morning Span*. 1963.

*135. *Embrown*. 1964.

*136. *17th Stage*. 1964.

*137. *Bridge*. 1964.

*138. *No Bid*. 1965.

139. *Shoot*. 1964.

140. *Flush*. 1963.

141. *Yellow Half*. 1963.

142. *Alongside*. 1967.

143. *Into the Hot*. 1964.

144. *Beam*. 1964.

145. Untitled. 1963.

146. *Absorbing Radiance*. 1964.

147. *Eight*. 1964.

148. *Sun Dried—Japanese Space*. 1963.

149. *Number Seven*. 1964.

150. *Aim*. 1964.

151. *Diamond Shaped Picture*. 1964.

152. *Color Temperature*. 1964.

153. *Drive*. 1964.

154. *March 22*. 1965.

155. *Tony's Gift*. 1966.

156. *Mr. S.* 1965. Acrylic on canvas, 61 x 61″. Susanne Hilberry Gallery, Birmingham, Michigan

157. *Alkis' Gift*. 1967.

158. Installation view of Noland exhibition at André Emmerich Gallery, New York, New York, 1964.

159. *Trans West*. 1965.

*160. *Mach II*. 1964.

*161. *Grave Light*. 1965.

*162. *Dark Sweet Cherry*. 1965.

*163. *Ambsace*. 1966.

*164. *Call*. 1966.

*165. *Saturday Night*. 1965.

*166. *Daydream*. 1965.

*167. *Transist*. 1965.

*168. *And Again*. 1964.

*169. *Return*. 1965.

170. *Southline*. 1966.

171. *Twist*. 1966.

*172. *Steps*. 1967.

*173. *Ado*. 1967.

*174. *Bright Ray*. 1967.

*175. *Shade*. 1966.

176. Installation view of Noland exhibition at Lawrence Rubin Gallery, New York, New York, 1969. Left: *Via Flow*. 1968. Right: *Via Token*. 1969.

*177. *Via Blues*. 1967.

178. *Wild Indigo*. 1967.

*179. *Lilium*. 1968.

*180. *Via Flow*. 1968.

*181. *It's Mine*. 1969.

*182. *Via Median*. 1969.

*183. *Air Beauty*. 1969.

*184. *Lucent*. 1970.

*185. *Intent*. 1970.

*186. Top to Bottom: *Untitled B*. 1971. *Untitled A*. 1971. *Enisle*. 1969. *Heptad*. 1969.

*187. *Little Rouge*. 1969.

188. *Appearance*. 1970.

*189. *Oakum*. 1970.

*190. *April Tune*. 1969.

*191. *Mexican Camino*. 1970.

192. *Out of the Red*. 1971.

*193. *Until Tomorrow*. 1971.

*194. Left: *Blue Intentions*. 1971. Right: *And Blues*. 1971.

*195. *Aires Solo*. 1971.

196. *Passion Flower*. 1972.

197. *Merge*. 1972.

198. *Twice Around*. 1973.

*199. *Over and Under*. 1972.

200. *Added Distance*. 1973.

*201. *Lineate*. 1973.

*202. Untitled. 1973.

*203. *Circum Grid Green*. 1973.

204. *Following Sea*. 1974.

205. *Pairs*. 1974.

206. Untitled (Diamond). 1974.

207. *Closing Meet*. 1974.

208. Untitled. 1974.

209. Untitled. 1975.

210. Installation view of Noland exhibition at Watson/de Nagy & Company, Houston, Texas, 1975. Left to right: *Curious Course; Voyager; Here-In*.

211. *Maker's Mark*. 1975.

212. *Blue Power*. 1975.

*213. *Gradient*. 1975.

214. *Eagle Yellow* (first version). 1975.

215. Installation view of Noland exhibition at André Emmerich Gallery, New York, 1975. Left: Untitled. 1975. Right: *Beam*. 1975.

*216. *Grayed Green*. 1976.

*217. *Pend*. 1976.

*218. *Ovaray*. 1976.

*219. *Halflong*. 1976.

*220. *Lapse*. 1976.

*221. *Edgeways*. 1976.

*222. *Determined Course*. 1976.

*223. *Burnt Beige*. 1976.

KENNETH NOLAND

3. Kenneth Noland in the grounds outside his studio/house, South Shaftsbury, Vermont, mid-1960s. Photo by André Emmerich

ONE

Kenneth Noland grew up in Asheville, North Carolina, where he was born in 1924.[1] Although Asheville had no museums or symphony, it was relatively sophisticated for a small southern town (its population was about 75,000 then).[2] Still Noland's family was unusual in being so involved with art. His mother played the piano, and his father was a Sunday painter who had had some formal training and did semi-Impressionist landscapes and still lifes. Noland recalls that paint and canvas were always around the house, and his parents encouraged the artistic interests of their four sons. Later, three of them studied at Black Mountain College at the nearby resort town of Black Mountain, North Carolina.[3] The oldest, Harry, became a photographer and art historian, and Neil, the youngest, is a sculptor who lives in New York.

Noland's father was also an amateur pilot, and he took the boys for plane rides at the local airfield.[4] Noland developed romantic notions about flying, and it was natural that, after graduating from high school during World War II, he would join the Air Force. He served in the armed forces from 1942 to 1946, first as a glider pilot and then as a cryptographer. Most of Noland's service was spent at air bases in the United States, but, toward the end of the war, he was stationed in Egypt and Turkey.

After his discharge in 1946, Noland took advantage of the G.I. Bill and enrolled at Black Mountain College, which was fewer than fifteen miles from his home. His brother Harry was already studying there, and the unconventional, progressive, and community aspects of Black Mountain appealed to them both.

Josef Albers, former member of the Bauhaus, was the head of Black Mountain's art department and by far the most powerful influence at the school. Because he was on leave when Noland arrived in the fall of 1946, Noland began working with Ilya Bolotowsky, Albers' temporary replacement, and only took a course with Albers—the first half of a two-semester design course—in the fall of 1948.[5] Noland did not take the second half of that teacher's course and continued to work with

4. Still life in oils painted by Harry Noland, Sr.

5. Kenneth Noland in 1931.
Photo by Harry Noland, Sr.

6. Kenneth Noland as a glider pilot in World War II

7. Kenneth Noland in his studio/house,
South Shaftsbury, Vermont, 1965

8. Kenneth Noland in the grounds outside
his studio/house, South Shaftsbury, Vermont,
in March, 1965, with his children.
Left to right: Lyndon, Cady, and Bill

9. Kenneth Noland in 1976. Photo by Bill Noland

Bolotowsky, who remained at the school through 1948.

Later, Albers felt that Noland had denied his influence, while Noland, for his part, thought that in emphasizing his relationship to Albers writers had not given enough credit to Bolotowsky, who had been his real teacher.[6] In any event it seems that Noland and Albers took a dislike to each other from the start. Noland found Albers uncongenial both as a teacher and personally ("too much the scientist," a "jeering manner"). After he had dropped out of Albers' class, Noland heard that Albers had a low opinion of him as a student and even wanted to have him dismissed.[7] A real rivalry existed between Bolotowsky and Albers—or at least between their respective "students" —and this atmosphere undoubtedly contributed to the attitudes that Noland and Albers developed toward each other. One may also point out that Noland was not the only independent-minded student at Black Mountain who reacted negatively to Albers: in fact, to many he seemed doctrinaire and rigid.[8]

On the other hand, despite the fact that he had relatively little contact with Albers at Black Mountain, Noland has always acknowledged that he learned a great deal from him and has spoken of his "perceptual insights," which he found "enlightening."[9] Noland familiarized himself with Albers' color theories, and, later, when teaching at Catholic University in Washington, D.C., he offered a course on the fundamentals of design patterned directly on what he had learned in Albers' class. In fact, any student at Black Mountain in those years could not help but be affected by Albers in one way or another. As Noland has said, "His influence was all over the school," and "I was very affected by the climate that he had created."[10] Martin Duberman, in his book on Black Mountain wrote,

> Those who weren't enrolled in Albers' courses not only heard about him constantly—art was a reigning topic at Black Mountain—but still more, saw and heard Albers himself in community meetings, at meal times, while lining up a row of seeds, or walking a mountain path. His views were continually quoted and argued about: Did preoccupation with the past, as Albers claimed, produce imitation and prevent creativity? Did a hankering for individuality lead to conform-

ity? Was fashion the enemy of honesty? Did words betray feelings and introspection atrophy the senses?

> Finally, Albers' courses themselves were never narrowly technical; they involved principles and procedures applicable to a wide variety of activities—the need to be aware of everyday objects and their individual properties; the essence of primary experience, of direct seeing and feeling, of problem-solving out of one's own experience; the importance of economy, leanness, and discipline; the realization that form has meaning and that "foreground" and "background" shift value according to context. What Albers embodied above all was a search "to make some kind of order out of things"—some perfect order—a search many took to be emblematic of the purpose of the college as a whole.[11]

Much, but not all of this philosophy was straight from the Bauhaus. It certainly must have had its effect on Noland, and attitudes related to Albers' are easily discerned in his mature work; for example, art as problem-solving, the direct handling of materials, the lesser role of history and art history in art making, the use of geometry, and the emphasis on color and the way that Albers emphasized it—juxtaposing distinct, separate colors, holding a symmetrical and concentric design constant, and thinking about color not theoretically but in terms of intuitive feeling for relationships. It is difficult to assess how directly these features of Albers' art and teaching influenced Noland since he came to most of them only later and as the natural results of his own development. But, at the very least, Albers always served Noland as an important confirming example.

No doubt, though, as Noland himself insists, Bolotowsky exercised a more direct and personal influence on him.[12] Although, again, when it comes to specific features, this influence only became evident much later and operated most like a confirmation and precedent. Noland speaks about Bolotowsky with great warmth as a sympathetic guide and teacher. And Bolotowsky is of course the link between Noland's art and European geometric abstraction—especially De Stijl—of the first part of this century. Bolotowsky's painting derives directly from Mondrian and Neoplasticism, but he uses more secondary hues and more intuitive chromatic choices rather than Mondrian's severe use of primaries.[13] Less concerned with theory or metaphysics, Bolotowsky is also less restrictive in his use of geometry and has varied the shape of his canvases, employing tondos, ellipses, triangles, diamonds, and very narrow vertical formats.[14] Most of these features appeared later in Noland's work, although with a very different result. Always in Bolotowsky's pictures, and this is true of Albers' as well, there is a conflict between the motility of color and the rigidities of geometric design. It can be said that both took color as far as it could go within what was still an essentially cubist-designed picture. As we shall see, it was what Noland learned from the New York School that later permitted him to really bring color into its own. I might mention in this context something that I want to develop later: there is a sense that Pollock, in his allover, noncubist layout and with his stain technique (of his 1951 paintings), had developed a uniquely color compatible picture—a picture that he took as far as he could given that he was essentially a draftsman. From this point of view Noland can be seen as fusing and fulfilling these two strains.

If Bolotowsky uses bright, intense, and somewhat more varied color than had Mondrian, he is far less sensitive or inventive with color than was Albers. On the other hand, Bolotowsky's art demonstrates a certain openness and variety in dealing with geometric structure. And, coming from Neoplasticism rather than the Bauhaus, Bolotowsky is more concerned with strictly pictorial problems. Albers' paintings often seem

10. Josef Albers, *Homage to the Square: Apparition*. 1959. Oil on board, 47½ x 47½".
Solomon R. Guggenheim Museum, New York, New York

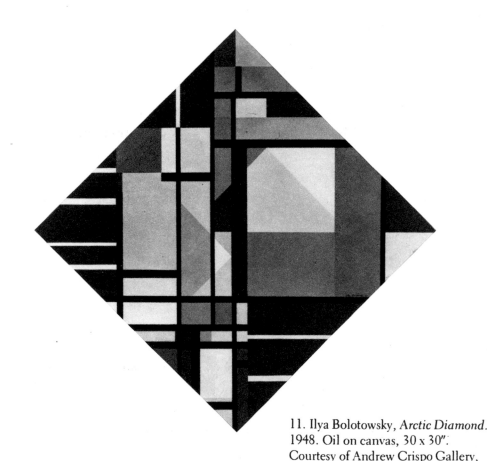

11. Ilya Bolotowsky, *Arctic Diamond*. 1948. Oil on canvas, 30 x 30".
Courtesy of Andrew Crispo Gallery, New York, New York

more like demonstrations than pictures. As Noland puts it, Albers "approached abstract art from a design point of view," while Bolotowsky "taught us a lot about cubism," i.e., about *pictorial* architecture.[15]

But what Noland liked most about Bolotowsky was his "permissiveness within abstract art,"[16] his openness to his students working in many different ways. Noland has also stated that "Bolo was more unsymbolically abstract."[17] By this Noland does not mean that Bolotowsky's pictures were more abstract than Albers' but that his conception of art was more purely abstract. For example, Albers, at least in his teaching, retained certain Surrealist or Dada attitudes from his Bauhaus days, such as playing with juxtapositions and combinations of materials, something that greatly influenced the most famous of his students, Robert Rauschenberg, and helped lead to Happenings and to Pop Art.[18]

But despite these important differences and speaking more generally, Noland's experience with these two teachers meant that from the very first his education was completely with nonobjective art. Both the Bauhaus and De Stijl, Albers and Bolotowsky began nonobjectively; that is to say that they began not with visible reality or by abstracting from visible reality but by a study of the elements of art—line, form, color, etc.—conceived of abstractly.[19] Noland is one of the first major painters to be educated entirely in this way, and he never had an extended figurative or representational early period. Both Bolotowsky and Albers were models of intense, focused, and uncompromising commitment to abstract art. And the basic approach common to the painting of both artists—eliminating variety of shape in order to work solely with variety of proportion—certainly had a deep influence on Noland. Also, unlike the abstract artists of the first quarter of the century, Albers and Bolotowsky did not surround abstract art with explicit philosophical or semitheological ideas. If their approach to abstraction was to a large extent still limited by cubism, they nonetheless were of a second generation of nonobjective painters who were more empirical, intuitive, workmanlike—less ideological than such pioneers as Kandinsky, Mondrian, and Malevich.[20] Noland inherited this experimental and workmanlike attitude. It prepared him to assimilate the far more radical working attitudes that he was later to learn from Jackson Pollock and from David Smith.

The sculptor Ossip Zadkine visited Black Mountain in the summer of 1945, and a few of his students subsequently went to Paris to study with him. Noland, still on the G.I. Bill, decided to do this, too, and he arrived in Paris in 1948. Teaching mainly at the Grande Chaumière, Zadkine also held private studio classes, and it was these that Noland attended. Zadkine struck him as "another man like Bolotowsky who was really very committed to art and very idealistic about teaching and very, very generous, sympathetic...."[21] "I painted on my own but in class I made sculpture. My own work which I was doing in my own studio was mostly painting which he criticized and helped me with. He

12. Untitled. 1947. Oil on board, 18 x 24".
Collection, Christa and Harry Noland, Reston, Virginia

had a really. . .very strong cubist orientation. After having been at Black Mountain and gotten some experience in Bauhaus-type education which I think was based on more abstract principles—I remember I used to have to take with a grain of salt, as it were, some of the things he would say, or I mean some of the things he believed in. It was limited by the cubist orientation."[22]

Noland's experience at Black Mountain had clearly given him a certain sophistication. Albers and Bolotowsky were of course both direct links with European modernism and both were members of the American Abstract Artists, a group that in general was oriented to geometrical or semigeometrical painting and saw it as the most advanced and developed vanguard art. Noland took this orientation with him to Paris, and he was at least partly aware of Pollock and the Abstract Expressionists. All this prevented him from feeling like a provincial in Paris, and it even made Zadkine's type of cubism seem a bit old-fashioned. Noland later summed up the attitudes he held during his student days in Paris:

> . . .we [the young American painters in Paris] didn't really get involved in French cultural life so much. Mostly we stayed together, most of the Americans did. And to me it was just that we had a different idea about art. I think we were willing to find out more about how art had been in Europe than being interested in getting into it. . . .We wanted to find out about the past more. We'd had the advantage of having had a lot of the best European artists that had come to the United States. It was true at Black Mountain and it was also true in New York. Mondrian had been over here. We already knew that there was work being done by another generation of artists such as Pollock or even, say, the American Abstract Artists that somehow had absorbed a lot that had developed in Europe. So we weren't even that interested in, let's say, Picasso. We felt that it had been absorbed by an older generation, brought over here, and then picked up by, say, the first generation Abstract Expressionists. We were aware of that. At least I was. As a matter of fact, it was my impression that most of the young artists of my age who were there

[in Paris] then felt the same way. . . .the tradition. . .of avant-garde art had been broken in Europe. We'd had the advantage of having it brought over here and soon after getting it you realized that there wasn't an ongoing avant-garde; it had been broken up. We knew the ongoing avant-garde in the United States. That really in essence is what it was.[23]

From Paris, Noland wrote to his brother Harry, "It sure is a temptation to paint like Bolo, Albers or Mondrian. I'll have to find a direction of my own before I do abstraction again."[24] From this comment it can be seen that Noland's outlook and commitment to the avant-garde had been decided at Black Mountain and that he assumed he would eventually paint abstractly. Far from being overwhelmed by his Paris experience, he viewed it in a deliberate way as a chance to learn something from the earlier School of Paris—something that would help him make original abstract art. This viewpoint coincided with the most advanced attitude toward painting of those years: to go beyond geometrical painting, yet work abstractly.

The French artists whom he met "knew about Picasso very much, and about Matisse and Miró. But they knew nothing about Paul Klee or Mondrian. They really just didn't know who they were. And over here we had known about Mondrian and Klee and assumed that they were of equal stature with the so-called French School of Painting."[25] Already practiced in Bauhaus and De Stijl, Noland quite consciously saw his stay as a chance to learn from the modern masters of the School of Paris; he looked closely at Miró and even did some neoclassical figures similar to Picasso's, as well as some still lifes in the style of Matisse. Along with Matisse's color, what affected him most was the very physical and sensuous character of the School of Paris and especially its emphasis on métier. "I got onto Matisse when I was in Paris and realized that I was going to have to revise my thinking about how to go about making pictures. Up until that time, you know, it was coming out of abstract art of the Bauhaus-cubist kind, and I realized that I had to really. . .learn how to paint. Of course that came from Pollock too. . .how to use materials in a kind of hand way. The cubist abstract way of painting was

13. Piet Mondrian, *Composition with Red, Yellow, Blue, Black*. 1928.
Oil on canvas, 19 x 19½".
Private collection, Chicago, Illinois

more like a process of predisposition. . .you planned and you conceived it beforehand. To paint out of Matisse, or, say, to use color, you had to learn how to use the materials somehow. I think Pollock helped a lot with that because Pollock actually experimented more with using materials, with some kind of intrinsic qualities that you could find out of the use of the materials."[26] What Noland first glimpsed in Paris, then, was something that was later much reinforced by greater contact with Pollock's art: the importance of the direct use of the materials of painting. This knowledge was to modify the geometrical-cubist approach that he had learned at Black Mountain.

Toward the end of his stay at Black Mountain, Noland already had begun to move away from the hardedged and smoothly finished geometrical abstraction inspired by Bolotowsky. He was drawn to the art of Paul Klee, who, like all former members of the Bauhaus, was popular at the school.[27] Klee was to remain very important for him. "He's a great colorist. And he used cubism [in a] much more expressive way, still being abstract."[28] Noland already knew something about Abstract Expressionism at this time, which undoubtedly accounts for his interest in "an aspect of cubism that was more of a kind of expressionism."[29] But it was Klee who seemed to offer the "expressionist" alternative to geometric art. In addition to his color, Noland was fascinated by Klee's noncubist configurations, the result of his special use of subject matter. But at this point, at least, the most important thing that Klee offered was the same thing that he had already sensed in his contacts with Abstract Expressionism and the School of Paris—a more spontaneous and more physical approach to the materials of painting.[30] Although in many respects more open than earlier abstractionists, Albers and Bolotowsky were limited not only by their geometrical-cubist approach but also by their more ideal conception of the medium. Even though less bound by theory, they conceived of the elements of painting—line, form, color—in an abstract, ideal way. So, for example, Albers was relatively uninterested in paint quality and in the relation between it and color, while in Bolotowsky's pictures the brushwork is even less conspicuous than in Mondrian. Klee, the School of Paris, and Abstract Expressionism stress *handwork* and a more physical and spontaneous kind of painting. As I shall emphasize

19

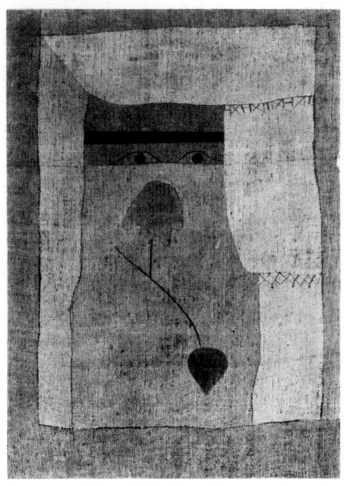

14. Paul Klee, *Arab Song*. 1932. Oil on burlap, 36 x 25¼".
The Phillips Collection, Washington, D.C.

at least in those pictures that were most personal and not experimental or mere learning exercises. Klee's expressionism was very much in evidence at Noland's first one-man show, held in April 1949 at the Galerie R. Creuze. "Exotic, almost barbaric color arrangements combined with 'graffiti' suggesting animals, huts and/or cathedrals," was the way one writer described the pictures that Noland exhibited, and the same critic added that color was Noland's real strength.[31] Also perceptive and indeed prophetic was Zadkine's preface to the show, "Il a dit adieu au Bauhaus, mais pour combien de temps? Car l'enfant a ses amours et ses anciennes amours, ver lesquelles il retourne pour puiser une vie nouvelle: Nous allons lui donner rendez-vous dans dix ans."[32]

Noland returned to the United States in the fall of 1949 and took a position in Washington, D.C., as a student teacher at the Institute of Contemporary Art.[33] Robin Bond,[34] who taught at the institute, reinforced Noland's enthusiasm for Klee, as did the room devoted to Klee's work in the Phillips Collection.[35] Through 1952 almost all of Noland's watercolors, drawings, and paintings show Klee's influence, but one also finds harbingers of his later paintings, as in an untitled oil of 1950 in which an irregularly drawn but unmistakable concentric circle motif floats in a field.

Noland returned to Black Mountain for the summer sessions, and at one of these, in 1948, he met Elaine and Willem de Kooning as well as Buckminster Fuller, Richard Lippold, Leo Amino, and Peter Grippe. The 1950 Summer Institute, which he attended, also included Theodoros Stamos, Paul Goodman, Clement Greenberg, and Helen Frankenthaler. Meanwhile, the Institute of Contemporary Art was about to close, and a fellow teacher, Alex Gianpetro, helped Noland get a job at Catholic University, where he began teaching full-time in the fall of 1951. Now married and a father, Noland made extra money by teaching ceramics to young children, driving a taxicab, and giving evening classes at the Washington Workshop of the Arts. This center for adventurous young artists in the Washington area had been organized by Leon and Ida Berkowitz. It was there, in 1952, that Noland met Morris Louis. "I knew a lot of other artists but I [only] really became a close friend of Morris' mostly because–our interests in art coincided. I felt an affinity with his preferences in art more than I did

later, Noland was to unite these two strains: the ideal and the physical, the geometric and the painterly.

Working on masonite, Noland began to use a thick build-up of paint, sometimes applied with a palette knife, and he occasionally scratched into the paint to get a graffitolike effect. Surprisingly one finds in these pictures, along with occasional figural elements, the whole vocabulary of motifs—concentric circles, diamonds, chevrons, and stripes—that were to appear in his mature painting.

Despite his study of Matisse during the year he spent in Paris, Klee remained the dominant influence on Noland's painting of that time—

15. *Inside*. 1950. Oil on masonite, 23⅛ x 29⅛".
The Phillips Collection, Washington, D.C.

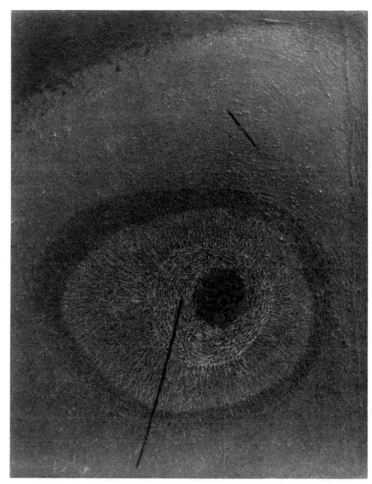

16. Untitled. 1950. Oil on board, 27 x 21".
Collection, Christa and Harry Noland, Reston, Virginia

with most of the other artists in Washington that I knew. So we became painting buddies...we'd see each other, oh, two or three times a week and we talked a lot. We were very close friends for about the first two years that we knew each other...he was very interested in Jackson Pollock, and so was I...he had arrived at this independently. I had arrived at this independently. I had arrived at it mostly through having had contact with Clement Greenberg. There was idealism, personal idealism...involved in that.... We were checking and comparing and bringing other kinds of information to each other—for instance we both liked Bob Motherwell's work."[36]

The progressive atmosphere at Black Mountain made the college receptive to all advanced artistic ideas and as early as the late 1940s there had been considerable talk about the Abstract Expressionists.[37] Interest though was confined to the "action painters"—Franz Kline, Willem de Kooning, and Jackson Pollock—and the work of these painters was known pretty much only in reproduction.[38] Noland at least saw few originals until he returned from Europe in the fall of 1949. The critic Clement Greenberg, whom Noland met in the summer of 1950 at Black Mountain, talked to him then about Pollock.[39] Soon thereafter in 1951 and 1952, Noland's work began to show the

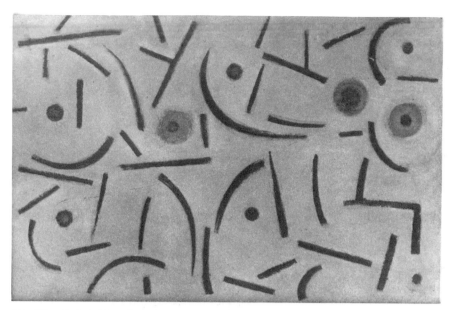

17. Untitled. 1951–52. Oil on board, 20 x 30".
Collection, Christa and Harry Noland, Reston, Virginia

18. Untitled. 1951–52. Watercolor on paper, 13 x 10".
Collection, Christa and Harry Noland, Reston, Virginia

influence of New York painting for the first time. Often done in blues and violets, with a fairly heavy build-up of paint and a repeating eye-like motif, the pictures of this time relate both to Klee (usually late Klee) and to Pollock, especially Pollock's work of 1944, such as *Gothic* and *Night Ceremony*.

In late 1952 and 1953, however, these pictures give way to larger canvases and to an even more vigorous painterliness; the influences now were de Kooning and Kline.[40] They reveal an even more "expressionistic" cubism, as it were. These were the sort of pictures Noland was doing when he met Morris Louis. For his part, Louis was working on his "Charred Journal" series, heavily influenced by Pollock and by collages made of dress patterns, which related to Motherwell's collages. This "affinity of taste,"[41] as Noland calls it, for "action painting," the painterly side of Abstract Expressionism, is what first drew the two artists together. Noland, although younger, was more worldly and savvy about painting, but both sensed the dedication, seriousness, and ambition in the other. At the beginning at least, there was a sharing and exchange—for example, Noland learned from Louis the use of magna paint (he had used only oils up until then). Sometimes the two artists would travel to New York to visit Greenberg. On the first such visit, in April 1953, Greenberg took them to the studio of Helen Frankenthaler, where they saw a picture by her, *Mountains and Sea* (1952), which greatly inspired them both (plate 20).

Employing a process derived from Pollock's work of 1951, Frankenthaler had stained soft washes of oil pigment thinned with turpentine directly into unsized, unprimed raw cotton duck canvas. Whereas with Pollock the results were large black and white drawings, Frankenthaler had seized upon staining as a way to get a light, airy, coloristic picture. The significance of *Mountains and Sea* for the two young Washington painters was summed up by Noland: "We were interested in Pollock but could gain no lead to him. He was too personal. But Frankenthaler showed us a way—a way to think about and use color."[42]

On the train back to Washington, they decided to try something radical, "jam painting, like jazz,"[43] both working together on the same canvas using various techniques in an effort to "break open painting."[44] What they had seen in Pollock and more accessibly in Frankenthaler

19. Kenneth Noland in his studio, Washington, D.C., c. 1952

20. Helen Frankenthaler, *Mountains and Sea*. 1952. Oil on canvas, 86⅞ x 117¼". Collection, the artist, on extended loan to National Gallery of Art, Washington, D.C.

was not primarily color—at least not at first. And they both knew that a new painting could not come from merely reproducing the look of Pollock's work. The problem was to find, as Pollock and Frankenthaler had done, new procedures, new techniques, new ways of working with the materials. Jam painting was an experimental effort to force the discovery of new procedures; for example, paint was often thinned down and applied with rags or in other unconventional ways.

After jam painting at the workshop for about three weeks, each returned to his own studio. Louis immediately began his "trellis" pictures, while Noland's work remained experimental and very scattered until late in 1957. Yet Louis did not really settle into his mature style until about the same time. In 1954, after the trellis pictures of 1953, Louis did about ten or so "veil" pictures, which show broad floods of stained pigments, layer upon layer, creating a rich colorism. These were small and less assured prototypes of his mature veils of

1958. But then, between 1954 and 1958, Louis reverted to Abstract Expressionism, lost direction, and finally felt compelled to destroy most of his works. In the period from 1954 to 1956 Noland also showed lack of a clear direction. His strongest influence by far at this time was Louis; he even began a series of poured pictures, which he subsequently destroyed upon Greenberg's advice because they were too close to Louis' 1954 veils. It can be said, then, that Louis, while still lacking assurance and clear direction, had painted a small group of original pictures and was clearly more advanced than the younger Noland, although neither completely jelled as an original artist until 1958.

Strongly drawn to New York painting, Noland was forced to remain in Washington, D.C.; he had very little money, and was able to visit New York only about every five months. But, as Greenberg has stressed, this relative isolation had its advantages. "From Washington

24

21. *In the Garden*. c. 1952. Oil on masonite, 19½ x 30″.
The Phillips Collection, Washington, D.C.

22. Untitled. 1952. Oil on canvas, 19¼ x 15¼″.
Collection, Vincent Melzac, Washington, D.C.

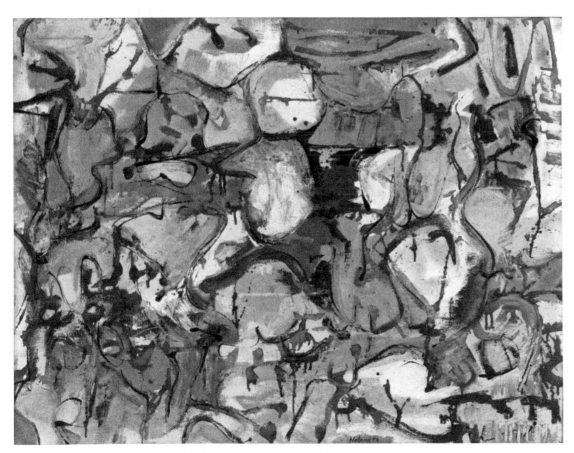

24. Kenneth Noland and the critic Clement Greenberg
in Greenberg's New York apartment, 1976

23. Untitled. 1953. Oil on canvas, 28 x 36″. Collection, Christa and Harry Noland, Reston, Virginia

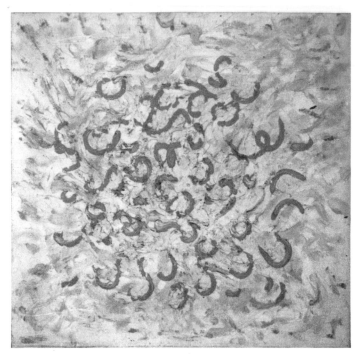

25. Untitled. c. 1956. Oil on canvas, 18 x 18″. Collection,
Mr. and Mrs. Robert B. Meyersburg, Bethesda, Maryland

26. Untitled. 1957. Oil on canvas, 60 x 54″.
Collection, the artist

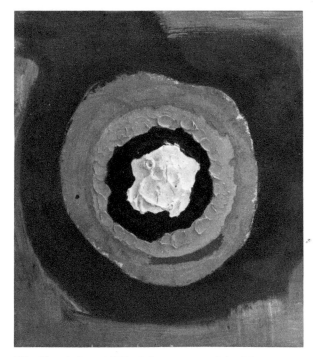

27. Untitled. c. 1957. Oil on canvas, 16 x 14″.
Collection, Christa and Harry Noland, Reston, Virginia

28. *Catherine*. 1959. Oil on canvas, 72 x 69 ¾″.
Whereabouts unknown

you can keep contact with the New York art scene without being subjected as constantly to its pressures to conform as you would be if you lived and worked in New York."[45] In the mid-1950s, the painterly abstraction of de Kooning so dominated New York that few young painters living there were able to evolve a fresh and personal style. Visiting New York, Louis and Noland saw what they did not want to paint; they maintained geographical distance for the sake of spiritual independence. Greenberg probably reinforced their own intuitions about this, for he had pointed to the dangers of the "Tenth Street Touch" as early as the early 1950s. (It was only after Noland had found his own way that he chose to move to New York in 1961.)

Greenberg must be counted as one of the most important influences on the careers of Louis and Noland. A sensitive friend and a means of contact with the New York art world, he was, above all, a respected audience with exacting standards.[46] In 1954, Greenberg included their work in the "Emerging Talent" show that he selected for the Kootz Gallery, and between 1959 and 1960, he made it possible for them to have one-man shows at French and Company, where he was serving as adviser. When the two artists had reached maturity, Greenberg wrote, in *Art International*, a crucial essay about their work in which he stated flatly that they were the only younger artists whom he considered to be candidates for major status.[47]

Another influence and source of encouragement was the sculptor David Smith, whom Noland met in 1950.[48] In particular, Noland credits Smith with giving him and Louis certain ideas about working methods. For example, Smith pointed out the advantages to the abstract artist of working in series, and he suggested that they always keep on hand a large store of materials so that they would not feel inhibited but free to take risks. More generally, the attentions of Smith together with his energy and ambition must have been an inspiration to the two still unknown young painters. During the mid- and late 1950s, Noland, much more personally outgoing than Louis, became an important catalyst for an emerging group of Washington artists. He served as their connection to Greenberg, Smith, and developments in New York painting. (Another connection was the magazine *Art News*,

which everyone read avidly.) The painter Thomas Downing has written, "Noland's appreciation of the mainstream of the new American painting, his understanding and insights into the work of Jackson Pollock, Still, Rothko and Newman provided a new orientation."[49] Anne Truitt adds, "Ken was important to us all with his vigor, enthusiasm, and intelligent talk about art."[50] Downing, as well as Ed Kelly and Howard Mehring, were Noland's students at Catholic University, where Noland also arranged exhibitions of the work of David Smith, Morris Louis, Herman Cherry, Lee Krasner, and Gene Davis.[51]

A painting by Noland was selected in 1956 by Dorothy Miller for a circulating show sponsored by the Museum of Modern Art, *Young American Painters*, and in February 1957 he had a one-man show at Tibor de Nagy Gallery in New York.[52] This was followed by a second one-man show at the same gallery in October 1958.[53] The pictures exhibited in these two shows were mainly influenced by Frankenthaler and Louis. Most of them employed thinned out pigment, and a few showed a tendency to organize around the center of the picture.[54]

By now Noland had fully absorbed all of the ingredients that were to be present in his mature art, and he was working with distinction in the most up-to-date abstract idiom of the time. He was ready for a breakthrough. And it was evident that this had come when, in the following year (October 1959), he showed at French and Company fully mature and totally original pictures; these were, of course, the concentric circles, which had an effect on Morris Louis and Jules Olitski, and which established Noland as one of the real innovators of abstract art.[55] Suddenly, he had returned to geometry and to the bright, juxtaposed color he had learned from Bolotowsky and Albers, but now completely transformed by what he had learned in the intervening ten years from Klee and Matisse, and especially from Pollock and New York painting. Six years later, in 1965, at the age of forty-one, Noland had become widely recognized and was given a retrospective at New York's Jewish Museum. In the following years, pictures from his chevron and circle series were chosen as part of the United States' representation at the Venice Biennale.[56]

TWO

In giving the primacy to color, Noland's art is part of a recent and very important shift in the tradition of the easel painting, which, from its inception, has given to color a subordinate role. Wishing to specify, locate, and give life to forms done from nature—and above all seeking to unify these same forms—painters of the fourteenth, fifteenth, and sixteenth centuries gradually worked out a consistent illusionistic space, a separate and self-contained world in which color had to know its place. Modeling of form and atmospheric perspective, for instance, meant the dilution and subordination of that purity and clarity of hue that one finds in Byzantine art and in Gothic art. I do not mean to say, of course, that our tradition of painting is—as is that of the Chinese, for example—primarily graphic or "tonal" or lacking in fine colorists. Quite the contrary. One only has to think of the Venetians. Even the chromatic luminism of Rubens and the Venetians, though, sacrificed frank oppositions of local hue. Bright flashes of color had to be carefully prepared for, and in general color was first of all a property of form and then orchestrated into a presiding light/dark structure. When the painterly colorism initiated by the Venetians culminated in Impressionism, pure hue—or at least what at the time seemed pure hue (actually almost all Impressionist colors were mixed with white) —returned as little touches applied so consistently and conspicuously as to flatten out the picture and create a contradiction between description of nature and chromatic effect. So the development had come full circle. The flattening caused by declarative surface and emphatic color now called into question that consistent illusionism that Western painters had so painfully worked out over the past six centuries—the same illusionism that had hollowed out the surface and held color in check. Nothing could have spelled out all of this more clearly than the late pictures of Monet. In many of these Monet canceled the contradiction or at least suspended it by driving Impressionism to its "logical" extreme, confining himself to a bit of nature, surfaces of water strewn with lily pads, which perfectly aligned itself—or almost did—to the flat

29. *That.* 1958–59. Acrylic on canvas, 81¾ x 81¾".
Collection, Mr. and Mrs. David Mirvish, Toronto, Ontario

continuity of the tactile and chromatic surface.[1] Chosen primarily for the sake of surface, Monet's subject matter nonetheless retained its inherent unity, integrity, or, more correctly, its own independent identity. Such other Late Impressionists as Bonnard had the same unquestioning respect for the identity of their subject, while choosing it with form mainly—if not solely—in mind. This certainly was not true of Cézanne, who both redefined Impressionist procedure and form, and who was also willing to distort the subject. He was the first to seek a *synthetic* solution to the Impressionist problem—to make both the surface and the three-dimensional illusion active and equally yielding partners in a fusion, instead of, as with Monet, only juxtaposing them as closely as possible.

Matisse and the Fauves seized upon certain features of Cézanne's art—his distortions and the way he used the inherent intensity, temperature, and value differences of more or less undiluted hues to evoke pictorial depth. What the Fauves themselves added and what, looking back, seems to have announced the new century was their willingness to simplify drastically. Van Gogh and Gauguin were important supporting precedents here. But while these two nineteenth-century artists remained fascinated by nuance and to that extent dedicated to the individuality of their subject, the Fauves, with a boldness rare among young painters, abandoned completely this presupposition of all nineteenth-century painting. Drawing became simplified, generalized. By enlarging his color areas and giving up the division of surfaces and shading, Matisse made one hue stand for the whole mass of an object. Moreover, this color was often descriptively arbitrary and functioned solely in terms of the internal demands of the picture. A simplified reality served as the implied spatial context within which these "local" colors could remain structural and relate to each other across a flattened surface. One has only to compare a Fauve painting with a typical Impressionist one to see what a dramatic difference all this makes. The Impressionist picture looks almost Old Masterly by comparison: it is tonal, the color still in the service of a preexistent, natural light internal to the picture. The Fauve painting bursts from the wall projecting its own light, a *literal* light, into the room. And color counts first as color—not since the fifteenth century had painting

showed such forceful oppositions of pure hue.[2]

For all their modernity and radicalness, however, the Fauves had not fully solved the problem that Impressionism posed. As with Monet, reality remained for them a more or less autonomous scaffolding, which was set against the flatness created by the autonomous means, color and paint. And since these means were now more explicitly themselves and reality was more explicitly only a scaffolding—more schematic because more simplified—the contradiction, rather than resolved, was exacerbated for being clarified (that the Fauves themselves knew this is clear enough from the worried remarks one finds in their letters about the potential decorativeness of their pictures).

It has not been stressed enough, I think, how the crisis that had been precipitated by Impressionism and then spelled out so lucidly by Monet and Fauve painting was the *same* crisis or problem that led to the cubist solution. Daniel-Henry Kahnweiler, the dealer and friend of Picasso and Braque, made this point, at least by implication, when he wrote that the goal of cubism was "to represent three dimensions *and color* on a flat surface, and to comprehend them in the unity of that surface."[3] And it is revealing that in order to work out a solution Picasso and Braque had to eliminate color, as their most intractable variable, and thereby redefine the issue as simply surface vs. depth, flatness vs. illusion, two vs. three dimensions. And this reduction and isolation of the problem *as a problem* meant that, for the first time in its history, the easel painting focused on the *process* of rendering nature conceived of explicitly as a problem or set of problems that as such could engage the painter.

In practical terms, all this meant working out a structure, a scaffolding, that retained three-dimensional illusion but was not itself autonomous; that, while allowing references to the visible world, was consistent only with the surface. To this end, the cubists borrowed Cézanne's version of the Impressionists' division surfaces—exactly that feature of his art that the Fauves had abandoned. From the Fauves, however, the cubists took the willingness to simplify or generalize the subject (even if, to them, this often meant generalizing the individuality of their subject, i.e., parody or caricature). And the end result, if not the artistic culmination of cubism's early development, was Synthetic

Cubism in which bright, intense, full-bodied color comfortably existed in a restructured picture. At the price of representation, or rather of its autonomy, the Impressionist crisis had finally been resolved and synthesis achieved.

Or was it? To be sure, color and surface no longer offered a system that was, at least potentially, separate from described reality. But the Synthetic Cubist enlargement of Cézanne's facets meant that plane, shape, drawing—and a rigid, rectilinear drawing at that—were now the vehicle of color. Moreover, although later cubism, like Fauvism, had eliminated shading and atmospheric perspective, the main impediments to pure color, it retained certain illusionistic survivals, especially overlapping. However, bright and pure Synthetic Cubist color still remained subordinated to shape and spatial placement, to drawing and illusionism. To the extent that it does this, color is prevented from becoming completely itself—from determining the structure of the picture rather than being determined by it. And this remained more or less the case with all cubist and cubist-derived painting. Here I count Mondrian and geometrical abstraction, in which color is a question of colored planes and forms, as well as the painterly abstraction that appeared in the United States right after World War II in the pictures of Pollock, de Kooning, Kline, and others. The latter, like the former, still based their art first of all upon a light and dark structure and gave to color a secondary place.

This was far less the case with Matisse's work and such Late Fauve painting as that of Milton Avery. At first it seems curious that that trend of modernist painting that stuck closest to representation would, at the same time, be the one that kept pure color—the most abstract of pictorial elements—most central. But in this, the Fauves remained close to their Impressionist beginnings. More properly, one should speak here only of Matisse, for it was he who made Fauvism into a viable style that could fully serve color. He retained reality as a structural alternative to the cubist division of surfaces, but one that permitted him to conceive far more broadly and boldly.

It was exactly because he did not break with the logic or structure of reality that Matisse's pictures seemed for a time less radical than the light-dark cubism of Picasso and Braque and the nonobjective painting that issued from it. So it was the latter with its concern with "forms" that dominated painting in the first half of this century. The painting of Robert Delaunay aside, only in the late 1950s was an attempt made to overhaul cubist style and to make it really serve color. Analogous to the way that Monet and, still more, Matisse had inverted the traditional relationship between color and description, Hans Hofmann, in his "floating rectangles," became the first and only painter to successfully fuse cubism and Fauvism by employing overlapping planes and depicted illusionism to permit color to become more completely itself—free, direct, and disembodied.[4]

I realize that the discussion so far makes it sound as if the achievement of a pure color picture is the hidden project or impetus behind the development of modernist painting. For our purposes this is a very useful way to look at things, although, taken alone, it is not able to explain the development as a whole. Nonetheless, such a reading does, I think, have a certain justification of its own. In terms of form and shape, Old Master art with its consistent illusionistic space allowed for a great deal more variety and complexity than does abstract painting. The flattened and often contradictory space of the modern abstract picture demands far more simplification. In terms of the range of form possibilities, abstract painting is no match for older art. And these possibilities were quickly exhausted. Yet at the same time, abstract painting is free of those restrictions on color that older art perforce imposed (the most obvious of these is, of course, the need to begin thinking in terms of shape and drawing). So here is an area where the demands of simplicity became an advantage, an extraordinarily rich and virtually unexposed area for discovery and invention—that is, an area in which the enormous pressures that modern individualistic society puts upon creativity can find release.

I want to continue this line of thinking for a moment. If Impressionist color initiated a devolution of Western illusionism, it is a devolution that is not symmetrical, not the exact mirror image of the evolution. The modern development differed in two respects—one radical and the other conservative. First of all, unlike past colorists, say the medieval artist or the Persian miniaturist, the modern painter is willing to compromise and, as it has turned out, to completely eliminate descriptive images. This is an important prerequisite for achieving pure color for it means that the modernist painter does not have to deal with any a priori shapes or forms. Even more important, the modern colorist is different from the abstract, decorative colorists of the past, such as the designers of Persian carpets, in that he remains bound by the terms of the Western illusionistic easel picture. He strives to make a consistent and autonomous (or perhaps one should say autonomous because consistent) picture with its own unique drama, capable of being seen "at a single glance." Color gradually came to have the upper hand, but it still had to constitute a *picture* in the sense defined by Western illusionism. It was not a question of just covering canvases with colorful pigments, but of making pure color pictorial; of giving it that unique unity and life that constitute the Western easel picture. And as we have pointed out, the Western easel picture defined itself in the first place by suppressing pure color. So color painting created problems, and these in turn became challenges to creativity— different, but analogous to those that the original development had offered. From this point of view, one might indeed call the creation of color painting a project, a historical project that could occupy not just one or a few artists but many artists over an extended period of time. And it does seem that historical projects of this sort—at least in intensely individualistic periods such as our own—call forth artistic creativity and exalted artistic feeling in a way that more static, less challenging historical situations—for instance, that that seems to exist currently in the novel and in photography—do not.

Other forces are at work as well. The drive toward pure color, like the impulse to flatness, can be seen as no more than a direct response to function and use. Modern society asks of painting only that it be art, that it fulfill no other need than an aesthetic one. And modern "authenticity" proscribes that the picture itself declare this fact. Now the pure aesthetic viewing of a picture *as a picture* involves a special mental set, a just and even distribution of detached attention, a nonpurposive, more optical, and flattening way of seeing in which the visual field itself structures what is seen. This is the attitude that every artist takes up when he narrows his eyes and steps back from his work in an effort to assess the overall distribution of visual weights, to savor the pictorial

unity of his painting. Since no other social tasks or requirements are placed on painting, it is no surprise that in the long run and with many twists and turns painting has shaped itself to conform with this purely aesthetic way of seeing. The most purely "optical" and most purely aesthetic pictorial property of all is, of course, color, and this, together with the fact that pictorial color is relatively unexplored territory accounts, I think, for its decisive role in the development of modernist painting. It accounts for the ease with which we can explain this development as a drive toward color.

Pure pictorial seeing also makes its demands on composition. So flatness and alloverness, the evenness of pictorial pressure over the whole surface, have, like optical color, been as if hidden objectives in the development of modernist painting—at least when this development is seen in retrospect. Beginning with the Impressionists, whose historical role it was to aestheticize naturalism, there was a search to identify the pictorial and visual fields (their so-called far vision) insofar as it is possible. But descriptive reality with all of its independent variety and recession had to be surrendered before flatness—which declares the literal, made character of the picture—alloverness, and optical color could exist alone, for themselves, each identified with the other. So it is perhaps no accident that alloverness makes its appearance almost immediately after cubism completed its task of dissolving the autonomy of descriptive reality into a system of abstract marks and signs. Abstract alloverness first appeared in Mondrian's plus and minus pictures of 1914. But having so quickly reached this point, Mondrian hesitated, for being primarily a draftsman, and limiting himself to horizontal and vertical lines, alloverness threatened his continued development as a painter. His solution was to renounce alloverness while retaining its two distinctive features: a holistic singleness of effect and the possession of the entire surface by the creation of an equalized surface tension.[5] Seeking the directness and explicitness of sharp edges, he dispensed with *passage*, the device that the Analytic Cubists had employed to relate forms across their flattened surfaces. Mondrian, instead, divided his surface with horizontal and vertical lines that repeated the edges of the rectangle; all was woven together, and the picture's wholeness as a single unit was forced upon the viewer in a new way. Rather than a balancing-out of shapes within a fictive depth, one saw, as it were, the picture balancing itself out; the painting, taken as a whole, now established that large coherence that was previously provided by a scene or image drawn from nature.[6] At the same time, despite their unprecedented flatness and lack of the slightest suggestion of shading, Mondrian's pictures do not seem thin and papery; the picture is perceived as a single, more or less evenly assertive surface, and thus something of the object character of the painting informs the final result. (Mondrian emphasized this by his handpainted, built-up surfaces and by bringing his canvases forward from the frame rather than setting them within it.) Moreover, the opaque, bright colors with their sharply contrasting values give an added assertiveness to the picture's wholeness. An effect that is usually called "presence," this is the abstract equivalent of the density older painting achieved through depicted sculptural illusion.

From one point of view Mondrian's paintings represent with diagrammatic lucidity the underlying structure of cubism—its logical conclusion: rectilinear drawing, flattened planes, and a light and dark grid scaffolding. In another sense they show a new kind of abstract structure. They are paintings in which all the essentials of the easel picture are preserved, but without any reference to reality: liveness, presence, and density are no longer the properties of the objects or of the forms depicted but of the painting itself, and in this sense the picture is, as Mondrian maintained, a "new reality." Until recently Mondrian's work has been seen in the first way rather than in the second—not as an advance but as an extreme formal limit. He himself was partly responsible for this since for purely ideological reasons— i.e., aesthetically extraneous ones—he restricted himself to horizontal and vertical lines and primary colors. So what seemed distinctive in his art was its sparseness and reductiveness of means rather than its compelling abstract presence.

Painterly abstraction, Abstract Expressionism rather, which emerged in New York and Europe in the 1940s, was reacting in part against what seemed the narrowness of Mondrian's art and the geometric painting that it had inspired. Beginning with Synthetic Cubism and especially Picasso's late version of it, the Abstract Expressionists sought to overcome the decorative thinness that often infected the large Synthetic Cubist picture by painting their planes with broad strokes of loaded pigment. Uneven densities of paint, together with the light and dark gradations caused by a loose mixing of this paint on the canvas, resulted in shading and with it an evocation of a more palpable space.[7] At the same time the thick build-up of paint created an assertive and sculptural surface that helped give body and substance to the large cubist-derived picture.

Nonetheless, painterly abstraction was constantly plagued by a conflict between self-declaring surface and emphatic depth. The painterly meant a breakdown of discrete edges evoking a *passage*-like space linking the forcefully shaded planes. But, at the same time, the covering of heavy pigment together with the increased size—made necessary by the broad athletic strokes—tended to flatten the picture and thereby abort the *passage* space; this in turn meant holes and isolating pockets.

Pollock solved these problems and in doing so rediscovered holistic design. In the early 1940s he was using a large image, a "totem" (e.g., *The She-Wolf* or *Pasiphaë*), on which to superimpose his painterly cubism. This image was much more flat and schematic than, for example, de Kooning's later "Women" (which is one reason why Pollock's pictures are so much more successful). As Pollock's painterly drawing became more energetically expressive and allover, it began to separate from or swallow up the underlying image, and it was at this point that he grasped another possibility for unity. Eliminating the image altogether, he let the continuous fabric of lines and blotches cover the entire surface and create a new focus, a new larger unity. In *Shimmering Substance* and *Eyes In the Heat*, done with dabs of paint often squeezed directly from the tube, variations of size and points of privilege are eliminated in favor of an allover evenness of attack. Yet in both paintings evenness seems to squeeze space out of the picture with a suffocating and heavy result.[8] The drip method, one of those perfect pictorial solutions, opened up the heavy pigment texture without diminishing its sculptural presence; literal immediacy is at the same time a disembodied, highly varied line. A continuous space is evoked not by *passage* but by the continuity of interlaced lines and transparency. Owing to the seeming monotony, the painted image is grasped instantly, synoptically, and thereby gains an intense force of presence as one thing. With these paintings Pollock had gone beyond Mondrian's plus and minus pictures to combine abstract alloverness with mural scale. In the best of his classical drip paintings there is a comfortable congruence between pure aesthetic regard and a surface more or less evenly articulated; between a just and even distribution of detached attention and an equalized pictorial pressure. The eye neither wanders aimlessly nor sticks at specific points, since there is a perfect harmony between the intensity of detail and the wholeness of the general aspect.

Yet, paradoxically, Pollock's allover pictures threatened the very existence of the easel picture. As Greenberg has written, "though the allover picture will, when successful, still hang dramatically on the wall, it comes very close to decoration, to the kind seen in wallpaper patterns that can be repeated indefinitely, and insofar as the allover picture remains an easel picture, which somehow it does, it infects the notion of the genre with fatal ambiguity."[9] If one puts it another way, one can say that the easel picture has always depended upon not only a unity perceived at a single glance but also on dramatic imbalance and marked variation of accent; the allover picture placed severe restrictions upon drawing, upon differentiated shape relationships, and upon marked figure-ground readings—features that can disrupt the even continuity and tight coherence of the surface.

But despite these limitations alloverness or at least its effects—wholeness and a more or less continuous evenness of pictorial pressure across the entire surface—have become imperatives of abstract painting; and since the late 1950s, it seems that young painters have had to engage with these features if they are to make significantly innovative pictures.

Despite this radicalness, Pollock continued to share certain essentials with Mondrian and cubism; line variation and a light and dark structure—i.e., drawing—remained the basis of his picture making; and as we have noted the allover picture placed severe limitations upon drawing. For this reason Pollock gave up alloverness and after 1960 sought to give greater accentuation and variety to his painterly draftsmanship by suppressing the tactility of paint—sinking thinned

black pigment into raw canvas. The result was large stained drawings in which the lack of textural change between painted and unpainted areas gave unity and tactile immediacy to the whole surface. At the same time the illusion became disembodied, detached from this surface in a curious way, so that Pollock's 1961 pictures, despite reversion to certain features of cubism and to totemic imagery, show a genuine freshness. What Pollock had done here became decisive for all the abstract painting that followed, and to that extent these 1961 pictures can be seen as being as important as his earlier drip paintings. The main point is that in the latter pictures an allover flatness established by emphasizing the material continuity of surface *as paint* is combined with allover articulation. In the stain pictures those two features are separated; here allover material flatness is established by the continuous materiality of the *canvas*, and this permits the incident—the paint—to depart from allover evenness of accent and become more differentiated and variable. Alloverness and flatness are given by staining itself and all at once; they are identified with each other and together constitute an entity that allows more variation in articulating the picture. More important still, the broad and continuous way that this new unity is established opens the way for the emergence of color abstraction. But Pollock himself, always the draftsman, was unable to move in this direction.[10]

All this can be viewed as the working out of the final consequences of cubism, which, seen in its extreme form in Mondrian's work, were drawing and value structure. The last and most fundamental impediments to color painting—i.e., to a painting in which color determines the structure—these features were also at the very heart of the Western easel picture, and consequently took the longest to eliminate. Pollock had created the conditions for doing so. In his 1951 pictures, structure no longer depended on a light and dark scaffolding, but on the continuous physicality of surface and on the identity of this surface with the illusion. To the end, however, Pollock continued to think in terms of value contrasts and of drawing.

This was less true of Helen Frankenthaler, who took her cue from Pollock's paintings when, in the early 1950s, she began spilling and splashing delicate washes of color into raw canvas. Lacking sharp changes of value and achieving a new kind of transparency, these

30. Jackson Pollock, *One*. 1950. Oil, Duco, Dev-o-lac, and aluminum paint on canvas, 106 x 209⅜". Museum of Modern Art, New York, New York

pictures looked less like drawings than watercolors; diaphanous and nontactile painterliness here admitted color, and the porous weave of the canvas insured that the color, no matter how intense, was filled with light and air. It was this sort of painting that inspired Louis and Noland when they made their first visit to Frankenthaler's studio in 1953.

Twelve years older than Noland, Morris Louis was the first to react creatively to Frankenthaler's art. In the following year he did his early veils, floods of thinned pigment, one over the other, which achieved a unity of physical surface while exploring the fluidity, and above all the transparency, of staining in a new way. Equally important was the breadth that he gained by this technique, the elimination of small-scale incident or any kind of wrist or even arm drawing (still present in Pollock's pictures). Finally all this—the breadth, the transparency —yielded a new kind of color: muted, but rich. Here, and even more in his 1958 veils, the pictures consist of a chromatic field contained within a large shape, sometimes sculpturally delimited, which looms before the viewer, imposing its singular effect. Louis had demonstrated that if alloverness limited drawing, it was especially adaptive to color painting in which it admitted a new breadth of range and variety. Seen from the point of view of the development sketched above, Louis had achieved something like an abstract equivalent of the chromatic alloverness of the Impressionists.

As I have noted, the Fauves, unlike the Impressionists, were primarily interested in that kind of color experience that results from the subtle modulation of color into color across the surface. Sharp changes of hue and value and also drawing—anything that will interrupt the continuous movement of color—are deemphasized. This type of color picture has usually meant some type of painterly application that results in broken color, such as the Impressionist touch or Louis' layerings or Olitski's spray. The Impressionist picture tends toward density and warmth as it also tends toward middle grayness and a monochromatic initial look; coloristic richness emerges only gradually. Overall tonality dominates, and changes of hue issue as fugitive, suggestive, evanescent, and nuanced. Due to the radically reduced value range, slight color shifts appear as identical with equally slight value shifts. The emphasis is not on the identity of individual hues but on a single, richly varied chromatic substance informed by an absorbent, inner light. Since the Impressionist type of color picture develops across the surface, the artist need not concern himself directly with composition, nor is he forced to continually step back to balance out his composition. On the other hand, the main difficulty encountered by the Impressionist type of colorist is that of accentuation and variety—of introducing sharp, pungent changes of hue and/or value. A secondary problem is of stopping the flow, or turning his field into a picture.

A motif drawn from nature helped the Impressionists deal with the problems of accentuation and pictorial completeness. Olitski's abstract solution to both of these problems resulted from his manner of application and from his discovery of the different nature of the margins of a flat, more or less uniformly accented abstract picture and its center. So, for example, with a few marks or strokes at the edges, he was able to introduce what are often abrupt, Fauvelike bursts of hue and value while simultaneously delimiting and declaring his fields as self-contained pictorial units.[11]

The Fauve type of color picture emerged full blown first in the work of Matisse and the Fauves, but the initial impetus had come from Van Gogh, Gauguin, and Cézanne. In it, the color effect is first all one of contrast, resulting from the juxtaposing of frank, pure, discrete hues all more or less clearly separate, each asserting its uniqueness, yet vibrating with the others into a pictorial whole. Sharp differences of value inherent in different hues at full intensity (e.g., blue with yellow) are often accepted for the sake of the vigor and optical energy that their contrast evokes. Far brighter and far more obviously colorful than the paintings of the Impressionists, the Fauve pictures stressed declarative immediacy and the individual identity of each hue. White was often included to heighten and to help unify an optical dazzle, and light seems to bounce off or be reflected from the picture rather than, as with Impressionism, being located within it. Such pictures live by vivid, ringing complementaries or else by unexpected juxtapositions.

With staining an Impressionist type of painting can be achieved by layering as in Louis' veils; but Impressionist modulation of color into color *across* the surface, especially of bright oppositions of red into green, for example, is difficult to achieve without muddied gray or more usually brown areas. For this reason staining when used with Impressionist alloverness tends toward monochrome as one can see in Louis' veils or Olitski's 1964 curtain pictures. So, too, the Fauve picture with its prismatic hues goes well with a stripped down surface and thin application—i.e., with neutralized or equalized tactile associations—such as one finds in Matisse's later work or in stain painting. Conversely, the Impressionist picture is usually built up of either small elements (dabbing, spotting, spraying, etc.) or by layering, and it seems to call for or at least admit more tactile effects. Important in this regard is the fact that stained pigment dries very quickly, and it is difficult to paint over an area later or when it is still wet. When interpreted positively, these technical limitations result in paintings in which no alterations or corrections were made, and in which decisive choice and spontaneity were at a premium. For these and other reasons staining has tended to suggest separate discrete areas of color and a Fauve type of picture.

In the next chapter we will discuss how Louis and Noland had learned from Pollock to take the materials and the procedures of painting as their only subject matter, to follow this subject matter, and to take their cues from it. For Louis the distinctive characteristics of staining were its transparency and its fluid, impersonal shapes. More essentially, I think, Noland came to see the inherent logic of staining in its potential for Fauvelike, side-by-side color. He was able to perceive this primarily because his personal sensitivity and genius is for this kind of color, but also because his experience with Bolotowsky, and especially with Albers, had prepared him to see this possibility in staining.

In any event, by 1958 Noland was painting pictures that were more intense in their color and more completely abstract than anything Louis had achieved up to that point. And so it was that by 1960 Louis was being influenced by the younger artist. But the reason that Noland took the lead at this point was not only his training and his personal color sensibility, but also the fact that Noland simultaneously had grasped that the release of color in this way was first of all a problem of design or layout.

The difficulties intrinsic to the Fauve type of color picture are those of unity, for the separate hues must be kept from canceling each other out and creating an effect that the Germans call *bunt*. The most frequent solution evident in the work of Matisse was to give clear dominance of one color in terms of area size, or else as in Noland's circles and then in Louis' "unfurleds"—which followed Noland's targets in this respect—to resort to a generous use of white. Since juxtaposed hues at full intensity bring with them clear edges and emphatic design, the Fauve type of colorist can only maintain the primacy of color by preventing this design from taking on an inert, filled-in look, from seeming merely posterlike and graphic. Also, since the eye first grasps differences of light and dark, he must so organize his picture that the sharp value changes present in full-intensity color do not balance out or read primarily as value accents but retain their full force as hue. Noland solved this problem with a device that was unavailable to the not-yet-fully-abstract painting of Matisse: various kinds of symmetry, i.e., a design that more or less obviates compositional decisions of the traditional kind.

Eschewing cubist overlapping or any device that would pin down his color areas and prevent them from finding their own place, Noland began to use repeating parallel bands. Color used this way, in its purity, is flat and thus calls attention to the surface—a surface that is of regular, geometric shape. And it is part of the "logic"—or of one of the "logics" —of staining, which identifies pigment with literal surface, that the design would also come to be so identified. Thus, Noland was led to place parallel color bands into a single, symmetrical geometric motif that is locked to the inherent geometry and lateralness of the support (the center, the sides, the corners, etc.)[12] His pictures thereby gain a sense of inevitability, and his hues a vivid presence. The solution in each case had been a compelling holistic layout that preserves the expanding openness that belongs to color and further serves to force color outward toward the viewer. Finally, since his pictures lack the traditional illusion of depth or a cubist *passage* to relate elements across the surface, the synoptic design helps bring multiple adjacent hues dramatically together. By using the word *holistic*, I do not mean to imply that a picture is exhausted by the initial dramatic impact. In Noland's pictures the indivisible singleness of his layout certainly admits pictorial indeterminacy and liveness, which come mostly from combining different color scales in the same picture and from such devices as varying the proportions and widths of the bands. The motif itself adds to this indeterminacy by creating a tension between openness and closure, or between the painted image and the picture's shape (for example, in Noland's off-centered chevrons and diamonds), by evoking multiple readings, or by the "ungraspable" character of the configuration (in the concentric circles, the chevrons, and the horizontal-stripe pictures). Phenomenally simple, Noland's pictures can aesthetically suggest richness and complexity. [13]

Almost always Noland's formats are dramatically expressive from a purely graphic point of view. In part this is also related to staining—its capacity to soften hardedged geometric drawing, thereby avoiding its potential brittleness while allowing geometry in turn to tauten the soft effect of staining. The rigidity of geometry and the relation of the geometric configuration to the literal support make the thin, nontactile character of stain more dense as it were. Hence Noland, and Louis followed him in this, evolved large, dynamic, hardedged designs to accommodate bright, high-contrast stained color. In both cases, the varied, nonallover articulation of design is made possible by the unbroken, i.e., allover, material unity of the whole surface, which, as Pollock had first discovered, staining creates automatically.

All of the essentials of Noland's solution were already present in the concentric circles pictures: they are geometric designs made up of hardedged color areas that are lucidly discrete parallel bands; the compositional function of each band is served by its relation to the support (i.e., the center), not by its specific hue or value or width or placement. Thus Noland is very free as regards relational possibilities. And since shape relationships are kept to a relatively uninteresting repeat, the viewer's attention is focused on the color. Repeating also creates the same kind of tightly coherent, even surface and sense of wholeness found in the allover picture. Organized solely in terms of the continuous surface the color areas have no inherent spatial role. And so impelling is the holistic effect that hues can be combined that contrast as to transparency and opacity, warmness and coolness, dullness and vividness. Still more important is the possibility of juxtaposing colors at full intensity and sometimes, therefore, of markedly different value.

Of course, working in series with a concentric, geometric motif came from Albers. [14] But the scale and breadth of Noland's concentric circles are a result of his engagement with Pollock's art. Along with the new material flatness that Pollock's pictures offered, Noland was also influenced by Pollock's allover expanding composition. The relationship between Noland's composition and Pollock's turns out to be something like the relationship between Mondrian's plus and minus pictures and those from his classical period. Like Mondrian, Noland sacrificed allover articulation for the sake of inflection while, nonetheless, retaining the holistic impact of alloverness together with its continuous, even, pictorial pressure, which possesses the entire surface. Mondrian had made this move to give himself more room to develop; to give greater force to line; and to readmit a dramatically balanced-out type of composition (what he called "dynamic equilibrium"). Noland employs the holistic picture as a way to accommodate a certain kind of color, which I have called Fauve, and he therefore places his parallel bands in symmetrical configurations as a way to *avoid* a balanced-out type of composition. But, as I have explained, he achieved this by means of Pollock's 1951 pictures, and via Helen Frankenthaler's. That is, he escaped strict alloverness of design by means of the broad, allover unity of surface that staining offered. To repeat, Noland's solution (and that found in Louis' Unfurleds) offers the abstract equivalent to the Fauve color picture, just as Olitski's spray paintings and Louis' veils give the present abstract equivalent to the Impressionist one. [15] Both are fully developed color painting and depend on the new continuous flatness that Pollock discovered but could not really exploit. And both unite pure color with alloverness or at least its effects: wholeness and an equalized surface tension. From this point of view, these artists can be seen as representing paradigmatic modernist responses to pure pictorial seeing—to a historical situation in which picture looking has become the sole touchstone for picture making.

THREE

The stylistic and formal relationships that we have just discussed between Louis and Noland and the previous generation can only be understood together with a fundamental change of attitude that Noland described to me in conversation: "The question we always discussed was what to make art about. We didn't want anything symbolic like say, Gottlieb, or geometric in the old sense of Albers. The Abstract Expressionists painted the appearance or symbol of action, the depiction of gesture. We wanted the appearance to be the result of the process of making it—not necessarily to look like a gesture, but to be the result of real handling. Morris achieved that before me." The change of attitude is a very momentous one. It amounts to a whole new subject matter for abstract painting. And, once arrived at, this became the subject matter of all subsequent color abstraction.

Louis and Noland had perceived that Pollock was the most advanced and radical artist of the previous generation and that his achievement promised a new kind of abstract art—a whole new development. This was certainly not the prevailing view. De Kooning dominated the New York avant-garde in the 1950s. Even by the leading members of his own generation, Pollock was thought to be "far out": a radical, certainly, but not a guide or model. And anyway it seemed impossible to work directly from his famous drip paintings without imitating them. (Louis' "Charred Journal" series shows the problem.) For most young painters it was de Kooning's art that offered the developable possibilities. De Kooning's look became the "in" look and the basis of a new academy.[1] To see Pollock the way that Louis and Noland did—and this is also true of Frankenthaler and Friedel Dzubas—was very unusual and, to a significant extent, the result of their friendship with Greenberg. Almost alone among artists and critics of the time, Greenberg argued for Pollock's preeminence as an artist over de Kooning; and he argued that Pollock represented the most advanced painting of the moment.[2] But if this was true, what exactly was it that made Pollock so important?

I have already described the central formal or stylistic features that

Louis and Noland eventually perceived in Frankenthaler's and Pollock's art: continuous, literal flatness and its potential for color painting. But even more important was the perception that this feature was inextricably bound up with a whole new attitude toward the making of abstract painting. Frankenthaler had combined much of Pollock's spontaneous application, the spilling and splashing, of his drip pictures with the stained procedure of his 1951 paintings. In this way she demonstrated how Pollock had pioneered an approach in which a new use of materials could itself lead to style, or equal style and artistic innovation. Going beyond Pollock or exploiting the possibilities he had opened up meant discovering new ways to combine paint and canvas that would simultaneously create a literal, allover flatness and a color experience identical with this flatness.

In line with this, Louis and Noland had to give up working with "forms" or shapes. They had to give up graphic or profile drawing since it would prevent a direct approach to materials; it would inhibit experimentation and prejudice the outcome in advance. And from the point of view of the result, profiled forms would undermine the identity of paint, color, and surface that constituted the new style. They did not want colored shapes. Neither shape nor shape relationships were to determine structure. That was Synthetic Cubism. Color was to be determining, and color was paint on canvas. Hence the relationship of paint and canvas unmediated by profiled shapes was to determine incident and structure.

Frankenthaler still retained profile drawing, as did Dzubas, but her accomplishment, uniting two different phases of Pollock's work, gave the two young painters the necessary distance to see his real importance. Benefiting from Pollock's innovations involved not dripping or even staining as such, but seeking a new approach to the procedures and materials of painting. The lesson of Pollock's dripping, staining, and his use of unconventional materials was the necessity for breaking down preconceptions about how pictures are to be made.

So it was jam painting, a most unorthodox and experimental procedure, that was Noland's and Louis' first reaction to Frankenthaler's work. One of the things that impressed them was how Pollock and Frankenthaler painted with their canvas on the floor. This made the canvas "more material—more a real surface and not an (ideal) picture plane."[3] And it encouraged them to think of paint and canvas in a very physical way: as wet and dry, or the canvas as a loose fabric unrelated to stretchers. One method they tried was placing objects randomly on the floor, draping canvas over them, and then pouring paint onto the surface. Settling into the valleys and creases, the paint would create unexpected configurations and pockets of space. They did not worry about establishing an image or flatness or a picture plane. As Noland has said in regard to staining, the picture plane, flatness, was achieved "just by stretching."[4] (The point here is that the new literal unity of surface achieved all at once and by the materials themselves now permitted the abstract painter to work away from, rather than toward, flatness.)

Physicalness meant interacting as directly as possible with the materials, giving the materials a more active role, following leads the materials themselves suggested. To use a term that Pollock had used, they wanted to get in "contact" with the painting as it developed.[5] This involved setting out to avoid all a priori conditions that might impede a sympathetic dialogic interaction with the materials; and it meant taking chances, keeping alert and open to surprises.

Now this very open attitude was not new. It came ultimately from Surrealist automatism and was also part of the ideology of "action painting," as it was called, the painterly wing of Abstract Expressionism. For example, in 1950 Robert Motherwell wrote, "The process of painting...is conceived of as an adventure, without preconceived ideas on the part of persons of intelligence, sensibility and passion. Fidelity to what occurs between oneself and the canvas, no matter how unexpected, becomes central.... No artist ends up with the style he expected to have when he began...it is only by giving oneself up completely to the painting medium that one finds oneself and one's own style."[6]

With the Surrealists and action painters, this open, experimental approach is usually associated specifically with chance and accident. Any ambitious artist wants to avoid the look of previous art, which means, in effect, escaping from his own taste, a taste that has been formed by what he has already seen. But in the past, the painter could

31. Untitled. 1955. Oil on canvas, 47 x 46″. Collection, the artist

rely on nature and then a specific theme or subject to stimulate his originality. Nature was a refractory and challenging stimulant, and by working to transform it into paint, the artist could, at least ideally, go beyond his predecessors and realize himself. With the friction, the resistance of nature eliminated, the danger of falling into style or taste is far greater; the abstract artist had to find ways to circumvent his own taste, to trick himself, as it were, into being creative.

Chance, accident, giving the materials their lead allow surprising and unexpected things to happen: one's own tastes can be challenged. Of course, taste always imposes itself in the end if only as the decision to accept or develop one accidental effect rather than another. But by using chance or accident deliberately, taste does not impose itself first, only later. By temporarily suspending taste, by putting its strictures off until the end, the painter gives himself time to get used to new effects and therefore to expand his taste. And this is exactly what new art must do to be creative: namely, it must expand taste.

So the artist begins without any a prioris, freely, loosely, and in such a way as to provoke unforeseen effects that might be exploited. This was the artistic idea behind Surrealist automatism and the use of chance. It became the doctrine of action painting in the 1950s.[7] Yet, despite a commitment to openness, many of the action painters and almost all of the young artists who followed them wound up painting very much alike. They did work more freely than their predecessors, but always they had in mind if not exactly a certain form vocabulary then a certain way of working: a loose hand or arm gesture with a loaded brush. And this in turn was because they thought of automatism and chance as means to express a predetermined subject matter: a uniquely risky, poignant, and heroic conception of "action." It was a subject matter that referred as much to a self-image of the artist as to the work.

What Frankenthaler, with her loose combining of Pollock's two different procedures, suggested was a more open and less ideological kind of action painting. Chance or accident became *merely* a way to get started, something to work from, devices to circumvent taste. More important, Pollock and Frankenthaler suggested an attitude for which no specific procedure was privileged, for which all a prioris were suspended—even chance itself. In fact, there were many ways to work

with paint and canvas. For example, if the materials and procedures that the artist was using led him in the direction of hardedged or even geometric configurations (which staining ultimately did), he went with that lead. But only by giving up allegiance to a specific vocabulary or technique—and their ideological justification—could the artist be free to follow up the lead that the *materials* presented. One might call this the demythologizing or radicalizing of action painting. In a sense, action painters had not fully accepted the implications of their own ideas. They had remained fixated on a certain look, certain forms, and a certain notion of action. They had not seen that the idea of action painting, more broadly and less dramatically conceived, meant a whole new subject matter for abstract art, a subject matter that remained with the painting and the processes of making it.

Stylistically, of course, Louis and Noland were much closer to such Abstract Expressionists as Gottlieb, Rothko, Still, and Newman, none of whom were action painters. As early as the 1940s, these artists had reduced the role of profile drawing and evolved the drastically simplified abstract color picture. Usually they worked in series and sometimes they used symmetry. Even more than the action painters, however, they continued to think of their configurations as abstract "images" that expressed or suggested an external subject matter. Their investment in certain particular abstract forms or effects as pointing toward a preexistent subject matter—usually "sublime" or "mystical" or "mythic"—puts these painters closer to Mondrian than to Louis and Noland.

In fact, most previous abstract painters were tied to their representational predecessors in that they took as their subject matter fixed and given forms that usually were thought of as having certain meanings or associations. (This, of course, was related to the continuing dominance of profile drawing.) The new approach, pioneered by Pollock but fully realized only in the next generation, meant beginning only with paint and canvas; it meant letting new and changing relationships between them become the subject matter. It meant consciously avoiding any preconceptions or assumptions that would impede the painter in following the dictates, the changing logic of this relationship.[8] I think it is fair to say that only with the emergence of this attitude does abstract painting really come into its own. No longer does it define itself negatively—as not using recognizable forms or imagery. Now it has a subject matter unique to itself. Like visible nature for older art, this subject matter is independent, not yet fully explored, and for that reason it can function as the source of stimulation and invention. It gives the painter something to develop in a way that abstract "forms"—geometric, biomorphic, painterly, or otherwise—cannot. The latter, especially when identified with certain external meanings, became a prioris that can inhibit innovation with and development of the materials.

This is the main reason why the color painters of the 1950s and 1960s—Louis, Noland, Frankenthaler, Dzubas, Olitski, Poons—developed from Pollock rather than from either de Kooning's kind of action painting or from the Abstract Expressionist colorists. Pollock had a more direct physical approach to the surface and a more open, experimental attitude toward the materials. Of all the Abstract Expressionists, he came the closest to taking the materials and procedures of painting as his sole subject matter.

To repeat, it was the material unity of surface with its concomitant potentiality for breadth and openness present in the pictures of Pollock that was the main *stylistic* or formal precondition for the color painting that followed. And it was the new approach to the materials, the new conception of subject matter, theoretically present in the ideology of action painting and concretely dramatized in Pollock's unorthodox procedures, that was the *attitudinal* precondition for the development of this abstract color painting.[9]

I want to turn now to Noland and ask what the new attitude, the new subject matter, has meant to him. We have already seen how in their formative years he and Louis adopted some of Pollock's radical methods and how they invented some of their own. The range and variety of Noland's 1954–56 work are expressions of the new, more open, and consciously experimental approach to abstract painting. Chance and accident play a large role in it as is true of Louis' contemporary work. Like Pollock, they often worked from above on a large canvas that was laid out on the floor. This not only meant a more material approach, but also it prevented them from continually step-ping back to see comfortably the progress of the picture and therefore from imposing their taste too early. Only later when the canvas was tacked up on the wall could they really assess what they had done. A related device was the one they had learned from David Smith: to always have at one's disposal a large quantity of paint and canvas so that one felt free to "waste" them, i.e., to take chances with a picture and not treat it preciously. These painters also remained open to the idea of turning a picture upside down or on its side or cropping it or cutting part of it once a painting was finished. Again, the critical or judgmental was postponed until last.

What is significant here is that both of these artists consciously adopted a new attitude. It boiled down to an effort to remain open at all costs, to question everything about picture making. But picture making itself was not questioned; an effect, no matter how arrived at and no matter how fresh, had to "work" in a whole, or, more correctly, to constitute a new pictorial whole. Without this commitment to a given control and resistance, openness, experiment, risk taking become abstract and merely experimental and, in the end, a matter of tastefulness.

At the time of Louis' early veils, Noland had not yet discovered his way, and this was to remain true for the next few years. The pictures that he did between 1954 and 1956 show no clear direction or tendency and display a variety of sources. Some have an allover, Pollock-like articulation; others a landscape feeling reminiscent of Frankenthaler; and, in a few, one may detect the influence of Still or of Sam Francis. But the strongest influence, or at least the one that occurs most often in these pictures, is that of Morris Louis.[10] Most of all Noland was looking for a new and personal way to apply paint to canvas—now it is put on thickly with the brush or fingers, now poured or stained in thin washes. Other possibilities were tried as well. Never before has the making of abstract painting been approached in quite such an open, freewheeling way as we find in these early pictures by Noland. There is no beginning subject matter drawn from nature, no favored vocabulary of forms as a preferred way of working. Like Louis and even more than Pollock, Noland gave himself completely to interacting with his materials and the processes of painting—relying on these alone for a personal style.

32. Untitled. c. 1955. Oil on canvas, 30 x 60″. Collection, Christa and Harry Noland, Reston,

The new attitude is by no means only a way to find an original style. It is also a way to remain original. After finding his personal style, Noland has continued to seek to organize himself so as to "act" creatively. He forces himself to improvise, to invent. Take his use of color, for instance. Occasionally Noland makes a small color sketch for a picture, but this is rare, and he never makes drawings as such. "I'd rather work directly in the actual size and actual materials that will be the result of what I'm doing."[11]

Usually he chooses the colors one after the other, improvising, letting the first suggest the second, the first two the third, and so on. "You can be fairly arbitrary about at what point you start."[12] The colors begin to suggest a logic of their own. As Noland puts it, "I pick a color and go with it."[13] It is the same with the sizes and proportions of the bands: "You can take any given size and let that size set the conditions for other proportions . . . so it's not as if you have to plan it out. You're already in it, if you are in it."[14] He deliberately tries to avoid set ways of working or forming habits and expectations. "I try very much not to determine what I might paint on any given day, whether light or dark or, for instance, warm or cool. I want the picture to come out of the experience."[15]

His technique also helps him to maintain spontaneity. Staining makes it difficult for him to paint over a color. ". . . it's very difficult. And I fail at it more often than I succeed because I've changed the texture of the color . . . and that extra density of a second application of paint will throw the tactile balance out of whack. . . . it gets too shiny, or too matte, or too rough. And then it will jump out of the balance that I have made."[16] This characteristic of staining led to what Noland has called "one-shot paintings."[17] "My idea is to make my paintings directly. I almost never paint over. That's my concept. It maintains the attention of the picture for me, my contact with what I am doing. Usually I throw away what I don't get right the first time."[18]

In addition to not preplanning the picture and not reworking it, Noland always looks for ways to refine his technique so as to work more simply and therefore more quickly and spontaneously. "Actually, since I want to get at color . . . I believe in working quickly and getting as simple a way of working as possible in order to put into practice . . . the

33. Untitled. 1956. Oil on canvas, 5 x 5'. Collection, the artist

making of pictures. So any way... I can figure out to do the work as easily as possible, to do more work, to get at the use of color, the use of materials the more I do it."[19]

In 1967 when he was working on the horizontal-band pictures, Noland sometimes used assistants actually to paint some of the bands. When the bands were even and undifferentiated, there was no need to work with his own hands since edge was defined by masking tape. Irregularities automatically created by the stained edges acted as "sensibility" (i.e., provided subtle variations and life, which avoided a static, rigid feeling). All of the inspiration, all of the feeling and invention were concentrated in Noland's color choices. To exploit this advantage and to force improvisation at this point he had to organize his working procedures so as to be able to make his choices as spontaneously as possible. Assistants helped here. They permitted him to work more quickly, more prolifically, and on several pictures at once. Like Pollock's dripping or working on the floor, it was another of those unorthodox, even outrageous, devices the discovery and exploitation of which are part of the creativity of abstract painting today. The use of assistants actually to paint parts of the picture is a simplification of technique that paradoxically permitted Noland to work more directly with the materials, to keep in contact with the painting. At this point, having to stop to spread carefully an even coat of paint for each band would only have slowed him down, in the same manner that cleaning brushes or rolling out canvas would have done.[20] From this point of view, the use of assistants is part of what I have called the demythologizing and radicalization of action painting.

Still another possibility that became available to Noland in the horizontal-band pictures was to paint a very large canvas and then to crop it into several smaller pictures. This was a reversal of traditional painting procedure in which the decision about the picture's format was the first one that every artist made—and it determined everything else. Now this choice was put off until last, and the picture's size, shape, and proportions became open variables. And after a picture is stretched, Noland has always been willing to hang it upside down or on its side if he feels it works better that way.

Noland describes his way of working as a juggling act: "It's based not so much on chance as on... juggling... I mean to handle simultaneously a lot of factors such as opacity of color, transparency of color, tactility, sheer quantity, scale, size. You are dealing with all those things [as if] thrown up in the air... and the final result is where you bring... them all into a certain accordance of size, shape, coolness, warmth, density, transparency.... If the painting fails, usually it fails on the basis of some color being too thin or too thick or too wide or too narrow, or the texture of the paint being wrong..."[21]

These words of Noland describe his approach to working with color once he already has a format or layout. A set layout, such as the target motif, the chevron motif, or the diamond, permits him to work in series. It is another means to work simply and quickly. It is what Noland calls planning "the conditions for color ahead.... I mean you can get together all the frame of reference(s) that will get you into the condition of using color in relation to shape, to size, to focus, to depth, to tactility."[22]

But naturally a layout or format can also become an assumption, an a priori. I think this was the case to a certain extent with such artists as Newman, Rothko, and Gottlieb. Each conceived of his characteristic configuration more or less as an image or a symbol that referred to some metaphysical or semimetaphysical meaning. For this reason it was harder for them to change their image. For Noland and Louis a configuration is simply a "layout," a motif to be altered or disregarded as soon as it has been fully exploited and ceased to challenge. "...the thing that bothered me about the Abstract Expressionists... was the fact that [these] painters had usually gotten set in [a] way of working. Morris and I talked about that. We figured that the best way to arrive at some kind of way of making art that was more personal was to get into a process of changing. We found that this was... different from Rothko and Clyfford Still, for example, because they arrived at one way of making paintings which they kept doing. So that was a lesson we learned from Abstract Expressionism:... we... learned... not just to [change] from one picture to another picture, but the necessity... at some point [to]... throw... everything into question... going back... to just rehandl(ing) the materials again."[23]

Here is the same conscious effort to avoid preconceptions or assumptions or habits, anything mechanical or uncreative, anything that will prevent Noland from remaining in contact with the materials. It is a "positivistic" attitude free of that posturing and murky references to meaning so characteristic of the public statements of the Abstract Expressionists. And given this matter-of-fact, workmanlike approach, open and experimental, it is not surprising that Noland's development is far more varied and complex than that of any of the Abstract Expressionists. His different motifs—the targets, the chevrons, the diamonds, the plaids, the horizontal-band pictures—each is the kind of layout with which many abstract painters built an entire career.

Of a piece with his willingness to change is Noland's intense self-criticism. Noland puts great value on studying, comparing, and evaluating his pictures. Talking about showing regularly he has said, "It . . . [is a] . . . tremendous kind of feedback. . . . By seeing your work in a one-man show you get to know that there are certain things that you're probably finished with; you can recognize that; or you can recognize that there are things that you want to push further. . . . So it's a good distancing means for your work."[24] Of course any serious artist has to distance his work in this way. What is new is the degree of self-criticism that Noland demands of himself and the way that he views it as part of the creative process. Anyone who has visited his studio knows how remarkably searching, open, and unprecious he is about his paintings. In the same way as working quickly and prolifically, constant self-criticism keeps the creative situation fluid, and in process. It keeps the pressure on, and it keeps his art moving, developing.

It is to Noland's development that I now turn. In large part it, too, will be a discussion of his attitudes, procedures, and the ways in which he deals with his subject matter.[25]

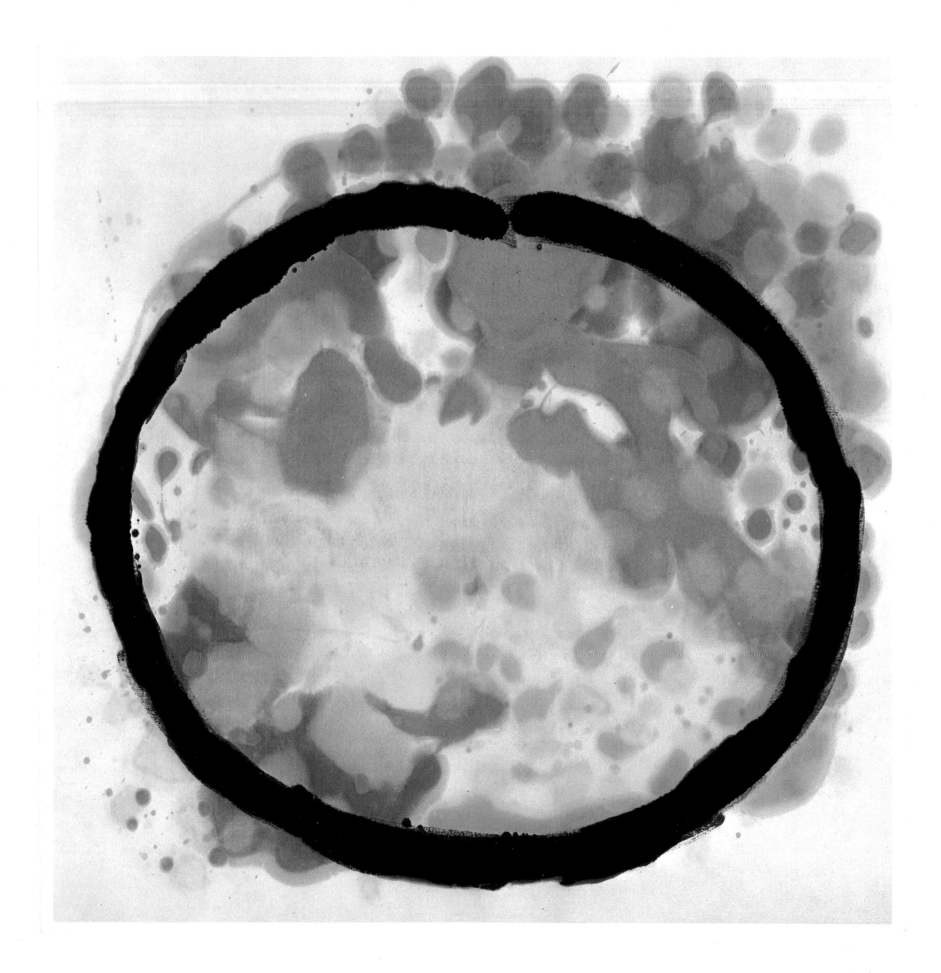

FOUR

Matisse once wrote, "I found myself, or my artistic personality, by considering my early works. I discovered in them something constant which I took at first for monstrous repetition."[1] Noland, too, found himself by isolating his own personal "monotony." This turned out to be a tendency to organize incident around the center of the picture, an unconscious impulse toward symmetry. And it was by emphasizing symmetry that Noland gained his own access to Pollock and released his own feelings for color.

Gradually, swirls of paint begin to orbit the center of the picture, or an even painterly attack is encircled by a wide band of color that flattens or pushes outward the area of looser handling. The key picture from the mid-1950s is *Globe*, 1956 (plate 34), in which thin washes of stained color are partly contained within a large centered black circle; the format is a square, and broad areas of the canvas are left unpainted. This work is clearly an attempt to combine the soft, airy, atmospheric color of Frankenthaler with the holistic impact and directness of Pollock's allover paintings.[2] Between 1957 and 1958, painterliness is gradually suppressed in favor of hardedged and more strictly centered motifs: discs, cruciform patterns, or lozenge shapes.

Pollock worked over or "in" his canvas, which had been rolled out upon the floor, a procedure that freed his drawing by enabling him to ignore the tyranny of the enclosing shape. And he would often see to it that the main incident did not quite attain the edges of the canvas, thereby giving to his images simultaneously the feeling of expansion and containedness; the continuous fabric of woven paint skeins could be grasped synoptically as an expanding whole. It is this expanding wholeness that possesses the entire surface and renders it evenly and continuously assertive that Noland saw in Pollock and that he discovered again in his own centered pictures. "Pollock was my biggest influence. After that allover painting that covers the whole surface, the only thing to do would be to focus from the center out—it is the logical extension—almost an inevitable result."[3] Noland, too, worked on the

34. *Globe*. 1956. Magna on canvas, 5 x 5'. Collection, Cornelia Langer Noland, Washington, D.C.

49

floor. He has said that by walking in circles around the periphery of his canvas he "discovered" the center. And by organizing a series of concentric circles outward from the midpoint, he avoided echoing the framing edge and to that extent neutralized it as an enclosing, confining shape; the picture opened outward, expanding from the center. The lack of any concession to gravity also helped Noland to escape the feeling of his picture being a container with shapes or forms within it, and it added to the sense of a *surface* opening outward on the wall.

At the same time, the holistic motif's anchoring to the literalness of the square format by sharing its actual midpoint gained a density and a powerfully focused presence. The Old Masters had usually sought to conceal or displace the actual center of their pictures because they knew that it had a tendency to isolate, to break the illusion. And this effect is even stronger in a square format, which, like strict symmetry, the Old Masters also usually avoided. Here is a case, and there are many such cases in modernist art, where something that was not possible or was problematic for representational painting becomes possible, positive, and for that reason the source of new feeling in abstract painting. The riveting force of the center can be seen in *Tip*, 1961 (plate 35), in which a very small motif generates great intensity and even plasticity without the slightest modeling or impasto.

Probably because they possess no arms that had to come to terms with the picture's edges, Noland's concentric circles far outnumber his crosses, stars, and pinwheels; the circles were more effective in loosening the relationship of color and configuration—they were, to use Noland's own expression, a "self-canceling structure. With structural considerations eliminated I could concentrate on color. I wanted more freedom to exercise the arbitrariness of color."[4] "Structure is an element profoundly to be respected, but, too, an engagement with it leaves one in the backwaters of what are basically cubist concerns. In the best color painting, structure is nowhere evident, or nowhere self-declaring."[5]

There are two senses in which the concentric circles can be called "self-canceling structure." First, they are an a priori general layout, which permitted Noland to work in series varying only the proportions, intervals, and hues. Secondly, their symmetry makes a very untradi-

35. *Tip*. 1961. Acrylic on canvas, 69½ x 69½".
Collection, the artist

tional kind of composition in that the picture does not balance out with hierarchies of dominant and subordinate areas. Hence, even abrupt differences of quantity—the width of the bands—or sharp hue/value changes from, say, black or blue to yellow read primarily as color rather than as compositional emphasis.

However "logical" the discovery of the center may seem in retrospect, it involved a long period of experimentation (almost four years) and courage; the very simplicity of the solution and the fact that the result did not look or feel like previous painting made the acceptance of the center an act of creative imagination, which is why it was simultaneously Noland's "breakthrough," for it freed his particular color sensibility. As Noland said, ". . .the thing is color. . .to find a way to get color down, to float it without bogging the painting down in Surrealism, cubism or systems of structure."[6]

The immediacy of the centered pictures permitted Noland to give up the kind of immediacy that he had previously obtained from painterly, impacted surfaces and to turn completely to staining, to soaking thinned pigment directly into unsized and unprimed cotton duck canvas. Greenberg has described the significance of this: "Colors are leveled down as it were, to become identified with the raw cotton surface as much as the bareness is. The effect conveys a sense not only of color as somehow disembodied, and therefore more purely optical, but also of color as the thing that opens and expands the picture plane. The suppression of the difference between painted and unpainted surfaces causes pictorial space to leak through—or rather to seem to leak through—the framing edges of the picture into the space beyond them."[7] Greenberg continued: "Noland. . .usually leaves much more of the surface unpainted, seldom going so far even as to whiten it with gesso. The naked fabric acts as a generalizing and unifying field; and at the same time its confessed wovenness and porousness suggests a penetrable, ambiguous plane, opening the picture from the back, so to speak. And given that Noland uses hard-edged, trued and faired forms, both the bare wovenness and the color-stained wovenness act further to suppress associations with geometrical painting—which implies traditionally a smooth, hard surface."[8]

As I have said, Noland was the first to see that hard edges and geometry tauten the effects of stain while staining in turn softens geometry, preventing it from becoming too rigid and brittle. And the effects of staining now dovetailed with his design: they both served to open the picture and to identify color with surface; raw canvas functions both as its literal self and as a kind of field, a space generating light, air, and atmosphere. "I do open paintings. I like lightness, airiness, and the way color pulsates. The presence of the painting is all that's important."[9]

Perhaps the most radical impact of the circles—especially the later ones—is their feeling of weightlessness, which comes not only from the absence of up or down, right or left, but also from staining itself and the flatness of geometrical design. Giving up the weight and density found in older painting, Noland accepts a certain thinness as positive, as lightness and airiness. This etherealness is very much part of Noland's personal sensibility; it is probably what first drew him to the work of Klee, and along with its potential for color, it is what interested him in the stain technique. But Noland's etherealness is always toughened by a crisp pictorial logic and by the tenseness of his unities.

In the circles, tension is generated between the evident flatness and riveted status of the circles on the one hand and their pictorial mobility—their revolving, advancing and receding, expanding and contracting—on the other. Symmetry and parallelism add a hypnotic opticality. When the rings are pulled apart leaving raw canvas circles between the positively colored ones, each color becomes more unique measured against a constant that in its turn changes tonally in response to adjacent hues. When the bands are closed, made contiguous, one is confronted with a concentrated, energetic disc spinning in a void.[10]

Once Noland said that there are two aspects of his work, the "general" and the "specific."[11] The general is what I have tried to describe: it is what allows Noland to work in series, a format that *permits* color to declare itself, to become structural, to have presence, to open up, to coalesce. Working out of such a format is certainly a creative act, yet it is the specific choices—the proportions, the intervals, and, above all, the hues—that fulfill this conception. Any given picture, of course, depends for its success or failure, for its unique feeling and expression, primarily on the specific.

The early Targets, those from 1958–60, often have a trail of freehand brushing as the outermost ring. Rendered in stain, without impasto, this ring seems like a shadow of a gesture or like color energy thrown off by centrifugal motion; it heightens the drama, wholeness, and almost plastic definition of the motif. Abstract Expressionist in derivation, this ring has a depicted and therefore illusionistic character, and it sets off the circles as a single configuration, a single thing. In 1961, Noland eliminated it in the interest of greater abstractness, that is, greater identification of the motif with the support. At the same time (1961–62), he started to make the ring configuration fill more of the square surface, and he now left wide areas of raw canvas between the rings, which became narrower and more even in width. Such 1961 paintings as *Sunshine* (plate 37), *Inner Way, Reverberation* (plate 114), and *Turnsole* (plate 81) exhibit these changes. Less like a target and more like a group of individual rings, the motif now locks with the ground like a stencil pattern, and the noncontiguous circles of color advance or recede more freely. Perhaps these later Targets are less intensely and tremulously expressive than the earlier circles, although they have a distinct feeling of their own: airy, elastic, and buoyant. The center dot or "eye" with its tendency to isolate—and which in the earlier Targets often had a diameter equal to or exceeding the width of the rings—is now smaller, more compact; tensely balled, it seems to be sending color pulses across the surface.

If one of Noland's objectives at this point was to effect an identification of image and support—the direction in which he seemed to be moving after 1958—then he was bound to be somewhat frustrated as long as he worked with round edges in a rectangular format. Neutral areas and thus a certain depicted illusionistic impression were bound to result. So the corners of the circles are at least incipiently more "neutral" than the raw canvas left between the rings. To achieve greater evenness of surface, greater abstract presence, he had essentially two options: either to alter the motif or to make the support itself curvilinear.

In 1961, Noland executed several tondos or concentric circle pictures with the corners eliminated. But, although several of these works are striking, I think the tondo raised more problems for him than it

36. *Plunge*. 1958. Oil on canvas, 70 x 71". Whereabouts unknown

37. *Sunshine*. 1961. Oil on canvas, 7 x 7'.
Collection, Dr. and Mrs. Jack M. Farris, Solano Beach, California

52

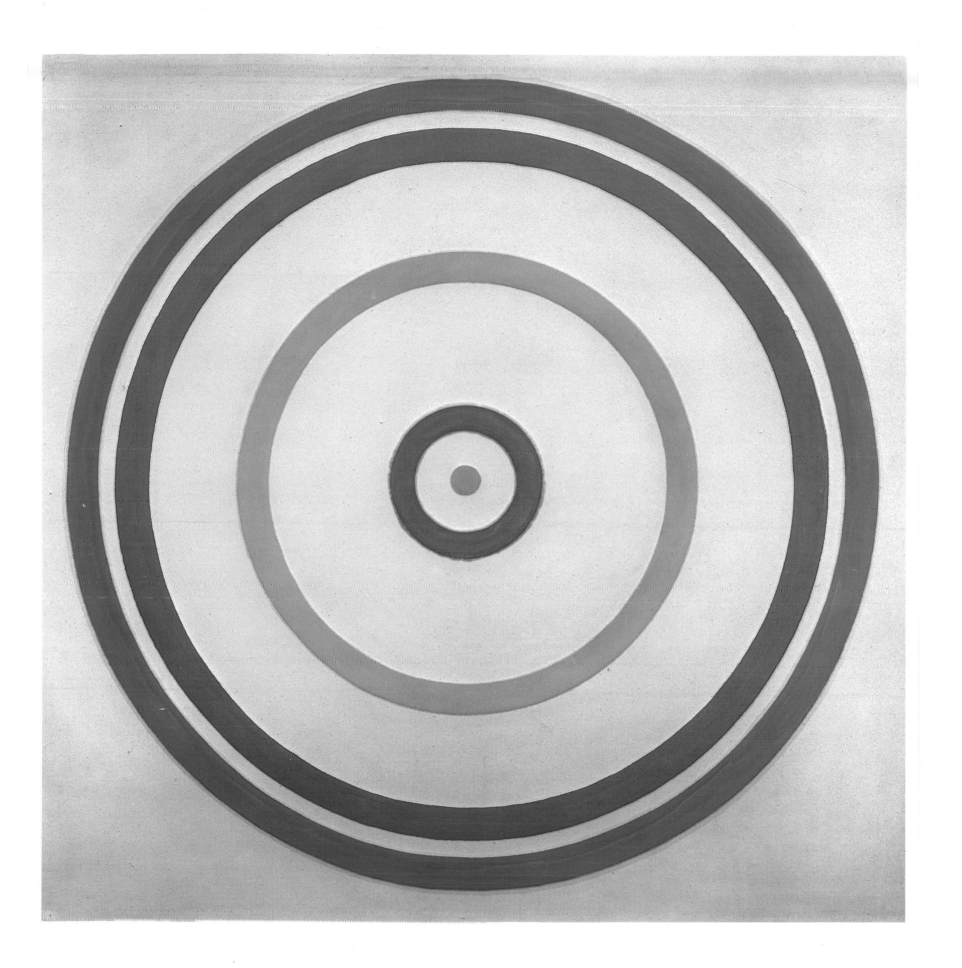

38. Robert Delaunay, *Disc*. 1912.
Oil on canvas, 53″ in diameter.
Collection, Mr. and Mrs. Burton Tremaine,
Meriden, Connecticut

39. *Tondo*. 1958–59. Oil on canvas, 50 x 50′.
Collection, Mr. and Mrs. Joseph Slifka, New York, New York

solved. Originally, the square support of the concentric circles functioned to give horizontal-vertical stability to the picture without confining or enclosing the whole. A tondo, however, when not stabilized by the internal articulation, seems uncontrolled; it appears to spin off the wall in an arbitrary way.[12] So, too, a completely concentric colored picture—as can be seen in the concentric square paintings of Albers and Stella—can be disturbingly constrictive to the eye, closing off color or locking it in. Noland once remarked that the tondo also limited him as to the extension of color—the ability to vary the width of his bands.

Unlike his contemporaries, but like Noland, Robert Delaunay was mainly interested in color, and, again like Noland, Delaunay was drawn to the symmetry and the expansiveness of circular forms as somehow an especially congenial vehicle for color. As far as I can determine, Delaunay only did one tondo, although he often used a concentric circle motif. If we look at this picture (plate 38), done in 1912 and one of the earliest nonobjective paintings, we can see that he felt compelled to sacrifice the autonomy of color rings to the stability of

the tondo. The in-and-out cubist space; the rather dense, "handmade" way that it is painted; the lack of any control of values, as well as the multiplicity of hues—all undermine his ambition to paint a pure color picture. The "simultaneity"(to use the term that was so popular at the time) developed by Picasso and Braque was a simultaneity of views, forms, planes; it was in direct contradiction to the "simultaneous contrasts" of color that Delaunay envisaged, but that Noland achieved only by going beyond cubism.

In terms of color, Delaunay always remained in the Impressionist tradition that conceived of color as generative of light. He shades and models with it à la Cézanne, and tends systematically to set complementaries, or warm and cool, in opposition. Noland does not think of color in terms of light, or the theory of complementaries or optical mixture or the color wheel.[13] His approach is not theoretical and ideal, but strictly empirical, intuitive, and open. In this he is far closer to Matisse than Delaunay.

A contemporary of Noland, Frank Stella, has also painted tondos as part of his Protractor series. In the version illustrated here (plate 40),

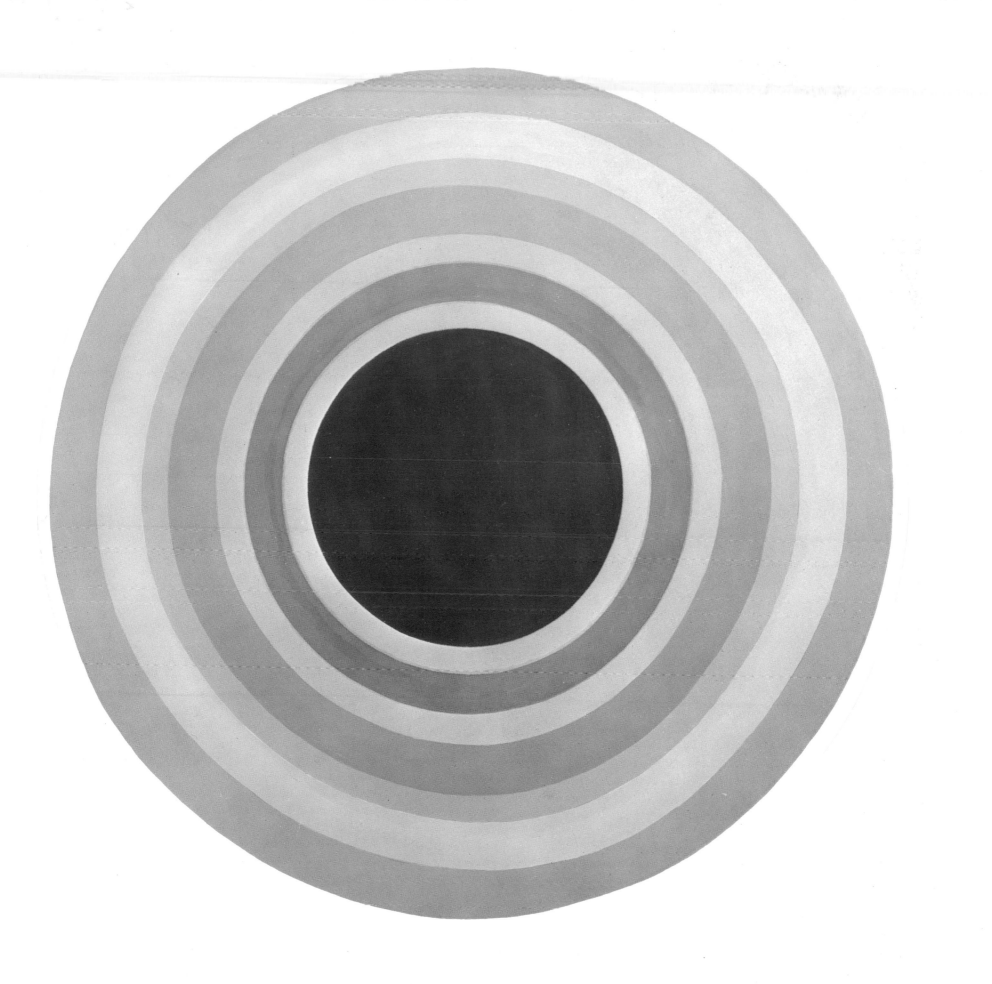

stability results from superimposing an illusionistically suggestive X-form over the concentric rings. In this picture, Stella creates a locked system, at once graphic and sculptural in character, in which color, for all its clarity, multiplicity, and aggressiveness plays a secondary role. (As anyone who has worked with color knows, it is not merely a question of brightness or colorfulness. The creation of *relationships* between colors is what really counts and what demands invention and sensitivity. Here is where a true colorist's feelings are invested.) As in Delaunay's case, Stella's design, although not precluding success with color, makes this more difficult and, if its constraints are accepted— which Stella does not—limits chromatic range.

Noland works in series as regards both format and color; within a single format he often explores one group of related hues and then moves to another. A change occurs when he finds himself acting uncreatively, as it were, failing to surprise himself with color. "You are involved with someone as long as something **is d**eveloping, changing or insightful. Painting is the same way."[14] And the same sort of consideration is most often behind a change of layout: he decides that, in a larger sense, color possibilities have become predictable.[15] Noland is one of the most inventive colorists in all of modern art—perhaps one should dare to say in the history of art—and the need to give his color full expression is the main impetus behind his development. He is most at home working comfortably with a flexible layout (like the Targets) that gives free play to his remarkable gift for chromatic invention. But the periods between compositional solutions when he is searching for a new format are often extremely painful and arduous. Sometimes, as in the tondos, or later, in 1964, in the square diamonds, he comes upon a layout that is more structural in emphasis, which inhibits color or does not offer many possibilities for color. These can be very successful, remarkable in their pictorial logic, but Noland does not stay with them very long. Yet they can lead to something more fruitful (for example, the square diamonds led to the needle diamonds, as we shall see). Sometimes too, Noland simply finds himself in a dead end or temporarily without direction, but it is his willingness to keep pushing his art, to keep challenging himself, and to tolerate the pain and chaos that this pushing necessarily involves that makes him the great artist he is.

40. Frank Stella, *Sinjerli II.* 1967.
Polymer and fluorescent polymer on canvas, 10′ in diameter.
Collection, Mr. and Mrs. S. Brooks Barron, Detroit, Michigan

And this willingness to radically change his art is, as I have noted earlier, of a piece with the new attitude toward abstract painting, the new subject. More specifically, to evolve a new layout, Noland usually concentrates on the limitations or restrictions of the composition he is currently working with. As he has said, "a breakthrough also means a limitation, a reduction of possibilities."[16] That is, however successful a solution, let us say the Targets, can always be subjected to new criticism. So, for example, a certain design may inhibit him as to the kind of color combination he can use; he may be unable to abut colors or combine opaque with transparent hues or vary the area size of his colors; sometimes he feels restricted to a certain canvas size or shape. Limitations such as these suggest different directions in which to move. Some of these prove fruitful, some do not. In retrospect, his development can appear more strictly linear than it was, and at any given point during one of these transitional periods—and some are much longer than others—Noland usually works with several different problems at once. There are often false starts, failures, and destroyed or discarded canvases.

All art, at least all serious art, depends to a great extent on compromise and subordination. Everything is not possible at the same time. Any style or mode, therefore, necessarily entails certain limitations and restrictions. Noland concentrates on these limitations and restrictions, makes an issue of them, sees them as a "problem." In one sense, this is a desire to keep his choices as open and as free as possible—to have maximum range—but even more important, it is what he paints about, his subject matter, and, as such, it keeps his art developing. Problems stimulate him by prompting him to find new "solutions," which, of course, then have their limitations.

If all of this sounds rather hermetically *l'art pour l'art*, it is not the static and ahistorical *l'art pour l'art* dreamed of by Whistler and the nineteenth-century aesthetes. Even Mondrian's approach had this static character because he felt he had isolated the reducible elements of painting—or vision—which then could be varied ad infinitum. Far more radical and open in this regard, Noland conceives of painting as self-criticism, as an open-ended series of linked problems and solutions. We might then want to call this an innovative and self-critical

l'art pour l'art, a modern response to our modern situation. Unlike cultures of the past, modern society does not set the artist problems or challenge him with tasks. If art is to keep developing, if the painter is to remain inventive in a thoroughgoing way, he must find both his own challenge and his own reponse, his own problems and his own solutions.

This approach to picture making has been implied in modernist art since Manet and is especially clear in the development of cubism and in early Mondrian. But until recently it was not the *sole* premise of picture making, and therefore it was not sustained and not fully self-conscious as such. Only with Noland's generation and within that generation, most purely in Noland's case, did this become true.

Noland's development, then, is self-contained and continuous in a dialectical sense; his "moves" have been determined by problems encountered in the actual process of painting, and only rarely by outside influences, and never by a priori considerations. All this is part of the new attitude toward making pictures. It demands a lucid and critical pictorial intelligence, an alertness and openness, plus a conscious effort to fight complacency.

What, then are the limitations of the Targets? I have already mentioned that the target motif left the surrounding areas more neutral. Also it can easily be seen that the Targets restricted Noland both as to the shape and size of his format; to preserve that centrality, these pictures had to be square, and if carried to a very large scale, they began to appear giantlike. Another restriction had to do with color itself. Large areas of bare canvas usually push a picture toward brilliance and coolness, whereas Noland sometimes wanted to be able to achieve a darker, warmer, and more glowing color statement. So, in certain pictures after the end of 1961, he began painting in the sides and corners or "leftover" neutral areas. To avoid an inert, filled-in design look, Noland occasionally reversed his previous procedure and covered the neutral areas with positive color while leaving the rings negative— raw canvas. But more usually he would close-value his colors or repeat the field color within the target to give the whole a readier pictorial unity.

Begun in 1962, the Cat's Eye pictures show an oval enclosing a repeated oval or circle that replaces the concentric rings.[17] One way to see the relationships of these pictures to the concentric circles that preceded them is to say that temporarily giving up his ambition to unite figure with ground, which had been the impulse behind the tondos (there were only a few of these, in any event), in the Cat's Eyes Noland wanted to make their relationship less a given one—something more active, dynamic. And he did this by dividing the center, as it were, differentiating between the horizontal and vertical axis of the picture. Pulled out along its horizontal axis, the motif is squeezed along its vertical axis.[18] If this makes the relationship between the motif and the support, incipiently at least, more a figure-ground one, it also makes it more actively reciprocal. And this means that Noland could now depart from the square and employ horizontally or vertically oriented supports. In the latter case, the "cat's eye," while maintaining lateral symmetry, was often moved above the vertical center as if to compensate for its horizontal extension and the now implied weight it took on as a more drawn, tactile entity.

Nonetheless, at this point, the more reciprocal relationship between figure and ground, effected by the use of the vertical axis as the main coordinate of organization, was less important in making available a wide range of formats than in allowing a new kind of color. The more active role of the fields invited Noland to treat them as a saturated expanse of prismatic hue. In such pictures as *Matter of Midnight* and *Hover*, it is as if color pressure is put upon the mobile drawing of the oval, which expands, fills, or rises in response—or again the displacement and vibrant hovering of the oval resonates the field color. (The two are related usually by means of a scumbled halo around the oval or a close valuing of the colors.) In any event, the paintings of this type have a very different kind of richness and intensity than the circles.

Begun in late 1962 or the very beginning of 1963, the chevrons are a greater departure from the circles than the Cat's Eyes. They continue the same approach of making the central vertical axis the main organizational coordinate, only now Noland uses straight, rather than curved, edges.[19] But this was not primarily a change of form vocabulary. It was a different way to relate parallel bands to the literal coordinates of the support, namely to the central axis, rather than the center

point. Straight-edged forms and a sharp-pointed configuration were the result. Noland does not think in terms of forms or shapes. He does not think graphically in terms of profile drawing. As regards layout, he is concerned to relate color to support.

So the central axis meant straight-edged bands, and in some of the early, more transitional examples, such as *Cadmium Radiance* (plate 41) or *Tripex* (plate 127), both 1963, the picture is developed formwise from the center axis. Emphatically dividing the picture down the middle, however, made it difficult to employ other than symmetrical color arrangements. A better system proved to be a series of parallel chevrons whose angles met along the center axis. This was more like the concentric arrangement of the circles and Cat's Eyes in that now symmetry encouraged rather than inhibited freedom of color choice.

Perhaps it was such a picture as *Cadmium Radiance* that suggested to Noland the possibility of stressing the midpoint of the bottom edge—anchoring there the bottom tip of his series of chevrons.[20] As pictorial edge or point touches literal edge, the whole motif is thrust forward. Here we have another of those effects available to the abstract painter that is denied to the representational painter. In the context of representational art, such a conjunction would too emphatically and abruptly call attention to the surface and consequently break the continuity of the illusion. Here it seems to snap out the motif and give it a dense force of presence.

In any event this layout had the disadvantage that the bands that occurred in the lower corners seemed to be cut by the frame in a way that the upper ones were not. They appeared to fall away from the rest, and although this could be compensated for by color, the need to do so seemed a limitation. Another possibility was to leave the lower areas bare while making the arms of the bottommost chevron, which was fixed at the midpoint of the lower edge, exactly bisect the upper corners. This had as a consequence an even greater flatness, an even greater identification of image and surface, for now the chevrons were even more explicitly tied to the picture's physical limits. Still another feature of these pictures is a new openness, since partly under the influence of Louis' Unfurleds, Noland here had used diagonal lines to release the picture at the top. No internal edge echoes or repeats the

41. *Cadmium Radiance*. 1963. Oil on canvas, 93½ x 95", Harry N. Abrams Family Collection, New York, New York

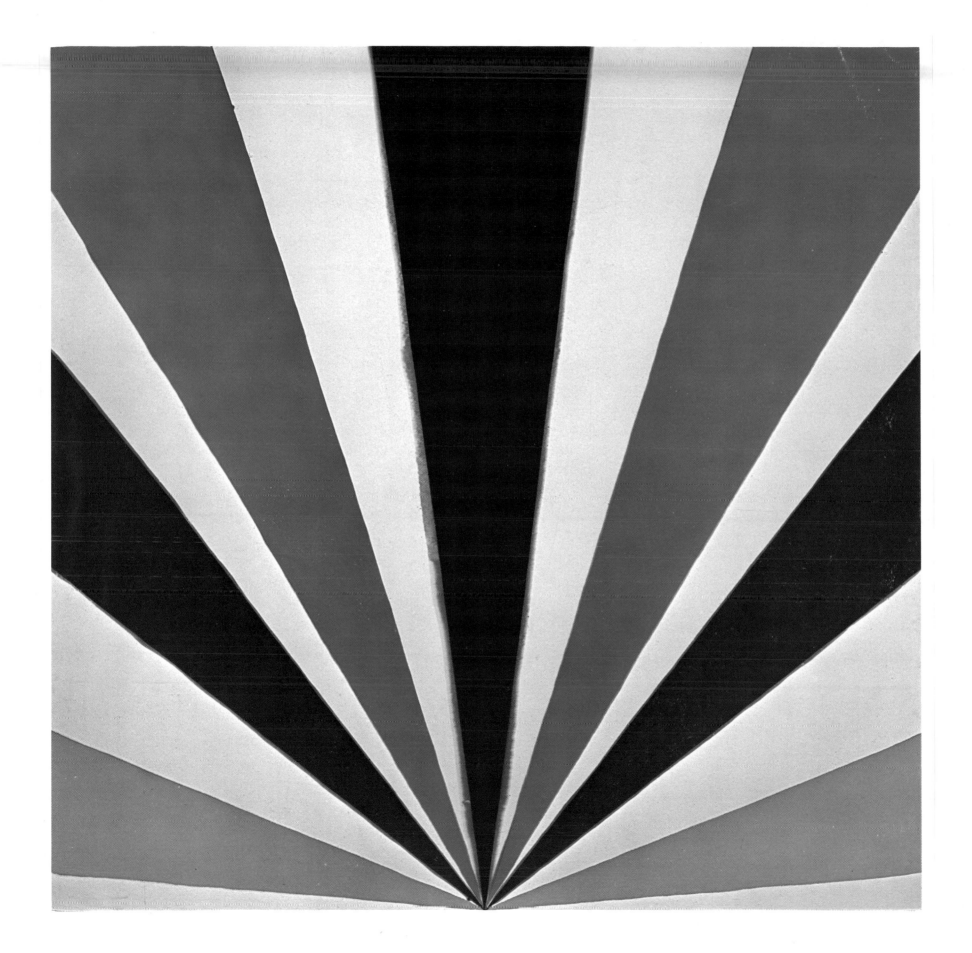

defining edges of the support; the bands seem cut from some larger and expanding chevron shape that, at the same time, is clearly delimited by interlocking with the picture's literalness. And so reciprocal is the interlocking that each expands laterally or vertically in response to the other. Thus Noland obtained a more flexible format and was no longer limited to the square.

Despite these advantages, the early chevrons, tied at three points to the picture's perimeter, could appear rigid and static, a bit over-structured—an effect that Noland tried to mitigate somewhat by raising the chevrons and letting the lowermost point swing free of the bottom edge. But this made the lower part of the picture, the area below the bottommost chevron, seem even more passive or neutral. As I have already noted, even in the earliest chevrons the two lower corners had only a secondary, simply triangular relation to the chevrons and could look spatial in an unspecified way.

In 1964, Noland created his eccentric or asymmetrical chevrons by swinging the whole motif offcenter and to one side.[21] This was very much like what he had done in the Cat's Eye pictures; a previously neutral area is made a responsive participant, thereby undermining a static figure-ground reading and giving greater unity to the surface. However, some of the larger centered chevrons fail due to too broad and unactivated areas of raw canvas. Also, the eccentric chevrons escaped all rigidity and sense of closure or containedness for their asymmetry eliminated that residual subordination to the lateral edges that biaxial symmetry still implied. The central axis was given up and pictorial logic is enforced solely by having the arms of the lowermost chevron bisect the upper corners. By twisting the whole painted image away from symmetry, Noland achieves a dramatic imbalance without reverting to a traditional, balancing-out type of composition. I noted earlier how alloverness challenged the identity of the easel picture; the same of course is true of symmetry. Noland gets drama into his symmetrical pictures by means of color; indeed, this is exactly the point of his symmetry—color becomes the life-giving variable. But the eccentric chevrons gain an added compositional drama and life without giving up any of the advantages of symmetry. It is generally agreed, I think, that these are among Noland's most original pictures. But they

42. Piet Mondrian, *Lozenge in Red, Yellow, and Blue*. c. 1926. Oil on canvas, 40 x 40". National Gallery of Art, Washington, D.C. Gift of Herbert and Nannette Rothschild

also reaffirm his continuous commitment to the easel tradition. And they make another point as well; I want to stress again how abstract painting, however much it gives up in the process, discovers new feelings and new expressions that were not available to older representational painting. In fact, what it gives up is a *precondition* of winning these new feelings for pictorial art. So, for example, total abstraction permitted Morris Louis in his Unfurleds to create a dramatically new feeling by emptying the center, exactly that area that in older art was the locus of meaning and importance.[22] His distinct kind of abstraction and weightlessness allows Noland here to invert the triangle, the hallmark of classical ordering and composition. I find the new feelings that this delivers difficult to characterize in words. But they certainly seem to be the very opposite of those traditionally associated with the triangle: weight, gravity, solidity, closure, repose.

The best of the asymmetrical chevrons are, I think, the square or vertical canvases, such as *Air, 17th Stage* (plate 136), *Bridge* (plate 137), *Sarah's Reach* (plate 133), and *Blue Plus Eight* (all 1964), in which enormous tension builds up between an implied spatial twist and utter flatness. At times the motif has a presence, an explicitness that makes it almost seem to lift off the surface, as if it had more force than the literal edge of the picture itself. And Noland often emphasized this by employing darker, abutted, or complementary hues at full intensity, blue and yellow, or orange, green, and red. As with the early circles, the chevrons often show a slightly tremulous irregularity of edge—here left by the roller. But the negative side of this greater immediacy was a pulling away of figure from ground that prevented Noland from covering the entire surface. Again, a felt limitation led to self-criticism and change; and again he was faced with essentially two options. He could alter his image to make it coincide with the rectilinear support, or he could change the shape of the support to make it coincide with the chevrons. The former possibility led eventually to the horizontal-stripe series, which Noland started in late 1965.

The other possibility, identifying the support with the chevrons, resulted in diamond-shaped pictures, which he began in 1963. He wanted to keep the immediacy of the chevrons as well as the tension and imbalance characteristic of the later eccentric chevrons (an asymmetric inside set against a regular support) but suppress all figure-ground relationships. A diamond or lozenge bears the same relation to the diagonal or chevron as a tondo bears to the circle: the motif and the surface can exactly coincide. Yet since the chevrons were not perfectly concentric and since a diamond automatically establishes horizontal-vertical axes, Noland did not encounter here the problems inherent in the tondos.[24]

The early diamond pictures, such as *Go* and *One Way*, are merely squares turned on end, like the diamonds that Mondrian had often employed after 1918. By then, Mondrian had already extended his horizontal and vertical lines to the edges and thereby flattened and opened up the cubist grid; the picture looked like a cutout from a continuous larger whole, and delimitedness, the frame, was, as it were, moved inside the picture. His lines now repeated rather than merely echoed the edges and thereby took on a force equal to or even greater than the literal edges. In this way the latter were deprived of their capacity to enclose. The whole seemed like a cut from some larger whole. By using a lozenge, Mondrian was going further in this same direction, giving greater independence to his lines—the horizontal and vertical—and escaping a sense of closure. No longer repeating the edges, the lines were now merely cut by them. This has to do with the fact that the diamond calls more attention to itself as a literal, cutout, whole *shape* while the perimeters of the more neutral rectangle act more like containing or continuing *edges*. Yet the open or noncontaining aspects of Mondrian's diamonds are of a traditional, illusionistic kind; that is, there is a strong behind-the-frame feeling. He thought of the outside of his picture as framing and therefore merely *opposed* to the inside, the horizontal and vertical. Noland thinks more abstractly, and, characteristically, he *interlocks* the outside and inside. The diamond is used to accommodate not lines but colored bands in chevron formation; these reflect two adjacent sides and are cut by the two others. At once open and delimited, they have no unambiguous, behind-the-frame feeling; they seem to be simultaneously a cutout from a series of larger chevrons marching off in one direction *and* a completely self-sufficient picture object.

But the abstract logic of its structure notwithstanding, the square chevron diamond format was not one of Noland's most successful series and is best seen as an intermediate step in his development. Too much "given," too much a shape, the square forces more involvement with explicit structure than is usually the case in Noland's pictures. Also color choices are severely limited: for instance, it becomes difficult to abut colors, or to cover the entire surface with color, or to vary their area size.[25] At least this is the case when the structural aspect is stressed, as in *Go* and *One Way* (both 1964). Here, too, Noland was virtually forced to arrange the colors according to a continuous value scale. Otherwise, color could be used more freely at the small end of the horizontal axis, leaving the rest bare (as in *Day* and *Halfway*, both 1964). But this, too, did not give color the prominence that is characteristic of Noland's best pictures.

Soon Noland began to broaden the diamond shape, pulling out opposing corners so that they formed acute angles. Just as in the Cat's Eyes and eccentric chevrons he sought an active relationship between motif and field, so here he sought the same active, reciprocal relationships between the inside of the picture and the outside. With this he undermined the a priori independent givenness of the square diamond. So in such pictures as *Dark Sweet Cherry* (plate 162), 1965, and *Strand* and *Ambsace* (plate 163), both 1966, it no longer seems as if the inside is determined by the outside—the feeling one gets with the square diamonds—but the reverse.[26] These pictures expand and spread out upon the wall without that tight restrictiveness of the square chevron diamonds.[27]

Until now, Noland had avoided echoing edges, but in both the concentric circles and the chevrons this had meant a certain depicted feeling, and when colors were abutted there was always the danger of evoking a single, monolithic image. In the diamonds, with their identification of motif and support, there is a new relationship between the literal edges and painted bands; the latter neither escape nor echo the former but merely repeat them. Taken together, the bands decide, constitute the literal shape of the picture; or can seem to do so if the outside is not rigidly square and the bands are larger and few in number. So in addition to greater openness and logic, this layout gives to the individual color bands a uniqueness and a greater presence than

ever before—because their edges now take on the same force and function as the literal edges themselves.[28]

The next group of pictures kept this feature and were an even more original transformation of the diamond format. As I said, the circles and early chevrons limited Noland to a square picture. In 1964 he began to focus on the "problem" of how to do vertically- and horizontally-oriented paintings.[29] Some of the Cat's Eyes and some of the eccentric chevrons are verticals. But only the chevrons offered possibilities for a horizontal picture and the last, 1964 chevrons, works such as *Karma* and *Bend Sinister*, have a long horizontal sweep. *Tropical Zone* (plate 43), a transitional picture also from 1964, shows two opposing stacks of chevrons meeting in the center of a long, horizontal picture.[30] It was only a short step to straightening out the arms of the chevron and thereby identifying the bands with the shape of the support. And so it was that in the winter of 1965–66 Noland painted a series of canvases that showed parallel bands, identical in width, usually arranged in a value sequence. Some of these he stretched as diamonds, some as horizontally-oriented rectangles; hence these pictures have identical measurements (2 x 8') despite their different shape. In both, the stripes *make* or constitute the surface, which is pulled taut by dramatic extension. In the diamond version the bands parallel opposite sides of the diamond rather than, as in the chevron diamonds, adjacent sides.

Throughout 1966 Noland experimented with this scheme, sometimes using a square diamond, sometimes a broader one, but he eventually settled on the original eccentric diamond shape (1:4, usually 2 x 8'). These came to be called the needle diamonds and appear to make a perfect cut from a larger dramatic sweep of diagonal stripes.[31] The bands twist diagonally away from symmetry while the horizontal-vertical axis of the outside enforces balance and equilibrium. As with the eccentric chevrons, dramatic imbalance is achieved without reverting to traditional balancing-out types of compositional choices. Outside is identified with the inside in that the outside seems like the natural limit, the result of the diagonal stripes. Simultaneously, however, there is a tension between the inside, diagonally-arranged bands sometimes value-stepped into perspective (they can appear to be ob-

43. *Tropical Zone*. 1964. Acrylic on canvas, 83 x 212½". Collection, the artist

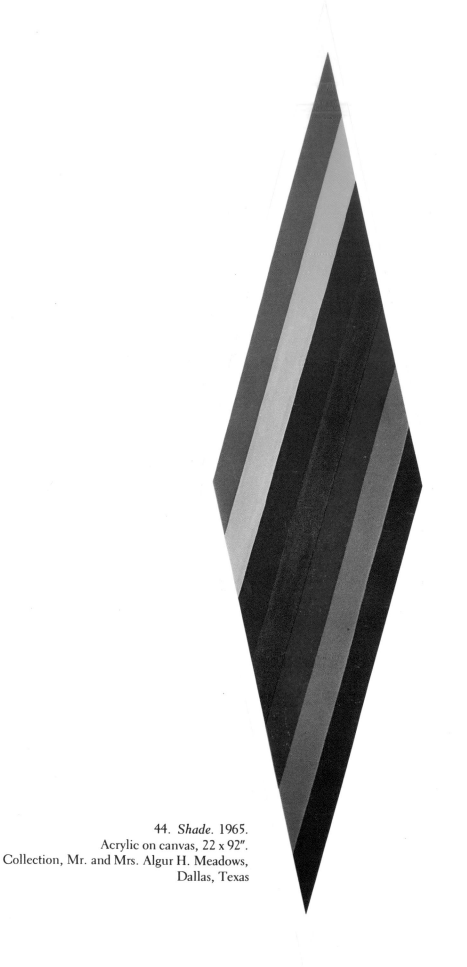

44. *Shade*. 1965.
Acrylic on canvas, 22 x 92″.
Collection, Mr. and Mrs. Algur H. Meadows,
Dallas, Texas

liquely viewed squares), and the outside, the diamond with its symmetry and arrowlike acute angles pulling the inside tautly flat and frontal. This tautening of the surface in turn demands and emphasizes a justness of color intervals unequalled in Noland's art before or since. I have in mind here the value stepping, the inspired adjustment of light and dark intervals or entirely different hues that occurs in many of these pictures. This sustains the taut continuity of surface established by the shape. When first shown in 1966, the needle diamonds disappointed those very critics who until that time had been most excited by Noland's art. Some found their surface area too small to sustain a significant color experience while for others the value stepping "subverted" the exterior shape in a detrimental way. These reactions turn out to be, I believe, a measure of the originality of these pictures. They prove once again how truly innovative art can upset and disturb the expectations of even the most sensitive and sympathetic eyes. Part of the triumph of the eccentric diamonds consists of precisely the fact that such a small area can evoke such a large and expansive virtual space. Since the limits or point-to-point dimensions of the needle diamonds are much larger than their edge-to-edge dimensions, these paintings command far more space on the wall than they actually occupy. But the bands imply extension beyond the frame, and the support itself thrusts sharply outward. Everything about the structure is expansive, but paradoxically this creates a countervailing compression of actual area. The point here is that the smallness of the area and the pressure that it puts on the exterior shape are parts of the expressive tension between inside and outside. And while it is true that color is restricted to a relatively small surface area and by the necessity of keeping to only a few bands usually regular in width (and often arranged in a value sequence), there is a compensation or advantage in that the *presence*, the immediacy of the individual colors, reaches a new pitch. If it can be said that in the square chevron diamonds the outside dominates the inside, and that in the later chevron diamonds the two are more or less in equilibrium, in the needle diamonds the inside, the color bands, has the upper hand and seems to be more dominant. In this they are the culmination of the diamond series and, at least in my view, they constitute, together with the Targets, the eccentric chevrons, and the horizontal-band pictures that followed, Noland's most successful series to date.

Although Noland works with a set layout, I think it is clear by now that the structure of his pictures is not simply a passive receptacle or only enabling in relation to color. Nor is it merely the result of his use of parallel bands. Each format makes color structural in a certain way and has different potentials as regards color. The structure stimulates him to discover and exploit these possibilities. Since Noland does not use a balanced-out type of composition, it is ultimately color that has the dramatic role; interlocking with the design, it unbalances a symmetrical picture, releases it at the top, closes it off, or establishes a directional sequence. Having its own "key" and logic, it interlocks with the logic of the structure, which, in turn, is locked to the support. Finally, and this is very important, being tied by the design to the picture's literalness, the bands—the color—gain a heightened sense of presence, a sense of vivid immediacy. So Noland's concern with figure and ground or interior and exterior is simultaneously the impulse to give color greater life, to force it outward toward the viewer. Even when Noland has evolved a structure in which the range of color possibilities is limited or in which color seems subordinated to structure (which is often true of the diamonds), this vividness keeps color out front, as it were. If one adds to this the fact that a picture, any picture, usually succeeds if its color succeeds—in pictorial art, felt color can justify almost anything—then one can see why Noland, with his extraordinary ability with color, has had at least some success with virtually every format he has used.

Yet if color painting means so devising a pictorial situation that the painter has maximum freedom of color choice—freedom to exploit what Noland calls (somewhat misleadingly) "the arbitrariness of color"—then the horizontal-stripe pictures, begun in 1965, represent his most perfect solution. They are, as he himself has said, "the payoff. . .no graphics, no system, no modules, no shaped canvases. Above all, no thingness, no objectness. The thing is to get that color down to the thinnest conceivable surface, a surface sliced into the air as if by a razor. It's all color and surface, that's all."[32]

The horizontally-oriented format and the diamond format were developed simultaneously, but it was not until late 1967, at the end of the diamond series, that Noland began fully to explore the possibilities of the horizontals.[33] Now the most obvious difference between the two was that the rectangle, even if very long and very narrow, is a less conspicuous shape than a diamond. So tension between the inside and outside was reduced, and Noland was free to use more colors and to vary their area size (i.e., their quantity), and in general he had a potentially larger, more variable surface with which to develop color. Equally important was the fact that the color bands now had a decisive role in determining not only the shape but also the size of the work.

Mondrian opened up the cubist grid by moving the frame inside the picture. By eliminating any reference to the horizontal, Newman went even further than Mondrian in opening up the picture, in making it less involuted and containerlike. The lateral edges were robbed of their capacity to enclose. On the other hand, Newman usually conceived of his bands as narrow entities placed in or on or in front of a field area, and to that extent he still thought of his pictures, for all their openness, as receptacles. With Noland, the bands make the surface, *are* the surface, and, therefore, aside from achieving far greater lateral openness due to Noland's use of horizontal bands, the pictures are flatter and more untraditional. Further, taken in itself, the vertical is, like a human body, more easily comprehensible as an object. This, together with the fact that Newman was more a draftsman than a colorist, pushed him in the direction of sculpture, of realizing his bands in three dimensions. This "graspable" character of the vertical also severely limited him as to the number of colors he could use in a single picture (although Newman did not have much range as a colorist in any event).

Compared to the vertical, the horizontal is far less specific or connotative of objects. One can easily see this at the seashore where the horizon's rim, except where interrupted by a ship, appears to be at no measurable distance from us.[34] It is this ambiguous or allusive character of the horizontal that let Noland create with it an indefinite, unspecifiable space within which color, sheer opticality, can comfortably exist; and, as with Pollock's allover paintings, the lack of internal points of focus encourages the viewer to grasp the picture as a whole.

Given Newman's concept, he could maintain pictorial logic only by placing the bands either at both sides, at one side, or in the center.

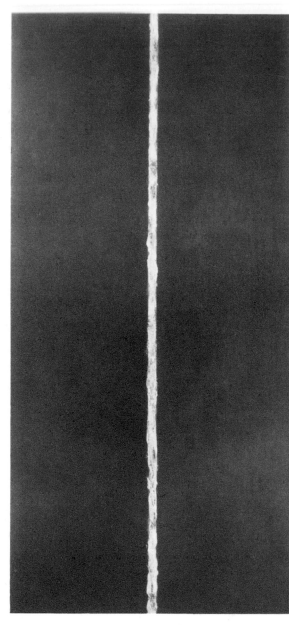

45. Barnett Newman, *Onement #3*. 1949.
Oil on canvas, 72 x 34". Collection,
Mr. and Mrs. Joseph Slifka, New York, New York

Naturally, variations were possible, but these were his main coordinates. Noland's horizontals have their coordinates, too. In general the
surface could be covered with bands more or less evenly (i.e., an allover
effect) or they could occur at the top and the bottom of a larger,
uninterrupted central area. The main advantage compared to Newman
was that Noland could use more colors and more value changes. But by
repeating only one dimension, the horizontal or the vertical, both
artists were able to paint much larger pictures than Mondrian had been
able to paint.[35] Taken together, the works of Noland, Newman, and
Mondrian spell out what a powerful convention the easel picture is.
Not only does it clearly limit our field of vision, but also it does so by
means of the horizontal and vertical, those underlying coordinates with
which we organize the visual field itself. Hanging on the wall, the easel
picture's surface parallels the upright stance of the body. The radical
solutions of these three painters are unthinkable without the entire
Western tradition of the easel picture. Indeed, their radicalness resides
in large measure in their choosing to make pictures solely out of the
barest conventions of this tradition. At the same time, however, there is
a sense in which their explorations of the inherent logic of the easel
picture result in a directness free of distorting cultural influence; that is,
their pictures are at once extreme art historical limits and paradigms of
pure aesthetic vision. This conjunction that is implicit in all abstract
painting becomes most explicit in the work of these three artists. It helps
to explain the persistence of the easel picture as a modernist genre, its
strength and longevity. For despite the frequent predictions and an-
nouncements of its demise, the modernist easel picture continues to
support an extraordinary amount of invention and new feeling, and it is
not fininshed yet.

The real originality of the horizontals—or perhaps, more simply, the
critics' desire to have something new and startling to say—accounts for
some of the inane comments that have been written about them. A few
of these statements, at least, need to be corrected. First, one looks at the
horizontals as one does at any picture in the Western tradition. No
matter how large they are, they never substitute themselves for the wall,
but, as with any easel picture, they distinguish themselves from it.
Similarly, they are meant to be seen as having discrete limits and never

46. Installation view of Noland exhibition at André Emmerich Gallery, New York, New York, 1967

as extending beyond the viewer's field of vision—that is, they are not "environmental," nor does one surrender to their opticality as sheer phenomena. (Those of Noland's pictures that force such effects are failures.) One backs away from them, just as one does from any other picture, in order to see them *whole*. Also, the only relevant way to view these works is from directly in front. (For some critics they invite an oblique viewing.) Second, the horizontals are not "chopped off" by their vertical edges. Because the stripes are not behind the surface, but make the surface, there is no need to acknowledge explicitly the vertical edges. They become merely neutral, determined by an intuitive sense of the capacity of the interior, the color to sustain expansion. Toward the center of the picture the bands have an unfocused free existence, whereas at either end where horizontal meets vertical they become specified, literal, flattened, pulling the eye back across the bands. The real difficulties in the horizontal-band pictures occur at the bottom and especially at the top edges where an arbitrary "framed" effect can result if the proportions are not exactly right. Noland usually accents the uppermost and lowermost bands with marked changes of value or hue that deprive these horizontal edges of their force, insure against loss of intensity at these crucial points, and give the picture a strong sense of internal delimitedness. Most striking about this format is its dramatic sense of extension and openness.[36] Interlocking of painted incident with literal support means that actual length equals aesthetic breadth and sweep. The proportions of the horizontals range from 1:16 to square, and unlike most of Noland's layouts they can become very large without seeming overheavy or gigantic. As Greenberg has pointed out, the large picture has a special importance to the color painter because it can come to occupy so much of the viewer's field that it loses some of its character as a discrete tactile object and thereby becomes much more purely a picture, a strictly visual entity.[37] But the horizontals can also become long and narrow.[38] Above all it is the *range* of format, of color, of feeling that is the most important characteristic of the horizontals.

All things considered, the biggest single problem Noland or any other Fauve-type painter faces is preventing juxtaposed hues of strong intensity from reading as value. As if to dramatize this, Noland pushed the horizontal format to the very limits of hue variation in a series of pictures done in 1967, some of which show as many as thirty different colors and almost as many widths. Some of these pictures have too many unstructured values and seem cut in two, or overoptical, or overspatial; allover evenness and continuity of surface tension are disrupted. But others, such as *Via Blues*, just make it and are dazzling. As if in reaction to these pictures, Noland next began to repeat the same or very similar sequence of colored bands over the entire surface. Another possibility was to key narrow tracks of sharply contrasting hues occurring only along the top and bottom edges of the picture to a broad center area of a single color. Jules Olitski had led the way in this latter kind of field painting when he discovered that abrupt changes of hue and value can be insinuated in at the margins of an allover "field" picture, introducing dramatic inflection without breaking unity and continuity of the surface. But Noland's horizontal-band version of this kind of "field" painting is very much his own. In a way, he was merely pushing to an extreme the Fauve device—common enough in Matisse's work—of dramatically contrasting area size so that a large expanse of a single color quiets and is in turn set off by multiple, small areas of bright, contrasting hues.

Leaving large areas of bare canvas is one way that the stain painter can strengthen the identification of color and canvas fabric. When fully covered with a single, positive color, this identity—and thus the textural or tactile unity of the whole surface—is less strongly felt, and this is especially true when the surface is large. So it was that at this time, when working with the broad centered horizontals, Noland began to experiment more with various tactile effects; for example, teasing and scrubbing his broad center field in order to get a rich, velvety, suedelike texture. For the first time variation and inflection began to appear within his color areas. Only tentative at first, this direction eventually led to something new—soft, painterly color and mottled hues. Although in some of the wide-band pictures the central area becomes a solid block of glowing color, in others it seems transparent or a powdery pastel that is stiffened, made taut or crisp by the bands at the margins; then the atmospheric scumblings and bleedings of "gorgeous" hues make their appearance. These pictures have about them a sense of release, even indulgence; they show a freedom and confidence that

47. Jules Olitski, *Seventh Loosha*. 1970.
Oil on canvas, 107½ x 78″.
Private collection,
New York, New York

belong to a major artist working at the height of his powers. And they reveal a sensuality not present before in Noland's work.

Stapling his canvas to the floor, Noland painted in the field and then added a sequence of stripes at the top and bottom. After a period of gestation, the picture was marked for stretching; some of the bands at the top and bottom were usually eliminated, and the exact dimensions were determined. Again, it is the immanent capacity of colors to sustain extension without exhausting their particular intensity or their ability to constitute a convincing whole that dictates where Noland crops his pictures. Matisse said that his way of working was so closely tied to his expression that he could only conceive in relation to a surface of specific size and shape.[39] But however revolutionary, the outside of Matisse's pictures still determine the inside, the conception. In Noland's horizontals, the outside of the picture, its size and shape, is not a cause, only a result. Choices about it are made last and solely on the basis of the "inside," the colors; that is, the inside of the picture determines the outside, again an approach pioneered by Olitski, but inherent in an open, abstract painting.

Louis, of course, had painted stripe pictures, and, while in the hospital just before his death in 1962, he had designated that a few of

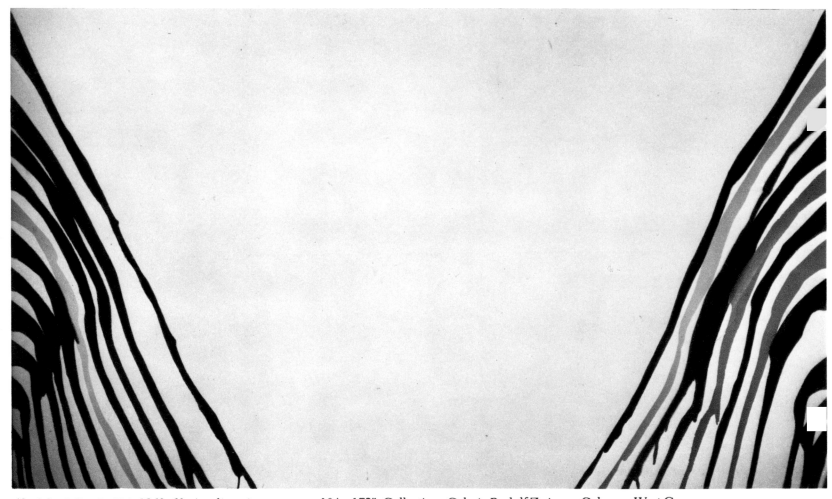

48. Morris Louis, *Ksi*. 1960–61. Acrylic resin on canvas, 104 x 172″. Collection, Galerie Rudolf Zwirner, Cologne, West Germany

49. Morris Louis, *Horizontal VII*. 1962. Acrylic resin on canvas, 27 x 96½". Private collection, Washington, D.C.

these be hung horizontally. This is perhaps as convenient a place as any to discuss the relationships between Noland's art and Louis'. In general Noland has tended to "go with" the staining procedure, identifying parallel, sometimes masked bands in geometric configurations with the inherent geometry of the support.[40] This gives his pictures a disembodied, weightless effect. Louis, on the other hand, wanted to give more variation and irregularity of edge and more plastic feeling to his figuration, which is never identified with the support in the inevitable way one finds in all of Noland's paintings. Louis conceived of the support and his color configuration separately, and the latter almost always relates one way or another to gravity. The result is that Louis' work always has a feeling of weight and density. Louis simply did more drawing, either by masking (never with tape but with other pieces of canvas, some of which were probably cut to size) or with a flat stick covered at one end with cheese cloth with which he guided and pushed the liquid pigment. At no point did either artist do outline drawing, but edge and configuration were more important to Louis, even in the stripes. By comparison, Noland's geometry and taped edges and the way he subordinates his stripes to the support tend to flatten and to thin out the picture.

In terms of color, Noland is more willing to vary area size and the number of colors he will use in any one picture; in general, his work shows a much larger range of color choice and only rarely and very deliberately does he repeat the same color in the same picture. Louis, on the other hand, did not mix colors and stuck pretty much to a set palette; he liked the optical dazzle and force of multiplicity as such—many colors, all with roughly the same area size, presented at once. His range is perceptively more limited, and he often repeats the same hues. Louis never used white because he wanted to contrast his color, which he conceived of as prismatic, with the raw white canvas. Noland likes to fuse the two, and not only does he often use white—and he is a master with it—but also he treats raw canvas more as color. Noland likes to combine colors from different scales and of different tactility. Louis' colors, at least in his best pictures, all seem to exist on the same level and have a uniform sheen.

Finally, Noland, by locking his incident to the literal support, was able to get much more variety in the size and shape of his pictures.[41] As early as the Targets, the square is drawn into the experience of the picture. In this respect, they are shaped pictures, although, as I have pointed out, the square shape is simultaneously neutralized. Nothing like this sensitivity to shape occurs in Louis' pictures until *Hot Half*, 1962 (a painting that was almost certainly influenced by Noland). On the other hand, no other painter, including Noland, has been able to paint so many successful very large pictures as Louis.[42]

71

FIVE

Between 1967 and 1970, in fewer than four years, Noland painted more than two hundred horizontal-band pictures; and, in general, he is extraordinarily prolific as compared to earlier abstract painters. His large output relates to his very untraditional attitudes about making abstract art. He is not precious about his work. He does not think of any one picture as his "masterpiece" (that is, of course, not to say that he has not painted masterpieces), but merely paints along, picture to picture. If he has momentum, he works quickly, letting the work itself determine his pace, never trying to make things difficult for himself or trying to make the painting look difficult.

Noland prefers to make many pictures quickly because this pace forces him to be more spontaneous, to improvise. By not overinvesting in a single picture or group of pictures or an image, he can be more inventive, open to those possibilities that his pictures, critically construed, continually make available to him. And it is this same attitude, this belief in his own inventiveness, in creativity as such, that gives Noland the confidence and security to forgo the seductive securities of style.[1]

As I have noted, at any given point in his development, Noland has been, to a greater or lesser extent, conscious of the inherent restrictions and limitations of the kind of pictures on which he is currently working. Gradually, as he exhausts the possibilities, he simultaneously becomes more aware of these limitations, and, when he finally feels compelled to make the change of layout, the limitations have sometimes become virtual obsessions. Toward the end of the horizontal series, for example, he stretched and hung in his studio a bare, vertical canvas. Obsessed with the idea of painting vertical pictures, he wanted to study how one *sees* a vertical surface. Someone suggested that he hang one of his horizontal pictures vertically, but Noland said that would be "too easy"; verticality had to be achieved, not imposed.[2] It was as if he wanted to get at verticality itself, its essence.

But a desire for verticality was not the only or even most important impetus to change; mainly, it had to do with a new kind of color. The great differentiation of color made possible by (and suggested by) the horizontal format included big differences in the number of colors in a single picture, in the type of color from picture to picture, and also in the size of the bands—the area of color—within a single picture. Also at this time he began to differentiate more sharply from area to area in terms of the consistency of application and texture. Noland had always done this to some extent but he now began to do it more noticeably and systematically. For example, some pigments were mixed with varnish or gel or pearlescent powder so that the bands would lie opaquely on the surface, and others, usually those in the large center area, were mixed with detergent, making them more transparent and letting color stain through the canvas.[3] Noland calls this kind of differentiation the "tactility" of color; it gives him colors that could not be gotten any other way, and it also lends a new and varied tactile presence to the different hues.[4] More important, it suggested to him certain possibilities for figure-ground painting, an area that he had largely avoided until then.

This also has its counterpart in Fauvism—namely, in the change between early and late Fauve painting. About 1906 Matisse found he could discipline and smoothly unify clamorous Fauve color by using large differences in area size. In line with this, he also began systematically to exploit sharp changes not only of hue but also of consistency (even/scumbled, opaque/transparent) and tactility from area to area. This unlocked the surface of his flattened figure-ground picture; large, flat, radically-simplified, and graphic design could be made to yield pictorial mobility and life. Noland's stress on the differentiation of area size, consistency, and tactility in the horizontals prepared the way, and pushed him toward the introduction of figure-ground effects in his next series. This is the most important link between the horizontal-band pictures and the paintings that followed.

Before 1971, Noland had avoided traditional composition by obviating internally balanced-out or echoing incident. A motif of parallel bands either explicitly repeated rather than echoed the external edges (in the horizontal-band pictures and in the diamonds) or explicitly avoided any parallelism with them (in the Targets and chevrons), and he had explored the inherent logic of the rectangle moving from the center point, to the center axis, to the midpoint of the bottom edge, to the upper corners, to two adjacent sides, to two parallel sides. By the end of 1970, however, it appeared as if he had at least temporarily exhausted the creative potentialities of this approach. It was at this point that he began to use narrow horizontal and vertical crisscrossing bands.[5] These new works are the so-called plaid pictures. From one point of view, they can be seen in the context of Noland's previous development, for they resulted from the self-criticism of one aspect of his immediately preceding works, the horizontal-band pictures. These latter had permitted him a range of format from square to exaggeratedly long, but simultaneously had denied him the use of tall, vertical formats. The plaid pictures allowed, even demanded, exactly that. Second, the plaid layout meant working with figure-ground painting and hence the chance really to explore and exploit the chromatic innovations of the late horizontal-band pictures.

At the same time, however, the plaid pictures can also be seen as an important change in Noland's approach and a certain break in his development. For the first time in thirteen years, he was now working with a system of bands that were not all parallel. This had certain immediate implications: the picture became more involuted and less flat, abstract, and open. The overlapping of differently colored bands created right angles and rectangles that echoed the corners and the shape of the whole support. Most important, when narrow, the crisscrossing bands existed on or in front of a ground. They were figure-ground paintings and therefore a structural means to justify and explore the differentiation of area that he had evolved in the late horizontals. Most of the plaids show narrow bands of different degrees of opacity in a soft ambience that is thinly scumbled and therefore transparent and varied. So, in addition to their nonparallelism and overlappings, the plaids are also a departure in the more Impressionist-like color of their fields. Some of them even have the bleeding and fusion of different hues and the tendency toward grayness that Impressionist color always shows.

The compositional idea of the plaids was to interweave vertical bands with horizontal ones so that the whole surface is laced together. Like *passage* in an Analytic Cubist picture or the synoptic motif that Noland

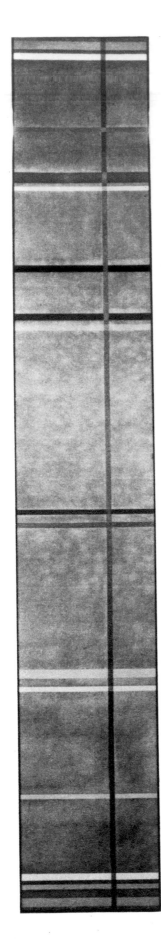

50. *Nursery*. 1972.
Acrylic on canvas, 103 x 16″.
Collection, Joanne du Pont,
New York, New York

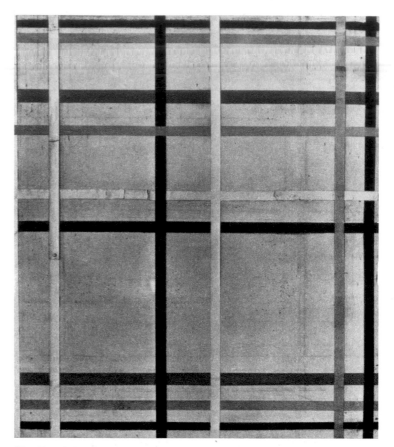

51. Piet Mondrian, *New York City No. 2* (unfinished). 1942.
Paper on canvas, 45 x 27″.
Collection, Sidney Janis, New York, New York

had used until then, the interlace is a way to relate distant parts, to give pictorial continuity across a flattened surface. Everything is kept frontal, and the layout suggests openness and encourages the spreading of attention, taking in the whole at a single glance. Not only does this involve overlapping of the bands and separation of figure and ground, but also it means that the bands now exist more as elements to be placed individually rather than as part of a set motif related as a whole to the support. So, along with its inherent complexity and spatiality, the plaid format often tempted Noland to balance the picture out, one band against another, and consequently push the picture even more toward a traditionally compositional feeling. For the same reason, the plaids are not—or at least not to the same extent—series pictures in that their

52. Installation view of Noland
exhibition at André Emmerich Gallery,
New York, New York, 1973

general layout is less determined in advance.[6]

At first glance it seems that with these pictures Noland is involved with issues similar to those that engaged Mondrian in his classic, post-1920s paintings. By extending his horizontal and vertical lines to the edges, Mondrian had managed to flatten and open the cubist grid. Essentially a draftsman, Mondrian was motivated to increase the literal presence of his lines and of the picture as a whole; he employed only primary colors, colors that do not relate but simply contrast, and only for their brightness and as visual weights. That is, he did not use color chromatically but as equivalents of and as counterbalances to black and white.

Noland, of course, is primarily a colorist and his grid type of layout is

not something received from cubism but something chosen. He accepts the traditional feeling that it has in the context of his own work for the sake of verticality and color. The new chromaticism has to do first with the differentiation of color—types of color, the tactility of color—which now becomes central. The plaid layout offers greater possibilities for adjacent relationships; individual hues "get at" each other more than was the case in those pictures that showed solely parallel bands. Second, the new layout along with the absence of raw canvas as a unifying and partly neutral constant means a more exclusive engagement with relationships between intensities. Finally, one is now faced with a much more complex-looking picture. There is still one large, dominant field—usually an atmospheric wash—but the other

75

color zones, which now show sharper differences in placement and size, are more able to assert their individuality. And for the first time in his mature work Noland combines Impressionist and Fauve color. In terms of stimulating Noland to a new range of color, a range totally unprecedented in his work (or in the work of anyone else for that matter), the plaid pictures were very successful. Indeed, there are some very beautiful plaids that have to be counted among Noland's masterworks. Nonetheless, there are, I think, fewer than in his other series.

The problems with the plaid layout all had to do with structure and were serious. To begin with, the plaids lack the inevitability and clarity of Noland's earlier work. Mastery of color has to carry the whole burden of success or failure. The overlapping creates especially difficult problems of space, one band reading unambiguously as in front of the other. (This is a problem Mondrian did not have to face as long as he kept to all black lines.) The intersections of the bands create a small square that can seem uncontrolled in terms of color and also can create disturbing optical afterimages.[7] Present between the bands the "background" has to be so handled as to keep it on the same visual level as the bands or at least to keep it from falling away too far behind them. Close valuing helped here as did keeping the picture relatively narrow. And Noland sometimes partially bled the background wash *over* the bands. Another alternative was to eliminate the background by enlarging the stripes into blocks and larger bands of opaque color, which lock together to make up the surface. But in the few canvases in which Noland tried this, the different sizes and orientations of the blocks and bands create a structural or checkerboard effect; too much is given up to value contrasts, and color becomes less visible, harder to see.[8]

Also, unless a plaid picture is very narrow, bands in or near its center tend to be disruptive, cutting away from adjacent areas too emphatically, creating an overexplicit figure-ground illusionism and a discontinuous surface. This had also been a problem with the horizontal pictures, and—as with them, so with the plaids—Noland was again driven to move the bands toward the edges, to empty out the center.

The problematic crisscrossing of the bands comes to exist only at the corners where, of course, it is far less conspicuous. The spatial implications of the overlappings are reduced, and abrupt shifts of hue and value

are relegated to the very margins of a luminous and now more-or-less monochromatic wash field; here, at the edges, field and bands begin to respond with bleedings of deeper saturation reinforcing the sense of an internal frame.

At this point—his show at the André Emmerich Gallery, New York, in February 1973—Noland found himself deeply into territory already occupied by Olitski. There is no question of influence; by following the logic of his own art, Noland had run into Olitski's, and by accepting this, even temporarily, Noland showed considerable courage. On the other hand, deliberate avoidance of Olitski at this point would have meant, paradoxically, losing touch with himself.[9] And as we shall see, it was the "alloverness" of these pictures that eventually led Noland back to those touchstones of his art, centrality and symmetry.

The thin parallel bands that run all around the perimeters of the open field seem to contain the whole, to box it in, and they also can make the picture seem a bit too patly ordered. In terms of color, these pictures seem more like a throwback to the late, empty-centered, horizontal-band pictures than something genuinely new.

The alternative to emptying the center was, of course, to stress it because in either case symmetry eliminated any suggestion of an internally balanced-out composition. So in 1973 Noland began symmetrically clustering his crisscrossing bands around the middle point of a much smaller picture. One ought to see this step as essentially the same as Noland's deduction of the circles from Pollock's alloverness; the difference is that now he is dealing with bands that are parallel with the edges but not all parallel with each other. While eliminating all balancing-out, centering made the small right angles and rectangles very conspicuous and the echoing of the support all the more insistent. Thus Noland immediately decided to change the shape of the support to either a diamond or a tondo, two regular shapes that radiate outward from the center point, but that have a nonechoing relationship to the crisscrossing configurations within. Again, Noland achieved several notable successes, especially with the diamonds. (The tondos could seem *too* unrelated to the crisscrossing lines.)[10] At the same time the plaid diamonds exaggerated the main difficulty with the plaid layout: the space created by the bands overlapping each other, and especially by their overlapping or lying on top of the field. No matter how those bands were managed, they made the picture—at least potentially—a container or traditional space box. Yet in these last plaids with their symmetry and return to Fauve color, I think Noland was realigning his painting to his own sensibilities. (In some of these he even worked again with raw canvas.) The color, if lacking in breadth and not quite as aesthetically visible as in most of Noland's earlier pictures, is no less creatively chosen. Above all, these pictures have that crisp lucidity characteristic of his best or at least most personal pictures. They represent a realignment then, a realignment that became the basis of his next major series, the shaped canvases.

Until recently—and despite its extensive use after 1960—the shaped canvas has remained a limited, even failed, idiom. It has seemed arbitrary as a form and marginal to the central development of abstract painting. Only with Noland's shaped canvases, begun in 1975, did this form yield major quality, and, too, it is the first time that the shaped canvas seemed really relevant and necessary. Also these pictures are "mainline" Noland. As in the 1960s, he once again worked with a format that permitted him an assured and expansive realization of his great personal gifts. At the same time, he was, in these pictures, able fully to integrate the figure-ground painting that he had first come upon in the horizontal-band pictures.

The popularity of the shaped canvas in the 1960s and 1970s is a byproduct of the new, literal, material flatness of the modernist picture and the allover layouts that, like the flatness, were the legacy of Pollock. As can be seen in the work of Olitski, these features tend to push profile (i.e., shape-defining) drawing out of the center of the picture, leaving room for it only at the sides. This kind of drawing exists there near the edge, or, as some of Olitski's early spray paintings show, *as* the edge, i.e., the edge is experienced as pictorial drawing, and the picture itself as a pictorially defined whole shape.[11] In these paintings, shape plays the role of stiffening or tautening the interior incident, and it remains subordinated to that incident, to the inside. Olitski has always used regular supports, and when it turned out that dependence on the shape of the support limited him to tall, vertical layouts, he began to introduce interior, drawn lines and edges at or near the actual edge, which,

among other things, gave him more flexibility. In his painting, as opposed to his sculpture, Olitski remains uninterested in shape as such. This is also the case with most of the major painters who emerged in the 1960s. Louis, Noland, Olitski, and Larry Poons are primarily color painters, and the new flatness and allover design has aided them in realizing their ambition. Because it interrupted or confined color and the natural properties of paint, contour or profile drawing became something to be avoided.

But other artists tried to hang onto profile drawing while asserting modernism's new flatness.[12] At the beginning of the 1960s, Frank Stella and Ellsworth Kelly, seeking to overcome the decorativeness of their large, flat, and graphic designs, shaped their canvases away from the simple rectangle. Now, as the sculpture of Anthony Caro demonstrates, a sculpture can dispense with an enclosing profile, and its parts need relate only to each other and to the floor. This is made possible because sculpture possesses the larger coherence that existence in three-dimensional space automatically confers. But seen as a three-dimensional entity, a painting is relatively uninteresting, a flat object suspended on a wall.[13] It escapes this status by creating its own larger coherence, a unified and autonomous virtual space. This space may become ambiguous, contradictory, and radically flattened out; indeed, it may be only implied, so long as it remains *internally* consistent. A regular framing or enclosing shape does not call attention to itself, but sets off this virtual space precisely in order to help the work escape its status as a three-dimensional object. But the more a canvas departs from a regular format, the more it calls attention to itself as a literal object hanging on the wall. To overcome this, it needs a new principle of unity, a new virtual space. If this is not to be merely the wall itself taken as the passive ground for a figure, or pattern, or relief, then the exterior shape as a whole has to be justified by the inside and drawn back into the virtual space of the picture.

This point has been grasped by Ron Davis, one of the few artists to handle the shaped canvas with some success. In his best pictures to date, those from 1966, virtual space no longer exists within the picture; rather the picture as a whole is put into an implied virtual space created by perspective. The irregular shape of the support and perspective

53. Ronald Davis. *Two-Thirds Yellow*. 1966. Polyester resin and Fiberglas, approx. 6 x 11'. Janss Foundation, Thousand Oaks, California

54. Installation view of Frank Stella exhibition of Irregular Polygons at Leo Castelli Gallery, New York, New York, 1966

interlock. Thanks to the design and the reflective plastic surfaces, the painting is seen holistically and appears to float weightlessly within its self-created illusion.[14] A more or less consistent perspective incorporates the literal shape into this illusion; and the tight completeness of the integration of declarative literalness of edge and emphatic pictorial illusion allow Davis to separate his declarative, literal, reflective surface from the same illusion, and hence to vary the textures and colors of the areas within.[15]

Frank Stella, the best-known practitioner of the genre of the shaped canvas, remained insensitive to the necessity of creating a vital tension between the whole shape of the painting and the pictorial illusion, between inside and outside. This was not altogether true of Stella's first shaped canvases, the Aluminum pictures of 1960. There, the repeating bands pull the discretely but nonetheless conspicuously notched literal edge into the picture where it lends some of its sculptural force to the purely depicted edges. Also it gives sculptural force—like the result of a cookie cutter—to the picture as a whole hanging on the wall. Stella discovered that this effect could be strengthened and flat design given further substance by deepening the stretcher bars (as Gorky and Rothko before him had done), making the viewer even more aware of the picture as a solid, slablike object hanging on the wall. If these pictures do not quite achieve major status, they remain Stella's most successful works to date. At least this can be said of those in the series that depart least from the rectangle.

In all of Stella's subsequent shaped pictures, he loses a sense of reciprocal relationship between the shape of the picture and the interior. The outside becomes merely the passive result of the interior or merely identical with it, and it retains no identity of its own. So the 1962 Copper series that followed the Aluminum pictures, as well as the Magenta series of 1963, falls into a kind of artistic limbo. Despite their ostensible rigor, they are, in the end, arbitrary objects hanging on the wall or mere fragments of larger but unspecified wholes. The Copper pictures reach out for an imaginary rectangle, while with the Magenta series self-containedness is achieved at the price of a kind of cosmeticized objecthood.

The strict repeating relationship between inside and outside, established first in the Aluminum series, meant that Stella had to restrict his drawing in an extreme way. The Notched-V series of 1964, in which the same unit is repeated in various combinations, is an attempt to get more variation within this limitation by stressing the diagonal and the angles rather than straight-edged parallel lines. But for the most part these pictures are little more than handsome but inertly decorative cutouts that are never galvanized into substantial pictorial art.

In his Irregular Polygon series of 1966, Stella tried further to free his drawing by linking interior to exterior by a drawn continuity rather than through parallel repeating. This meant even more eccentrically-shaped canvases, now made up of shapes, all of which shared at least some edges with the literal edge and therefore some of its three-dimensional force. But in the presence of these works there is rarely a feeling of inevitability either with regard to the whole or with regard to the specific parts (or for that matter, with regard to the color). If flat, asymmetrical, and eccentric shapes are to subvert the sense of a continuous enclosing edge, then some larger principle of discipline or order seems required to govern their behavior. Since the outside does not have an autonomy or identity of its own, pictorial unity and tension are basically a question of balancing out the individual hardedged shapes, one against the other, on the passive ground plane of the wall. Unlike the Copper pictures, some involution is achieved in the Irregular Polygons (though the feeling that the picture is a fragment is not wholly eliminated) but only by lapsing into Synthetic Cubist thinking.[16]

Despite his use of tondos, diamonds, and elongated formats, Noland has never been interested in the shaped canvas as such, i.e., as shape, as drawing.[17] For example, his diamonds are simple, regular, geometric forms that accommodate parallel, diagonal color bands. Noland has always framed his pictures with stripping, never has he deepened the stretcher bars, and until the mid-1970s did not work with irregular formats.[18] His art has been based on relating flat, parallel color bands (the simplest way to avoid shape interest and thereby present bright, frankly contrasting hues) to a regular geometric support. He wishes to make this relationship seem logical and inevitable as well as open and expansive. And he wants to contrive for himself maximum flexibility as regards the size and shape of the picture and as regards color range. But above all, Noland follows the inner logic of his own development even "against the grain," as it were; and often it turns out that the results are not against the grain after all. The logic of Noland's art sometimes suggests to him the exact opposite procedure to the one he has been using. This was the case, for instance, with the change, just described, from the empty centered plaids to the centered ones, and it is also the case with Noland's next move, his most radical to date, from symmetry and parallelism to their opposites.[19] Perhaps symmetry and parallelism seemed exhausted for the moment. What is most interesting, however, is the way that Noland makes a new principle out of their negation. In the spring of 1975, Noland did a series of diamonds, developing out of the plaid ones, but now for the first time showing all diagonal, non-parallel, asymmetrically-placed, straight-edged areas.[20] Mostly vertical in orientation, these areas did not seem to overlap each other, and their diverging edges reduced the effect of a ground. More all of a piece, the surface became immediately flatter and hence more related to the preplaid pictures. Also, Noland painted his areas in different ways, some sprayed, some stained, in an effort to render them all positive and thereby to eliminate still further the sense of a negative ground.[21]

Now the problem was how to relate the asymmetric, divergent, nonparallel areas to the support. The diamonds did not offer a satisfactory solution, but they are very interesting transitional pictures, and all the more so in that they seem to improve in quality when hung slightly askew, i.e., with the axes, like the edges, not parallel with the limits of the wall.[22] The interior incident now seemed justified for it shared asymmetry and nonparallelism with the support while acting with it to give balance to the whole. Noland did not immediately grasp the implications of this. But he did grasp something else: the possibility of reversing the procedure that he had followed since 1958, the possibility of using nonparallelism as a consistent principle of placement. This he did in a series of large, horizontal rectangles in which ray or wedge-shaped bands move off in contrary directions. The edges of these bands are not parallel with each other nor are they parallel with the edges of any of the other bands. Some of them suggest mutually contradictory suggestions of perspective, which together create a very tense whole; all is then judiciously framed by the rectangle. It became immediately apparent that, as with the diamond framing, the rectangle left areas, usually at the corners, that isolated and could not hold their own with the rest of the surface. At this point, Noland simply cut these areas off. Still not satisfactory, this attempt at a solution led to something that was. The cutting usually made the picture look inertly rectilinear, and therefore arbitrary, but it also made the same point as hanging the diamonds ajar: The nonparallel and asymmetrically placed rays asked for nonparallel and asymmetrical literal edges. It meant a shaped canvas.[23] With the cutoff rectangular format, the main edges of the support were still parallel with the floor and wall. The edges of the diamonds—more radical in this respect—were merely parallel with each other. Nonetheless, like the cutoff rectangles, the diamond format, even when hung ajar, retained the feeling of a given, imposed, a priori shape, and hence a choice perceptively separate from those evinced on the inside.

With his shaped pictures, Noland created a completely irregular, asymmetrical, but still straight-edged shape that avoids the static, a priori character that the rectangular and diamond shapes still possessed.[24] Horizontal-vertical balance is not given by horizontal edges or axes, but created by making the outside and inside equivalent as intuitively-arrived-at, dynamic configurations, which, together, establish a tense equilibrium. The corners of the literal edge act as pointed thrusts that reinforce or counterbalance the thrusting rays inside. Everything is positively engaged, and there is a sense in which the picture is more autonomous, self-referential, i.e., abstract, than any pictures before by Noland or anyone else. That he uses contrasting or at least nonrepeating colors adds to their extraordinary sense of openness and dispersal; everything diverges from everything else and usually away from the center and beyond the frame.[25] The inside is pitted against the outside in such as way as to draw the outside, the support, into the picture and prevent it from reading as an inert shape on the wall. But at the same time, it no longer offers merely neutral limits but is allowed to call enough attention to itself to declare, as a more central part of the work, that it is a framed, flat surface on the wall.[26] This means a flattening or tautening of the surface, which then readmits or even demands certain kinds of illusionism that had previously become problematic due to the modernist need to flatten the traditional rectangle. Stressing the object character of the picture, plus the presiding tension established between the outside and the inside, makes the latter more of a piece, more of a flat surface, and in turn permits or calls for the figure-ground implications and the perspective suggestions of the rays.

To repeat this point, it is the object flatness together with the overriding relationship established between the exterior as a whole and the interior, the illusion, as a whole that opens the way for more flexibility within the picture. This, I think, will turn out to be the most influential and fruitful aspect of Noland's shaped pictures. Once again in modernist art another given convention of the traditional easel picture, in this case the regularity of the support and its orientation to balance, is made conscious and controverted, and its negative yields a new convention—and a new area of development—for abstract painting.

Almost always a change in format suggests to Noland a change of color, and the shaped pictures are no exception. They seem to admit dramatic hue-and-value contrasts and the use of primaries that recall the color of the Targets and the chevrons. This is not surprising if one considers that the Targets—centered, symmetrical, and square—are the exact opposite of the new pictures—empty-centered, asymmetrical, and irregular. That is, they have an opposite but complementary kind of structure and drama. And, like the chevrons, they call for a few broad, diagonally-oriented areas of uniform color. But now the figure and the ground are more chromatically responsive to each other.

Stella's Irregular Polygons of 1967, his best works after the Aluminum series, bear a superficial resemblance to Noland's new paintings. But Stella's pictures depend on shape, on having the depicted shapes share edges with the literal support and, consequently, some of its blocky three-dimensionality. The colors, despite their declamatory assertiveness, serve only to identify and to distinguish the shapes one from the other and have no chromatic relation or internal harmony. The interlocked shapes balance each other out against the ground plane of the wall and its horizontal and vertical limits, which

55. Installation view of Noland exhibition at André Emmerich Gallery, New York, New York, 1975.
Left: *Inverted Mordent*. 1975. Acrylic on canvas, 110 x 180″. Right: *Beam*. 1975. Acrylic on canvas, 96¾ x 172½″

the shapes in part obey. In all of this, Stella remains within the confines of traditional composition and design with velleities toward three-dimensional relief.

With Noland, the outside shape is not conceived of as directly continuous with the inside, but, as with Olitski, the inside as a whole is set against the outside as a whole. Instead of the balancing out of shapes, such as one gets in Kelly's shaped canvases or Stella's Irregular Polygons, drama is achieved by putting an expansive inside into tense balance with a delimiting but thoroughly responsive outside. The perimeter retains a sense of continuity and identity of its own, but not as a known, graspable shape. It shares and reflects the nonparallelism, directionality, and asymmetry of the inside; at the same time, it is set against the inside as a different order of edge definition—i.e., literal v. depicted. So the exterior shape has its own autonomy (unlike Stella's Copper pictures or Irregular Polygons), but on the other hand it does not stamp out or declare shape as such (as in Stella's Aluminum pictures). All given, a priori sense of shape, of a gestalt, is avoided because it would interrupt the continuous and reciprocal tension between the inside and the outside. Together they create an achieved, rather than given, balance and orientation to horizontal and vertical stability.[27] Drama and order are the result of pulling all edges apart and of making the literal and the depicted separate but related coequal

determinants of the whole work of art.[28]

Ron Davis succeeded with the shaped canvas by reverting to traditional perspective. Stella, on the other hand, was driven to the shaped canvas by following the logic of modernist flatness. But his simultaneous commitment to profile drawing meant that eventually he was driven back to traditional cubist space (the Irregular Polygons and Protractor series) or to traditional relief (in his work of the mid-1970s). That is, in the end he gave up his effort to unite modernism and contour drawing and opted for the latter over the former. Noland comes to the shaped canvas not for the sake of shape, but as a way to relate the support to a certain type of color bands.[29] This ultimately forced him to cancel the picture's shape and, paradoxically, to gain involution by means of dispersal. His shaped canvases are the first irregularly-shaped canvases that are both fully modernist and fully successful major art.[30]

It has been pointed out by Donald Judd that the shaped canvas is an intermediate step between abstract painting and minimal sculpture.[31] This is true enough, but it is only true of the shaped canvas conceived of as a vehicle of shape. As I have tried to show, it has been conceived of by Noland far more fruitfully as a new way to suspend shape and therefore deal with issues of balance, illusionism, and color; as a way to open up a new range of *pictorially* viable aesthetic choices.

56. *Splay*. 1976. Acrylic on canvas, 104 x 111½".
Collection, William Hokin, Chicago, Illinois

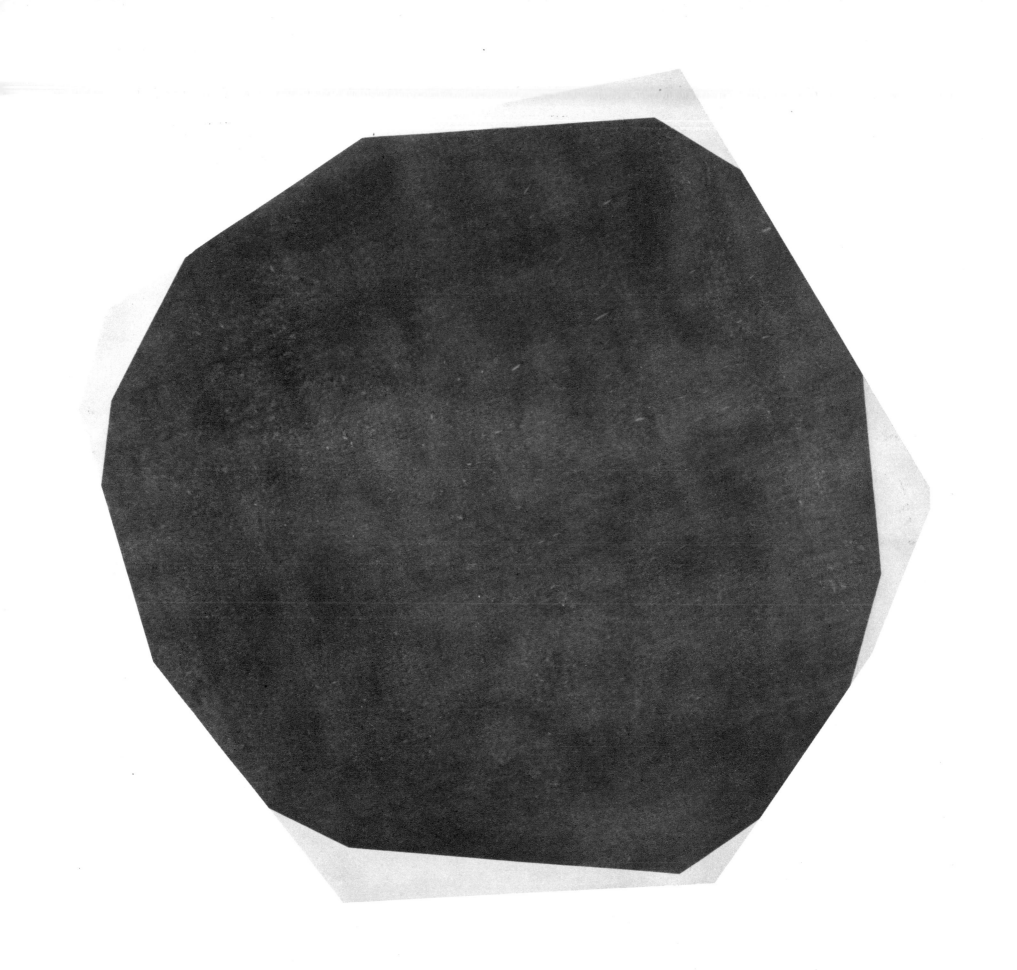

57. Kenneth Noland supervising two assistants
in his studio at South Shaftsbury, Vermont, 1975

SIX

Taste, even it seems, "educated taste," has more difficulty recognizing creativity and feeling in color than in drawing and in design. Therefore, Noland's paintings have sometimes been characterized as "only optical" or as arresting and attractive but emotionally empty, decorative patterns. (Oddly enough, it is often the same critics who find Noland "too intellectual" who also find his work merely sensual or merely attractive.) The lack of personal handling in his pictures; his use of geometrical, hardedge configurations; his preference for working in series; and his rigorous approach to pictorial problems—all these have been taken as signs of a cold and calculating temperament.

For this reason I want to comment here on the "content" of Noland's paintings. At the beginning of Chapter Three, I described the new attitude toward making pictures that became evident in Pollock's work but that was fully realized only by Noland and the other color painters of the 1950s and 1960s. I said that this new attitude amounted to taking a new subject matter for abstract art. In Chapter Four and Chapter Five, I tried to show in detail what this meant in Noland's case: how he took the new subject matter, the materials and procedures of painting, and followed it; how he developed the logic of stain, of color, of the support.

Subject matter is what the artist makes art about. It is not the same as content. For example, in the Sistine Ceiling, the Book of Genesis is the subject matter. The content, on the other hand, is Michelangelo's unique feeling for representation in general and his subject matter in particular; his feelings were expressed through, or, more correctly, *as* the form (taken in its broadest sense). It is the same with Noland. His subject matter, too, is something independent, something objective by which he is limited, by which he is led, by which he is stimulated. The content is his feeling for that subject matter: his conception, and his imaginative, felt choices of color, texture, proportion, and edge, and, above all, the relationships between these. More generally, one might characterize the content of Noland's paintings as the tension between the splendor of color and its taut control, or between clarity and immediacy of presentation and the pictorial indeterminacy that results. In the horizontals, for example, the viewer relates colors vertically against the repeated horizontality, which pulls everything taut. The resultant tension can be unnerving after five hundred years of seeing pictures in terms of stable shape definition. Sequences slip away while others form; color becomes an ungraspable, sheerly optical property while at the same time possessing a vibrant abstract presence. "Imagine yourself looking across a street at a crowd of pedestrians; suddenly one of them glances your way; that quality of connection is what I'd like those colors to have—but abstractly."[1] Tension, presence, openness, and ungraspability are the very structure of subjectivity, feeling, and personal contact. As such, these features are often found in great portraiture of the past; they are also present in Noland's pictures—but abstractly.

More than one critic, however, has been dissatisfied with characterizations of Noland's content on this level of generalization and has wanted to say something more specific; so his pictures have been described as "cheerful," "brooding," and "introspective." But abstract forms and colors, like musical notes, have no fixed, conventional meanings. The import of the meaning of most musical compositions or abstract paintings is the result of their expressive structure, their symbolizing what Suzanne Langer calls "a pattern of sentience," "a logical expression." Langer also says that "we are always free to fill its subtle articulate forms with any meaning that fits them; that is, it may convey an idea of anything conceivable in its logical image. So although we do receive it as a significant form, and comprehend the processes of life and sentience through its...dynamic pattern, it is not language because it has no vocabulary."[2] The critic may, of course, record his particular private associations that will turn out to be more or less evocative of the work's content; but what counts—what makes the picture a success or failure as art—is the expressive configuration that gives the original impetus to these associations.

Finally, it is the very nature of Noland's approach that he consciously avoids a prioris. He wants his "solutions" to be arrived at by feeling and by intuition and each time anew. It is simpleminded to

regard the use of hardedged or geometric forms as "intellectual" and the employment of soft, brushy ones as "lyrical." It is equally possible for the former to be full of expression and the latter no more than a safe conforming to preexistent taste. Of course, many works of art, especially many done in the last twenty years, are too intellectual (in the sense of being wilfully contrived); but whether or not this is true of any specific artist or picture is not something that can be decided in advance on the basis of technique or morphology alone.

Some critics have complained that in his emphasis on color, Noland neglects too many other elements of painting as it has been traditionally practiced. They see his work as being too narrow. I would not deny that modernist art has meant a certain narrowing compared to representational art. As I have tried to show, however, it is exactly its rejection of representational art with all of its complexity that permits abstract painting to discover new feelings, new kinds of pictorial experiences. Since the beginning of this century, Western illusionism has appeared to be exhausted, no longer able to produce fundamental innovation. And it is innovation, or at least the possibility of innovation, that stimulates the most creative minds. One can have creativity or representation—one cannot, or so it seems, have it both ways. But one thing is sure: modernist art, by isolating "problems" and pushing to extremes, can open up entirely new, unsuspectedly rich areas of content.[3] For the sake of color and light, Monet was willing to confine himself to a single point of view and to a single moment in time; he suppressed value contrasts, the foundation of traditional pictorial structure, and he suspended descriptive content. Yet who today will deny that, in an important way, art is richer for his reductions.

Like Monet, Noland is a radical artist rather than a synthetic one; unlike Cézanne or the later Picasso, he has not been anxious to fuse modernism and tradition. While accepting the challenges of the greatest achievements of the past, he has called into question all conventions for the sake of color (all conventions except seriousness of intent, pictorial unity, and that particular aliveness or drama that distinguishes painting from decoration). In precisely this way, he has gained conscious control of all the coordinates of painting: composition, shape, size, proportion, color, paint quality.[4] He may temporarily hold certain of these coordinates constant, but nothing is taken for granted or assumed—all limitations are self-limitations and positively expressive.

Seen from this point of view, Noland reminds one of Mondrian in the single-minded way he has borne down on the inherent logic of the pictorial surface; and no other artist, except Mondrian, has produced successful paintings that are as abstract in feeling as his. Saturated with aesthetic consciousness, the pictures of Noland and Mondrian show an extreme identification of sensibility with conception—the nakedness of artistic choice becoming one with the expressive essence. A kind of moral rigor, lucid intelligence, and forthrightness is felt both in their developments and in their individual paintings.

Noland's work should also be seen as relating to two other modern masters. I have already stressed that he has created the abstract equivalent to the Fauve color picture. Of all modern painters Noland is closest to Matisse in his purely intuitive and innovative use of color. A second and less obvious precedent is Klee. Probably the most radical aspect of Klee's art is the way he combined a very physical approach to painting with a disembodied illusionism—an elimination of the density and weight of depicted form. His scratchy, dimensionless line and his thin, watercolor washes of color both drained the easel picture of body and weight; yet his surfaces, as fragile and delicate as they are, always make a certain tactile appeal. Noland organizes stained color solely in terms of the flat surface, usually without any overlapping, and he uses nonsculptural, geometric drawing. And as with Klee, his disembodied illusion is one with an affectively, if subtly, tactile surface. In this way, Noland—whose strongest early influence was Klee—wins for large-scale, abstract painting the same delicate weightlessness and airiness that first drew him to Klee's pictures. I have called this Noland's etherealness and noted how geometric logic and the tenseness of his unities—the heritage of Mondrian—stiffen this etherealness and are softened by it.

If Noland can be said to unite three strains of modern art—Matisse and Fauvism, De Stijl and Mondrian, and the work of Paul Klee—he is hardly eclectic about it, and not at all interested in consciously reworking the past. These strains are simply one with his sensibility. Noland's sole conscious attitude toward the past has been radical: to go beyond his own immediate past—first the necessity to work through Pollock and then to follow the inner logic of his own development. The Abstract Expressionist generation, and Pollock in particular, reached a potential for a new kind of abstraction and especially for a new color painting, which, as I have tried to show, has been as if a natural objective of modernist painting all along. But in the main, the Abstract Expressionists were unable fully to realize this themselves. They had devised new structures and techniques that were as if made for color; and they perceived, or at least Pollock did, a new way of making abstract art—a freedom, an openness, a lack of predispositions in dealing with the materials. It was the historical role of Noland (and Louis and Olitski as well) to bring this new kind of abstraction to fruition.

If pointing out these relationships helps to locate Noland in the history of modernism, it can also obscure his originality, an originality that lies not only in his unique fusion of these strains but also above all in the personal character of his color and in the way he has forced us to see color and experience a picture in entirely new ways. No small part of Noland's originality is the extraordinary range of his color—his capacity continually to surprise us with new and unexpected chromatic inventions.

Like color, quality in art is impossible to grasp with words; one can only point. But I think Noland has already established himself as one of the real master painters of our century. Few modern artists have achieved the level of quality that he has attained and even fewer have maintained it in so many pictures. At the age of fifty-two, Noland now has a great new challenge: to sustain a standard of quality in abstract painting that he himself has helped to establish.

58. View of Noland's sculptures in the garden adjoining his residence, South Shaftsbury, Vermont.
Left to right: *Loom*; *Shadow*; *Homage: David Smith*; and *Jenny*

A NOTE ON NOLAND'S SCULPTURE

After 1959 Noland was a close personal friend of the English sculptor Anthony Caro. Noland somewhat influenced Caro's early sculpture and methods of working. For his part Noland feels, "I've had the longest and most confirming relationship I've had with any artist with Tony Caro. I've had not only the revelations of his work but also those of his friendship." Caro often came to South Shaftsbury to visit Noland, and over the years the surrounding area, including nearby Bennington College, became a center for making constructed sculpture.

Noland had not made any sculpture since his student days in Zadkine's studio, but stimulated by the sculptural activity around him he began in 1968 to work in three dimensions. He made three groups of sculptures. One consists of wooden beams and some bronze and steel. Based on a grid, they are directly related to the plaids (*Jenny*, 1970,

plate 60; *Vermont*, 1971–73, plates 63, 64, now in Yarkon Park, Tel Aviv, Israel). In another group (1973–76) he used stainless steel pieces inherited from David Smith (*Homage: David Smith*, 1973–76, plate 69). Most recently, Noland completed three pieces in Cor-ten steel that have much in common with his shaped pictures (although they were begun before them, in 1971). One of this group is *Loom*, 1971–74 (plates 65, 66) and another is *Ridge*, 1974–76 (plate 71).

Noland's sculptures are all large, ambitious, and quite original in conception. They strike one as a painter's sculpture in that, except in the stainless steel pieces, he began with a relatively simple idea or gestalt, usually related in one way or another to flatness or to the rectangle, and then worked away from it toward indeterminacy through a series of slight adjustments.

59. *Around*. 1968. Stainless steel, approx. 4½ x 6'.
Collection, the artist

60. *Jenny*. 1970. Wood and metal, 14' x 16' x 8'1¼".
Collection, the artist

61. Anthony Caro, *Shaftsbury*. 1965. Steel painted purple,
2'3" x 10'7" x 9'. Lewis Cabot Collection, Boston, Massachusetts

62. Kenneth Noland and the sculptor Anthony Caro in the grounds
outside Noland's studio/house, South Shaftsbury, Vermont, 1975.
Photo by André Emmerich

63. *Vermont*. 1971–73. Wood and metal.
Photographed at Noland's residence, South Shaftsbury, Vermont

64. Another view of V*ermont*, at Yarkon Park, Tel Aviv, Israel

65. *Loom*. 1971–74. Cor-ten steel, 6'4" x 11'10" x 11'.
Collection, the artist

66. Another view of *Loom*

91

67. *Shadow*. 1973–76. 5'10" x 20' x 8'
Collection, the artist

68. Another view of *Shadow*

70. David Smith, *Voltri* V. 1962.
Steel, 85¾ x 36 x 25″.
Joseph H. Hirshhorn Museum and Sculpture Garden,
Smithsonian Institution, Washington, D.C.

69. *Homage: David Smith*. 1973–76. Stainless steel,
4 x 12 x 7′. Collection, the artist

71. *Ridge*. 1974–76. Cor-ten steel, size unknown. Collection, the artist

NOTES TO THE TEXT

CHAPTER ONE

1. The text of this book is an expanded and much revised version of three articles that I published in *Art News* and *Art International*. See the Bibliography.

2. Thomas Wolfe's descriptions of Asheville make this evident. In the 1920s, Asheville was a center for tubercular care and attracted considerable wealth. International bridge tournaments were held in the town, and there was a great interest in jazz.

3. Martin Duberman notes that Noland, along with two of his brothers, was among the few natives of the Asheville area ever to attend Black Mountain College, in his *Black Mountain: An Exploration in Community*, New York, 1972, p. 428.

4. Noland has said that his father was an "early bird," one of the first hundred or so people who learned to fly. Interview with Paul Cummings, December 9, 1971, *Archives of American Art*, p. 2. Hereafter referred to as *Archives*.

5. According to Noland's memory, he entered Black Mountain in the fall term of 1946. Albers was away and did not return until the midterm of 1947; Noland only took a course with Albers in the fall of 1948, i.e., in the last year of his stay at Black Mountain. If this chronology is correct, Noland had been working with Bolotowsky for a year and a half before he personally encountered Albers. The art department in 1946 at Black Mountain was small. It consisted of Mary Gregory (woodworking), Franziska Haas (weaving), and Bolotowsky (painting and drawing). No instruction was offered in sculpture. No one taught design during Albers' absence because that was considered Albers' specialty.

6. In the 1960s Albers was sometimes credited with being Noland's teacher, e.g., *Time*, April 18, 1969. Bolotowsky claims the role of being Noland's teacher and insists that Noland and Albers never got along personally. Duberman, *op. cit.*, p. 474.

7. Duberman, *op. cit.*, p. 428.

8. Duberman, *op. cit.*, p. 62.

9. Duberman, *op. cit.*, p. 70, and in conversation.

10. *Archives* and in conversation with the author.

11. Duberman, *op. cit.*, p. 73.

12. "As a teacher, Bolotowsky was also more permissive than Albers: he let the art students paint in whatever style seemed to attract them and then criticized their work from that viewpoint, be it naturalistic, surrealistic, or whatever." Duberman, *op. cit.*, p. 301. Bolotowsky, too, felt that Albers molded his students excessively—to the point where few successfully went on to develop their own styles. Far more than Albers, Bolotowsky usually established a warm and very personal relationship with his students. See Duberman, *op. cit.*, *passim*, and *Archives*, p. 4.

13. Nonetheless, Bolotowsky's color is very limited. He often confines himself to tints and shades of the primaries and never uses green. After the early 1940s, he no longer worked with the diagonal and limited himself exclusively to the horizontal and vertical. Following Mondrian, Bolotowsky characterized his art as Neoplastic, which limits itself to the right angle in distinction to Geometric Art, which explores the potentiality in all geometric figures. See *Ilya Bolotowsky*, Solomon R. Guggenheim Museum, New York, 1974, pp. 19, 20. Noland has noted that although Bolotowsky was more concerned with color than Mondrian that "he still paints in terms of value." See *Archives*, p. 11.

14. At the time when Noland was studying with him, Bolotowsky was going through a particularly Mondrianesque period. It was exactly at this time, 1947, that he also was experimenting with a diamond-shaped canvas.

15. In conversation.

16. *Ibid.*

17. *Ibid.*

18. The Surrealist or Dada side of Black Mountain owes something to Albers. It had been a part of the Bauhaus (e.g., Kurt Schwitters), but neither Albers nor Bolotowsky liked Surrealism as such, and there was not much interest in it at the art department of Black Mountain in contrast to the music department where John Cage, the Dada composer, was one of the main figures. Noland studied musical composition with Cage one summer. Duberman, *op. cit.*, *passim*, and *Archives*, p.8.

19. In terms of art history, Albers was, of course, against teaching it at all. Bolotowsky "Just took us back... as far as Impressionism when we were beginners and through cubism into a kind of Neoplastic abstract art, and Surrealism. So the education was fairly avant-garde." *Archives*, p. 33.

20. For example, Albers taught a version of Johannes Itten's "Vorkurs," which had been taught at the Bauhaus, but he "purged it of Itten's cultist, mystical overtones." See Duberman, *op. cit.*, p. 64. As for Bolotowsky, "I don't know whether Mondrian ever worried about the Ying and the Yang, the sex idea behind the horizontals and verticals. Since the idea is so prevalent and everybody is assuming everything, you might as well ignore it. In other words, if everybody is immersed in such basics of human psychology, and if Mondrian had it just like everybody else, then it's nothing special, so let's just skip it." See *Ilya Bolotowsky*, p. 31.

21. *Archives*, p. 6.

22. *Ibid*.

23. *Archives*, pp. 7, 8.

24. Letter to Harry Noland, undated (1949), in the possession of Harry Noland.

25. *Archives*, p. 10. For his part, Noland has said (in conversation) that he remained unaware of such French vanguard painters as Dubuffet, Mathieu, and Fautrier.

26. *Archives*, p. 11. What Noland means here, I think, is that it was in Paris that he first perceived that the way beyond geometrical painting was through working with the materials—that is to get away from beginning with the elements of painting—line, form, color—as ideally conceived entities, fixed and separate, which were then to be somehow combined. Working with the materials meant *arriving at* line, color, scale, and texture through experimenting with the physicality of the medium. It meant thinking of the elements as inseparable from one another, as dialectically interrelated.

27. Albers himself had, of course, been influenced by Klee.

28. *Archives*, p. 10.

29. *Archives*, pp. 10, 11.

30. It may sound odd that Noland should single out Klee as an "expressionist" alternative to geometric painting. In the end, I think Klee's version of late, more painterly cubism appealed to Noland because of his own sensibility for a delicate, fragile, weightless feeling. This is something that is already present in Noland's early watercolors after Klee and, of course, is very much the expression of his mature style.

31. John Devoluy, "Art News in Paris," New York *Herald Tribune*, Paris, April 29, 1949.

32. Announcement card for the exhibition *Kenneth Noland*, Galerie R. Creuze, Paris, 1949; see also "The New Expatriates," *Life Magazine*, August 22, 1949, p. 87, in which Zadkine singled out Noland as an especially promising young painter.

33. The Institute of Contemporary Art, run by Robert Green and Robert Richmond, was a school for part-time students; it held mostly night classes and offered no degree. Instruction was given in drama, design, ceramics, painting, sculpture, film, poetry, and literature. Performances of dance and theater were often given at the institute.

34. Robin Bond was an Englishman whom Noland mentions along with Bolotowsky, Greenberg, and David Smith as having had the most effect on him. Bond had taught at the A. S. Neil School at Summerhill, and it was through him that Noland first went into Reichian therapy. Noland credits Reichian therapy with "opening him up" and having an important effect on his living and working attitudes. *Archives*, p. 19.

35. Noland has remarked to me that he was very interested in the paintings of Augustus Vincent Tack (1870–1949), whose pictures were also to be seen at the Phillips. The many Impressionist pictures in the Phillips Collection were especially important for Washington color painting, as has been noted by Gene Davis. See Barbara Rose, "A Conversation with Gene Davis," *Artforum*, vol. 9, no. 7 (March 1971), pp. 50–54. As a boy of fourteen or fifteen, Noland had been taken to the National Gallery of Art by his father, especially to see the Monets.

36. *Archives*, p. 17.

37. In conversation.

38. The color painters Rothko, Newman, and Still were known only as names.

39. Greenberg introduced the two, and Noland once visited Pollock at his home in East Hampton.

40. It is not clear if Noland began these de Kooning-influenced pictures before or after he met Louis.

41. In conversation.

42. James McC. Truitt, "Art-Arid D.C. Harbors Touted New Painters," Washington *Post*, December 21, 1961, p. A20.

43. *Ibid*.

44. In conversation.

45. Clement Greenberg, "Louis and Noland," *Art International*, vol. 4, no. 5 (May 1960), p. 27. Noland has said, "It gave us some distance to reflect upon things that we could see happening in New York, which was the center. It gave us a little objective distance." *Archives*, p. 17.

46. Noland's relation to Greenberg, which has continued for more than 25 years, has been the subject of much speculation and rumor. But Noland himself has clarified it. "... He's been accused of telling people how to paint. But of course the record itself... [denies] that... for the very simple reason that the kind of art that he's thought to be the best is not necessarily alike. I mean certainly Pollock is not the same as, say, Newman or Rothko or David Smith. Each... is... uniquely different. The record proves that. So it's not as if he tells anybody the way they should paint or anything that they should do. He doesn't do that. He has the ability to look at the work in its own terms and see what's going on and see certain things that are more unique to your work that he can point out or where you may be hedging some things in your own frame of reference. Well, I don't know—it's just that there's nobody quite like him... he can point things out so that you can see for yourself and it gives you that second sight. I think it's a very good relationship. I think historically that all painters have had one or two people whose eye they trusted...." *Archives*, pp. 35–37. The view that an artist can never benefit from any critic's suggestions is, of course, the result of the nineteenth-century romantic conception of the artist.

47. Greenberg, *op. cit.* Sometime in early 1954, differences arose between Louis and Noland. They saw very little of each other until 1958 when, after meeting at French & Company, they resumed their relationship, but on a social basis only.

The last pictures that Louis showed to Noland in his studio were the trellis paintings of 1953. Noland saw Louis' early 1954 veils at Greenberg's apartment. He also saw several shows of Louis' pictures and especially remembers one of these at the Washington Workshop of the Arts (October 1955—the pictures Louis showed there were not Veils and were subsequently destroyed). Louis was Noland's biggest single influence between 1954 and 1958 despite the lack of personal contact between the two men.

48. Like Greenberg, Smith made frequent trips to Washington, D.C., in these years, and it turned out Noland's first wife, Cornelia, and David Smith's first wife, Jean, were friends who had gone to Sarah Lawrence College together. Cornelia was a painter and had been a student of Smith's at Sarah Lawrence. Noland introduced Louis to Smith in these years, and they were often together with Greenberg.

49. In the catalogue, *The Washington Color Painters*, Washington Gallery of Modern Art, 1965, p. 30. Downing is mistaken in mentioning Newman, whose work was not known to Noland until 1959.

50. In conversation. See also the catalogue, *Art in Washington: Twenty Years*, Baltimore Museum of Art, 1970.

51. Noland had shown occasionally in local group shows at the Corcoran Gallery of Art and at the Phillips Collection. He had a few one-man shows in Washington (the Dupont Theater Gallery of Art, 1952; the Margaret Dickey Gallery of Art, District of Columbia Teachers College, c. 1955; and several times at Catholic University), and two in Philadelphia (Dubin Galleries, 1951 and 1952). In 1958 he showed at Alice Denny's Jefferson Place Gallery, and in 1960 he again exhibited there, this time with his concentric circle pictures.

52. The dealer Betty Parsons had called Dorothy Miller's attention to Noland. For reviews of the first Tibor de Nagy show, see *Art News*, vol. 55 (February

1957), p. 10; and *Arts*, vol. 31 (February 1957), p. 65. Noland showed *Globe* (plate 34), *Bed Spread, Elmer's Tune, Opal,* and *Royal Envelope.* Helen Frankenthaler helped Noland get his first show at the Tibor de Nagy Gallery. See *Archives*, p. 20.

53. For reviews, see *Art News*, vol. 57 (October 1958), p. 13; and *Arts*, vol. 33 (October 1958), p. 57. Among the pictures Noland showed were *Season, Outskirt,* and *Lavender Blue.* Noland had shown the early ring picture *Globe* (plate 34) in 1957, and by October 1958 he had begun the concentric circles. Yet he was still unsure about them, and the pictures that he exhibited, some stained, some done with thicker surfaces, were not circle paintings.

54. Noland feels that his 1956–57 pictures are close to Abstract Impressionism, a trend that was noticed by several critics of the time. See, for example, L. Finkelstein, "New Look: Abstract Impressionism," *Art News*, vol. 55 (March 1956), pp. 36–39+. The painters who were most often mentioned as Abstract Impressionists were Philip Guston and Milton Resnick. Others included in this strain were Hyde Soloman, Michael Goldberg, Miriam Shapiro, Wallace Reiss, Vincent Longo, Ray Parker, Ernest Briggs, Rosemary Beck, Cajori, Wolf Kahn, Neil Blaine, Joan Mitchell, Robert de Niro, Stephen Pace, Friedel Dzubas, and Helen Frankenthaler. See also T. Hess, "U.S. Painting: Some Recent Directions," *Art News Annual*, no. 28 (1956), p. 83 ff.

Abstract Impressionism is a brief phase of American painting that has largely been forgotten, having produced little of real importance. But in retrospect, its significance is that it was the first movement that attempted to unite the two separate trends of Abstract Expressionism: the painterly application of the "action painters" and the color emphasis of Still, Rothko, and Newman. Abstract Impressionism usually shows broken color and a very physical build-up of surface. However, most of Noland's pictures of 1954–57 are thinly painted. Some have a thicker pigmentation, and these may have been influenced by Still or more likely by such 1953 Pollock pictures as *Easter and Totem* or *Ocean Greyness*, which Noland had seen at the Janis Gallery show in March 1954.

55. For reviews, see *Art News*, vol. 58 (October 1959), p. 16; and *Arts*, vol. 34 (November 1959), p. 58. Among the pictures that Noland showed were *Ex Nihilo* (plate 113) and *Plunge* (plate 36). The largest was ten feet square. Some were pinwheels, but most were circles or circles that had diamonds or ovals in them. One was a double target. A few showed large dripped forms and were close to Morris Louis.

56. In 1963 Noland had purchased a former home of the poet Robert Frost in Shaftsbury, Vermont, and had moved there.

CHAPTER TWO

1. Clement Greenberg, "The Later Monet" (1956), reprinted in *Art and Culture*, Boston, 1961, pp. 37–45.

2. Impressionism was clearly a painterly style. Fauvism fused the painterly and the nonpainterly. Neo-Impressionism also attempted a synthesis of these two possibilities when it separated the Impressionist touch and regularized its shape and size. This was done in order to reintroduce controlled modeling of objects, but very soon pure color began to impose its own logic. In the work of Signac and Cross, the stroke became progressively larger, the color and touch more conspicuous; and as this happened, the intervals between usually became more evident. The large strokes no longer mix in the eye or effect nuanced tonal transitions; and they relate far more to each other than to the motif. Fauvism carried over much of this (Matisse and Derain both had worked as Neo-Impressionists, as had most of the other Fauves); the difference was that the Fauves rejected the Impressionist and Neo-Impressionist division of nature's surfaces and made an enlarged area of single hue stand for the whole local color of an object. This was done to attain a still more purely chromatic statement, to achieve greater visibility of color. As Matisse wrote, "Neo-Impressionism, or rather that part of it which is called Divisionism, was the first organization of the method of Impressionism, but this organization was purely physical and often mechanical. The splitting up of color brought the splitting up of form and contour.

The result: a jerky surface. Everything is reduced to mere sensation of the retina, but one which destroys all tranquillity of surface and contour. Objects are differentiated only by the luminosity that is given them. Everything is treated in the same way. In the end there is nothing but tactile animation, comparable to the vibrato of a violin or voice." George Duthuit, *The Fauvist Painters*, translated by Ralph Manheim, New York, 1930, p. 57.

The larger color areas of Fauvism had a flattening effect that in turn demanded new means of lateral relatedness. (*Passage*, the cubist solution, was unavailable to the Fauves not only because they wished to hang onto reality, but also even more because their approach demanded broad, discrete areas and shapes.) Since the Fauves no longer depicted natural light, they needed an abstract, flat equivalent of pictorial light and space if their pictures were not to become merely decorative. Paint application and/or bare canvas, the more sensible presence of the physical surface throughout, helped accomplish these ends.

3. Daniel Henry Kahnweiler, *The Rise of Cubism*, New York, 1949, p. 7 (my emphasis).

4. W. Darby Bannard, "Hofmann's Rectangles," *Artforum*, vol. 7, no. 10 (Summer 1969), pp. 38–41.

5. The concept of wholeness was first adumbrated by H. H. Arnason in his introduction to the catalogue *American Abstract Expressionists and Imagists*, Solomon R. Guggenheim Museum, New York, 1961. This idea was elaborated by Lawrence Alloway in "Easel Painting at the Guggenheim," *Art International*, vol. 5, no. 10 (December 1961), pp. 26–34; by Donald Judd in "Specific Objects," *Contemporary Sculpture, Arts Yearbook 8*, 1965, pp. 74–82, and in various reviews in *Arts*, 1959–65; and by William Rubin in "Jackson Pollock and the Modern Tradition," *Artforum*, vol. 5, no. 6 (February 1967), pp. 14–22; vol. 5, no. 7 (March 1967), pp. 28–37; vol. 5, no. 8 (April 1967), pp. 18–31; vol. 5, no. 9 (May 1967), pp. 28–33. Rubin was the first to point to the holistic character of Mondrian's pictures. The idea of allover composition was first discussed by Clement Greenberg in 1948 in "The Crisis of the Easel Picture," reprinted in *Art and Culture*, pp. 154–57. See

also my *Jules Olitski*, Museum of Fine Arts, Boston, 1973.

6. Alloverness, or at least evenness of accent, continued to hurt Mondrian's pictures until 1927 when he began to give clear precedence to one area, usually the center. An exception to this is his first plus and minus painting of 1915, now in the Rijksmuseum Kröller-Müller, Otterlo, The Netherlands.

7. Clement Greenberg, "After Abstract Expressionism," *Art International*, vol. 6, no. 8 (October 1962), pp. 24–32; see also W. Darby Bannard, "Cubism, Abstract Expressionism, and David Smith," *Artforum*, vol. 6, no. 8 (April 1968), pp. 22–32, and "Willem de Kooning's Retrospective at the Museum of Modern Art," *Artforum*, vol. 7, no. 8 (April 1969), pp. 42–49.

8. William Rubin, "Jackson Pollock and the Modern Tradition," *Artforum*, vol. 5, no. 6 (February 1967), p. 19.

9. Clement Greenberg, "The Crisis of the Easel Picture," *Art and Culture*, p. 55.

10. In this respect, staining can be compared to fresco, in which the pigments are *in* rather than *on* the supporting surface. And like fresco, staining, by its very nature, creates a pervasive, softening unity.

The reader may note that in distinction to previous writers I stress as crucial the tactile, material character of stain painting. Aside from the pervasive role of the canvas weave other less obvious factors reinforce this effect. As the paint dries, it contracts slightly, creating a subtle tactile difference between painted and unpainted areas. And when an oil medium is used it creates a halo around the color areas, which also is a material, tactile effect (as well as a middle value).

11. See my *Jules Olitski*.

12. In 1960 Greenberg had pointed out that Noland's use of stain had solved one of the problems that plagued geometrical painting: brittleness and rigidity ("Louis and Noland," pp. 26–29). Actually Mondrian and Malevich had been very aware of this and by and large had kept their pictures small and had given them a marked handpainted character. But most later geometric painters, including Bolotowsky, Ellsworth Kelly, Vasarely, and many more, became less sensitive

to this issue, and their pictures show less variability of surface. They become smoothed out and often degenerate into design. Stain creates pictorial mobility automatically. In the introduction to his *Last Lectures*, New York and Cambridge, 1939, p. 35, Roger Fry points out how certain materials can automatically count as sensibility.

There is another sense in which Noland's paintings can be said to be the fulfillment of geometrical painting or—more correctly—to be the first really abstract geometrical painting. Late Kandinsky and Malevich used geometrical figures very much as if they were natural forms, placing them *on* or *within* the given rectangle. More abstract in this respect, Mondrian approached geometrical painting as *division* of the surface. What counted in his works was not the relationship between different, given geometrical forms and shapes but only different proportions. It was a truly abstract system in which a change in any one element automatically changed the visual character of all the rest. But Mondrian remained traditional, still tied to representational painting insofar as he took horizontal and vertical lines as given, unvariable "forms" independent of the picture, as entities with an independent meaning of their own. Noland does not think of geometry as something independent or separable from the picture, but conceives of both geometry and support abstractly—as seamlessly related, mutually responsive aspects of one whole system.

13. Sometimes Noland has erroneously been classified with the minimalists. But he never seeks simplicity for its own sake. On the problem of simplicity, see Clement Greenberg, "Seminar Six," *Arts Magazine*, vol. 50, no. 10 (June 1976), p. 90, where the author says, "Quality, the very success or goodness, of formal art (art which is given objective public form) derives, formally, from . . . decisions, from their intensity or density. The density or intensity of decision that goes into the making of communicable art has nothing to do with quantity or multiplicity."

14. The enclosed, involuted, space-box character of Albers' squares is due to the cubist conventions of edge-echoing and overlapping planes, both of which Noland avoids.

15. It is also worth noting that with the abstract version of the Impressionist picture the layout usually follows directly from the means of application. Examples include Olitski's sprays, Louis' Veils, and Larry Poons' pourings. But with the abstract version of the Fauve picture, design or structure—the way that the incident is related to the support—becomes a problem. Add to this the fact that stain, while identifying the incident with the canvas surface as a whole, leaves this incident curiously disembodied and without a structure of its own. So it is that stain requires that the painter conceive of a design or layout. Like the Impressionist colorist, he can work in series, but he needs to invent a composition to do so. For this reason, Noland's career—and this is also true of Louis—shows a sequence of discrete series punctuated by very experimental periods of intense searching. With such a painter as Olitski, and I am thinking of his poststain work, the pigment—its consistency, texture, etc.—and color are identical (that is, as we shall see, also true of Noland, but to a lesser degree), and one group of pictures leads naturally and smoothly to the next.

CHAPTER THREE

1. Friedel Dzubas often talks about how there were two camps in the 1950s: one following de Kooning and one following Pollock.

2. It is no accident that almost every major abstract painter who emerged in the late 1950s and early 1960s was close to Greenberg.

3. In conversation with Noland.

4. In conversation.

5. Bryan Robertson, *Jackson Pollock*, New York, 1960, p. 194.

6. Robert Motherwell, catalogue, "The School of New York," Perls Gallery, Beverly Hills, California, 1951, n.p.

7. See, for example, almost any issue of *It Is*, the organ of the action painters in the late 1950s.

8. When I speak of the logic of the materials—of color, of stain, of the rectangle, etc.—I do not mean to imply that there is only one logic of any of these any more than there is only one logic in the rendering of nature. But like representation, the materials when used in certain ways and for certain ends suggest certain directions rather than others. Staining, for example, suggested transparency but also the bright intense Fauve color. Some of these directions prove fruitful, others do not. My only point is that these directions or "logics" exist, and that searching out their possibilities and limitations is what this kind of painting is all about.

9. Next to Pollock, Clyfford Still was the most important precedent for the next generation. Like Pollock, he created a continuous physical surface, an allover flatness that presided over any suggestion of illusionism. And, like Pollock, he achieved this by an unconventional use of the materials (working with the palette knife throughout the entire picture). Louis and Noland were aware of Still's pictures in the early 1950s, but I do not think they really focused on them until about 1957. As I have pointed out elsewhere, Still's influence may have been present in Louis' 1958 Veils. See "Morris Louis: Omegas and Unfurleds," *Artforum*, vol. 8, no. 9 (October 1970), pp. 44–47. Noland feels that some of his 1956–57 pictures were influenced by Still.

Noland says that he and Louis had seen only a few pictures by Rothko and that they did not interest them much. In the end, Rothko was a tonal painter, more concerned with light than color per se. And, too, he liked to veil, i.e., glaze, his colors to give them a "mystical" remove. For this reason his pictures lacked the material directness and immediacy that attracted Louis and Noland to Pollock and Frankenthaler. In addition, Rothko was conservatively cubist in his layouts.

Barnett Newman's pictures were not known at all to Louis and Noland until his show at French & Company in the spring of 1959. Newman, for all the breadth of his color fields, remains essentially a value painter and draftsman. His color choices show little range, and he usually limits himself to two or at most three colors in a picture. Newman showed little sensitivity to paint quality or to the materiality of the surface. His layouts, which *were* new and radical, did influence Louis at one point. See my "Morris Louis: Omegas and Un-

furleds," *Artforum*, vol. 8, no. 9 (October 1970), pp. 44–47.

Noland has remarked that in contrast to Hans Hofmann and Adolph Gottlieb, Newman and Rothko were "not colorists in the full sense. Albers, Avery, and Matisse also used a wide range of color, keeping their hues distinct." Noland, who was to lead the way in this direction, was drawn to the work of Hofmann and Gottlieb. Louis, while liking these painters, "didn't think they were major" (in conversation). Noland's taste, as well as his art, was ahead of Louis' in this respect.

10. Noland often mentions being influenced particularly by a large red and black painting by Louis that showed both thick and thin, impasto and stain.

11. *Archives*, p. 13.

12. *Archives*, pp. 25–26.

13. *Ibid.*

14. *Ibid.*

15. *Archives*, p. 47. Noland's procedure may make one think of jazz, in which a premium is also put on improvisation and spontaneity. Often a theme is stated and then followed by a variation, which in turn stimulates the next variation. Noland likes this analogy, and he is very fond of jazz.

16. *Archives*, p. 27.

17. "Peacock Duo," *Time*, January 8, 1965.

18. "Hitting the Bullseye," *Newsweek*, vol. LIX, no. 16 (April 16, 1962).

19. *Archives*, pp. 25–26.

20. In a few years, Noland's color areas started to become more differentiated in handling, and therefore he had to give up his use of assistants and paint them in himself. Noland used masking tape, of course, not in order to get a mechanically straight line (which, strictly speaking, is impossible with stain), but more than anything else to keep the bands, the color areas, separate from each other while he was working.

21. *Archives*, p. 27.

22. *Archives*, p. 45.

23. *Archives*, p. 25. This quote has been slightly altered by Noland.

24. *Archives*, p. 35.

25. From the first Noland was schooled as an

abstract painter and consequently lacks many of the presuppositions that a representational training necessarily imposes (such as that one must begin with forms, or that a painting must have a palpable depth, or that a painting must be the product of much time or manual effort, etc.). His teachers Bolotowsky and Albers were both second-generation abstract painters who were more open and more nonideological than such of their predecessors as Mondrian, Malevich, and Kandinsky. Of all the modern artists before Pollock, I think one can say that the most "dialogic," the most open in his use of materials, was Paul Klee, and it was to Klee that Noland had been most attracted in his early years. If one adds to all of this the knowledge that Noland had gone through a de Kooning-influenced action painting phase at the very beginning of the 1950s, one can see that Noland was uniquely prepared to adopt the new approach to the making of abstract art that Pollock offered.

CHAPTER FOUR

1. Quoted in Lawrence Gowing, introduction to the catalogue *Henri Matisse, 64 Paintings*, Museum of Modern Art, New York, 1966, p. 9.

2. A tendency to center the incident is already discernible in some of Noland's pictures of 1956. He painted the ring in *Globe* freehand and at the suggestion of his wife, Cornelia.

Jasper Johns made his first target pictures in 1955, but Noland did not see any of them until January 1958, when one was reproduced on the cover of *Art News*. Soon after, in early 1959, he saw this actual canvas, as well as others, at the Leo Castelli Gallery and was surprised that Johns had done so many of them. Target-like configurations had appeared in Noland's work as early as 1948, and he had painted centered pictures as early as 1955.

As William Rubin pointed out in 1960, Noland's use of this format differs completely from Johns'; for Johns, it is first and foremost a target, i.e., an image, a visually static sign that takes on meaning by reference to the real world. For Noland, this motif is conceived of as mobile concentric rings or circles, a way to organize and "galvanize" the surface of an abstract picture. See Clement Greenberg, "Louis and Noland," p. 27; William Rubin, "Younger American Painters," *Art International*, vol. 4, no. 1 (1960), pp. 28–29.

Barnett Newman did some paintings and drawings in 1946 that show centered circles (see Thomas Hess, *Barnett Newman*, New York, 1969, pp. 29–30). But neither Louis nor Noland saw anything by Newman until 1959. Newman was the first effectively to center the picture. But when he began to insist on the center, in 1948, he was using stripes, not circular forms. By dropping a stripe down the center, he achieved, as did Noland later, a confrontational directness and a release of the picture at the sides, an unenclosed feeling. But the vertical occurring at the literal center tends to isolate in a sculptural way; Nóland avoided this by focusing on the center *point*—outward equally in all directions.

Albers was one of the first, if not the first, to center the abstract picture, and he did so with a concentric configuration. His work was a very important precedent for Noland's concentric circles, but, as I have pointed out, there were very important differences. Noland's circles are post-Pollock in feeling and intention.

3. "Hitting the Bullseye," *Newsweek*, vol. LIX, no. 16 (April 16, 1962), p. 108. Such a picture as *Untitled*, c. 1956 (plate 25), in the collection of Mr. and Mrs. Robert B. Meyersburg, Bethesda, Maryland, clearly shows the relationship of Noland's targets to Pollock's allover paintings.

4. Al McConogha, "Noland Wants His Painting to Exist as Sensation," *Minneapolis Tribune*, March 13, 1966, p. 4.

5. Philip Leider, "The Thing in Painting is Color," *The New York Times*, August 25, 1968, pp. 21–22.

6. *Ibid*.

7. Greenberg, "Louis and Noland," p. 28.

8. *Ibid*.

9. "Peacock Duo," *Time*, January 8, 1965.

10. "His working methods at this time were as follows: sometimes he would start to work directly on the canvas or sometimes he would begin by mixing up about forty jars of Magna (he had started using Magna in 1955 and says that he and Morris Louis were probably the first to stain with it). Then he would dip a Q-tip into some jars and put some rings of color down on paper. [Noland has remarked that he only did this sometimes.] This enabled him to see the color relations. From there he went to the paintings. Six foot paintings were made on sawhorses, larger ones on the floor. After marking the center of the paintings, he used circular shapes such as dinner plates or hoops to draw the rings in pencil. The rings were painted freehand with brushes. The center one was always painted first." Jeanne Siegel, introduction to the catalogue *Kenneth Noland, Early Circle Paintings*, Visual Arts Gallery, School of Visual Arts, New York, 1975.

The pictures were usually worked on tacked to a square stretcher. When finished, they were taken off the stretcher bars and rolled up. The exact dimensions were established later and intuitively when the picture was restretched, so that many vary slightly from a perfect square. They tend to be roughly 6 x 6's, a size that Noland has said appealed to him because it is "halfway between a mural and an easel picture." All in all, Noland estimates he did about 150 or so concentric circles.

In the very first concentric circles he used as a guide any round edge that he could find (plates, saucers, etc.). Later, he found a store that sold display hoops in many different sizes. With all of these round forms he made a light pencil mark that established one edge of a ring. As Siegel points out, the band itself was always painted in completely freehand, that is, the width of the band, and the edges were established intuitively.

11. In conversation.

12. Noland tried to overcome this difficulty in the tondos by moving his rings slightly offcenter and upward.

13. Of course, Noland has assimilated color theory. He says it is like a language. "You learn a language, but you don't use it structurally according to all the rules; you use it to say something." *Archives*, p. 43.

14. "Bold Embers," *Time*, April 18, 1969.

15. Sue Ginsburg and Andrea Levin, "Kenneth

Noland," an essay in the catalogue *Color*, UCLA Art Galleries, Los Angeles, 1970, pp. 28–29.

16. "Kenneth Noland at Emma Lake," in the catalogue *Ten Washington Artists: 1950–1970*, Edmonton Art Gallery, Edmonton, Alberta, 1970, pp. 10–11.

17. The first of these pictures is *New Problem*, 1962. The series runs through 1964 and consists of about 15 or 20 pictures. I am indebted to Michael Fried's discussion of these pictures in *Kenneth Noland*, Jewish Museum, New York, 1965.

18. Noland made these essentially the same way he made the late circles—sketching in the perimeters of the motif with pencil, using as a guide wholesale, commercial display hoops of different sizes, and then painting them by hand.

19. As early as 1958 Noland had used two concentric circle motifs, one above or beside the other, in the same picture, thereby stressing the center axis rather than the center point. Between 1958 and 1962 he did a number of these, but with the exception of one, *Alliance*, 1960 (plate 85), which was square and not a double square, he decided to cut them into two pictures (e.g., *This and That*, 1958, became *This* and *That* [plate 29]). Especially when the picture was large the double focus tended to compete and make it hard to see the color. *Alliance* is a small picture, as is *Red and Purple Octuple*, 1962 (plate 119), which shows two "cat's eyes," one above the other.

20. The relationship between the Cat's Eye pictures and the chevrons is discussed by Michael Fried, *Kenneth Noland*. My discussion of the chevron pictures is indebted to Fried's essay at several points.

21. For an interesting discussion of these pictures, see Rosalind Krauss, "On Frontality," *Artforum*, vol. 6, no. 9 (May 1968), pp. 40–46.

22. See my "Omegas and Unfurleds."

23. The earliest chevrons, such as *Yellow Half* (plate 141), *Blue-Green Confluence* (plate 131), *Blue Horizon, Flush* (plate 140), and *Purple in the Shadow of Red*, are, like the circles, approximately 6 x 6', and were shown at the André Emmerich Gallery, in New York, spring 1963. The chevron series continued into 1964 and consists of about one hundred pictures.

In painting the chevrons Noland used a straight edge to guide his pencil marks (now for both edges of a band). The smaller, earlier chevrons were painted by hand, but for the very big ones he used rollers. The later chevrons mark the first time that Noland was able to work in very large scale (bigger than 6 x 6'), and they also mark the point when he shifted from Magna to Aquatec paint.

24. Noland had used a lozenge motif in some of his earliest works done at Black Mountain College, and he had employed a diamond-shaped canvas in the early 1950s. At his first French & Company show in 1959 he had hung one of the circles as a diamond. Bolotowsky often used a diamond format.

Centered within a square format, a lozenge, like a circle, is a nonechoing, expansive motif. Used as a format, it diminishes the enclosing force of the edges by making the horizontal-vertical axes and the corners coincide; the sides become merely the arms of arrows. Like the concentric circles and the chevrons, the diamond has an inherent openness and weightlessness.

At various times Noland has also experimented with triangular and oval-shaped canvases.

25. Noland usually so proportioned the raw canvas areas between his stripes as to prevent them from reading as lines. The few exceptions to this, such as *Shoot* (plate 139) and *Color Temperature* (plate 152), both 1964, tend to function more in terms of design than color.

26. Like the square chevron diamonds, these pictures contain multiple illusions: a truncated pyramid in perspective, overlapping diamonds, framed chevrons. But the illusion is never singular; one cannot hold a single reading, nor are the illusions sharply exclusive of each other. Despite its initial simplicity, the picture has an ambiguous identity, a ghostly presence provoked mainly by the colors. If the chevrons tended toward striking oppositions of hue, these wide chevron diamonds often show an imaginative use of neutrals—grays, browns, and blacks.

27. Beginning in late 1963, Noland experimented with the square-diamond format, trying to assess the relationship between it and the chevrons (*Sun Dried—Japanese Space*, 1963, plate 148; *Day*, 1964; *Go*, 1964; *Eight*, 1964, plate 147; and *Absorbing Radiance*, 1964, plate 146). These were shown, along with several chevrons, in November 1964 at the André Emmerich Gallery, New York. The last chevron diamonds, those from 1966, such as *Ambsace* (plate 163) and *Strand*, were shown between February 23 and March 13, 1966, at the André Emmerich Gallery, New York, together with the first horizontals and the new parallel diamonds.

28. When the square chevron diamonds or the wide chevron diamonds are hung with the motif pointed down or up, both interior and exterior are symmetrical. Usually the square chevron diamonds, at least, are hung so that the chevrons point right or left. This creates a more dramatic and tense whole: an asymmetrical inside set against the symmetry of the outside. The next series, the needle diamonds, exaggerates this tension—first seen in the eccentric chevrons—no matter which way they are hung.

29. Noland has said that this was one of his main concerns at the time.

30. *Tropical Zone* (plate 43) is, of course, related to those pictures such as *Alliance* (plate 85) in which Noland doubles his motif in an effort to get a vertical or horizontal picture, i.e., in an effort to escape from the square.

31. It is not always possible to establish the exact sequence of Noland's development. He himself does not always remember the dates or sequence, and the location of many of his pictures is unknown. In any event, there are very few square diamonds with all parallel bands. The square-diamond format seems to have been even more of a problem here than in the chevrons.

As a small standard size, the 2 x 8' diamonds could be painted stretched, permitting Noland to work more comfortably on a table rather than on the floor. He did a great many of them. Many were painted vertically, and most are meant to be hung that way. A few, though, work equally well or better when hung horizontally. (Large 1:4 pictures, such as *Up Cadmium*, are, of course, horizontal paintings.)

All in all, Noland estimates that he painted 75 to

100 diamond pictures.

32. Leider, *op. cit.*

33. After doing his first horizontals in 1965 (*Shade*, plate 44), Noland knew that he could paint more of them but he "postponed" doing so at this point in order to concentrate on the diamonds.

34. Noland first drew this analogy with the horizon at sea in conversation. For an elaboration of this idea, see Krauss, *op. cit.*, pp. 45–46.

35. Mondrian's best pictures are almost all very small, usually no larger than 20 x 20". This size is smaller than, say, the average size of a cubist or Impressionist picture.

36. Following the logic of his drip technique, Pollock tried a number of exaggeratedly long horizontal pictures (*Summertime*, 1948; *Number Two*, 1949; *Number Seven*, 1950). Louis once remarked to Greenberg that Pollock should have hung these pictures vertically. Some of them, especially *Summertime*, are difficult to take in as a whole.

37. Greenberg, "Louis and Noland," p. 28.

38. Noland reached a standard size for these smaller pictures, roughly 6" x 8'. The artist made a great many of these paintings, and more than any other single group of pictures they cover the range of Noland's color.

He also did at least one painting that is 3" x 15' (1:60). Once he remarked to me about this picture, "It stays flat and does not become an object. If it were vertical, it would be a thing, an object."

39. Henri Matisse, "Notes of a Painter," in Alfred H. Barr, Jr., *Matisse, His Art and His Public*, New York, 1951, pp. 119–20.

40. Mondrian, of course, used masking tape after 1920 or so. Tape can leave slight ridges along the edges of the painted areas, which give a tactile presence to them. Both painters have exploited this peculiarity of taping.

41. Flexibility of scale is also a question of adjusting the width of the band to the size of the surface. In general, this meant that Noland had to use proportionately larger bands on smaller surfaces.

42. This statement includes Olitski and all of the Abstract Expressionist painters as well. If all of the great very large pictures of the twentieth century were counted, I believe most of them would be Veils and Unfurleds. In terms of direct influence, in 1958–59 Noland did a few canvases that showed a centered, floral-like motif (e.g., *Crystal*, 1959), and these might have had some influence on Louis' Florals, begun in 1960. Greenberg has written, "His [Louis'] art would have evolved anyhow, I feel, towards intense and more opaque color, and vertical stripings were already emerging from under his veils in the previous years. Noland's influence served, however, to speed their emergence, and his example also demonstrated the uses of the off-white of the unprimed cotton duck field on which to float vertical as well as concentric stripes." Introduction to the catalogue *Three New American Painters: Louis, Noland, Olitski*, Norman Mackenzie Art Gallery, Regina, Saskatchewan, 1963.

By opening his picture at the top in the Unfurleds, Louis in turn influenced Noland's chevrons. See Fried, introduction, *op. cit.*

As noted, Louis designated that certain of his late stripes, done in 1962, were to be hung horizontally, floated free in a raw canvas field. This floating of horizontal bands was surely influenced by Noland's floating of concentric ones. On the other hand, Noland had been thinking about painting horizontally-striped pictures before 1962, although he did not actually do so until 1965. One should not see influence in this case, except perhaps a confirming one, for Noland's horizontal-stripe pictures are a logical result of his enterprise, begun in 1958, of finding ways to place adjacent, i.e., nonoverlapping, color bands within the rectangle. Actually, horizontal bands have a very different meaning in the work of the two artists. Louis' pictures show a column of colors, isolated on a raw canvas ground; together they often have an almost plastic definition. Noland's horizontal stripes are flatly identified with the whole surface and indeed constitute that surface.

Finally, it should be noted that there was an important technical exchange between the two artists. Despite the fact that Pollock and Frankenthaler had used unsized and unprimed canvas, Louis and Noland did not at first work directly on raw canvas. They were afraid that the colors would fade and that the canvas would rot. Louis used a thin size of rabbit-skin glue and a thin ground of precipitated chalk. He taught Noland to use a thin size, and then they both gradually diminished the use of a ground. Only after he began the concentric circles in 1958–59 did Noland begin to stain directly into the canvas surface. Louis followed suit in his Florals.

CHAPTER FIVE

1. Noland's way of working is much closer to the Impressionists and to the cubists, modern artists who worked from nature, than to most previous abstraction.

2. In conversation.

3. Frankenthaler was using Grumbacher student-grade colors, oil paint thinned with turpentine, and, occasionally, commercial enamel paint, such as Pollock had also used. In 1953, Louis and Noland began working with all of these materials. Louis, who knew Bocour, was the first to use Magna, and Noland soon followed suit. Then, in 1955 or 1956, Noland bought some dry pigments and mixed them with Elmer's glue. This was the beginning of the use of water-soluble acrylic paint. Three or four years later, it could be bought commercially from Bocour.

Noland experimented with these materials, and by his early Targets of 1958 he had settled on Magna. He used it up through the 6 x 6' chevrons of early 1963, but when he was painting the bigger, later chevrons, he switched to the water-based acrylic available from Bocour. (In the mid-1970s Noland used some Magna in his shaped pictures.) The binding agent of both Magna and Aquatec is acrylic resin. Magna is oil-compatible, and Aquatec is water-compatible; either can be thinned without loss of color intensity, and both offer a new range of colors. Neither leaves the oil sheen or turpentine halo that results from staining with thinned oil paint. Moreover, Magna and Aquatec can be stained directly into raw cotton duck canvas without affecting the canvas fibers the way oil paint tends to do.

A few early Targets are not wholly Magna, but are

mixed media (Magna and the water-based acrylic Noland made himself). The use of admixtures helped Noland to achieve differences of tactility and, therefore, different colors. He was already sensitive to the fact that more medium or more turpentine varies the thinness and thickness of the pigment and permits, for example, combinations of washy color with dense, opaque color. (Louis was not very sensitive to this point. In general, he mixed all of his paint more or less the same way and did not change densities in the same painting.) Noland, on the other hand, was using such admixtures as silver and bronze powder as early as his 1954–58 experimental period.

But it was in the horizontals that Noland really began to give far greater attention to tactility and to the changes of color that can result from such various admixtures as pearlescent powder, varnish, detergent, and gel. (Noland credits Olitski with stimulating him in this.) Also it was in the horizontals that Noland first began staining through the canvas with one application as the field and then opaquely building up the bands. Taping made this possible without having to paint over a color and having to face the problems that involves.

Noland has also remarked that different ways of applying paint—with a squeegee, rags, a roller, a sponge—all give different "dispersion." Like differences of viscosity or quality of texture, it gives a different tactile quality and therefore a different color. *Archives*, p. 43.

4. Noland has noted: "You can only describe colors in tactile terms: thinness, thickness (which are visually tactile factors), transparency, opacity, mattness, dryness, sheen. These are all tactile terms." *Archives*, p. 43.

It is the presiding unity of surface achieved by stain that in turn throws up the subtle differences of *color* that can result from even slight tactile differences of surface.

5. The last horizontal pictures show very narrow pin stripes usually spaced evenly and painted *over* a soft field. These should be seen as the horizontals most related to the plaids, which follow.

6. To paint the plaids, Noland taped out the band areas, and then washed in the color of ground over the surface. After the surface dried, he scrubbed the surface with an electric cleaning or sanding brush to raise the nap and bring up the surface of the ground. Then he retaped out the field area, and painted in the bands with a brush and opaque pigment, usually with an admixture such as varnish or gel. Sometimes he wove the bands over and under, creating a true interlace. This two-step process was first used in the late, open-center horizontals, and was also used in Noland's shaped pictures of the mid-1970s.

7. Mondrian also had to accept an interweave or interlace effect in 1942 when he decided to use different colored lines (*New York City No. 1* and *No. 2*), but he did not have Noland's problem of ambiguous or muddy colors at the intersections because he used all opaque hues. The interlace did, however, render these paintings less flat than his previous pictures, and also made the white areas more passively ground. So Mondrian then flattened the picture by painting in the intersections or joinings of his bands. Next, to add variety and integration, he carried these little squares throughout the picture. In *Broadway Boogie-Woogie* and *Victory Boogie-Woogie* the picture became flatter and has an allover flicker that recalls Mondrian's own plus and minus pictures (which, as I have tried to show, are the basis of Mondrian's mature art).

I think Mondrian got this idea from the optical afterimages that are often present at the intersections of his lines. In this regard, it is significant that when he did paint in these little square intersections he used an optical gray.

It is also interesting, and another proof of the closeness of these two artists, that Noland reached the same conclusions—painting in the joints and distributing them over the surface in at least one picture (*Closing Meet*, 1974; plate 207).

8. Another way of saying this is that the more size and shape vary from color area to color area, the less does color have the predominant role.

9. Noland decisively influenced Olitski's painting in 1960. At that time, Olitski adopted Noland's use of round, concentric configurations; the stain technique; and his side-by-side Fauve color. They had first met the previous year, and the two artists have been friends ever since. A certain rivalry prevails between them. Noland puts it this way, "When there is an adjacent art, other painters working with the same sort of awareness, then you usually watch each other. This was true of Morris and me, and it is true of me and Jules." One might add that it was also true of the French Impressionists, the Fauves, and the cubists (or, for that matter, of Raphael and Michelangelo).

10. It is interesting to note that Mondrian started to use the diamond in 1918 right after his plus and minus pictures. He saw that alloverness calls attention to the shape of the support. Yet Mondrian did not have much success with the diamond until the late 1920s when he placed a few lines asymmetrically within it. Unlike the rectangle, the square diamond comes through as a powerful, somewhat static, symmetrical shape. Visually to justify its use the inside must show sensitivity to this fact. Otherwise, the picture looks arbitrarily "framed." The two most obvious possibilities are to make the inside emphatically asymmetrical (as in Noland's chevron square diamonds) or perfectly symmetrical (as in his plaid diamonds).

11. Clement Greenberg, "Jules Olitski," *XXXIII International Biennale Exhibition of Art*, Venice, 1966, p. 38.

12. The relationship between the shaped canvas and profile drawing was first pointed out by Clement Greenberg in "The Recentness of Sculpture," *Art International*, vol. XI, no. 4 (April 1967), p. 19.

13. As relief, a painting is also uninteresting because it consists of only one uniform level parallel to the wall and has none of the subtle play of real light over the surface that characterizes traditional relief.

14. Beveling the edge of his pictures back from the surface added to the impression that the pictures were floating away from the wall.

15. Given Davis' concept, perspective must remain internal to the individual pictures, i.e., not imply the wall around them. This is clearly demonstrated in Davis' unsuccessful attempts to arrange two or more of his irregular formats in a suggested perspective on the wall. Here the wall is made too much a party to the illusion, and pictorial involution is destroyed. The

result is a rather heavy decorativeness and inert figure-ground readings. Also, perspective tends to limit Davis' art almost as much as it helps it. The price that Davis paid for his identification of the whole shape of the picture and perspective was a sensible disjunction between the literal flatness of the fiberglass sheet and the illusion. Space existed not as continuous with the flat surface (as one finds in traditional painting or in the best abstract paintings) but behind it, as in a painting covered with glass. Or one could say flatness was not created by paint on support, but merely given as a material property of the fiberglass. Davis spent the next years seeking out various coloristic and textural ways to help flatten his illusion, which in turn led to disruptive effects and an undermining of his color. Hence, it is not altogether surprising that, in a series of very good pictures of the mid-1970s, Davis has given up plastic and the shaped canvas. Nonetheless, perspective always gives to his work a certain expected, traditional look.

16. That these pictures do not go beyond Synthetic Cubism can be seen by comparing them to the polygons done in the 1930s by the cubist painter Charles G. Shaw. The only real difference is that Shaw stuck to horizontal and vertical drawing while Stella makes liberal use of the diagonal. And it is exactly this difference that makes Shaw's works in my view more self-contained and sucessful on their own terms than Stella's. I should mention Dorothea Rockburne here, who did some interesting, unstretched, shaped canvases in the mid-1970s.

17. On the other hand, there is a sense in which Noland has always shaped his pictures and has been sensitive to their shape. By locking his configuration to the literalness of the support, he draws the shape of the support into the experience of the picture. For example, the concentric circles implied the square and were set off by it. The whole picture became a tightly coherent system. It was Johns and Stella who were the first totally to identify their images with the shape of the support. Noland has acknowledged that Stella's Black Paintings, which he saw in 1959, "made the problem explicit" and were "the first shaped pictures I ever saw."

But all this does not mean that Noland, like Stella, is interested in the experience of shape as such. He always wants to open his picture and to that end he *neutralizes* its enclosing character—and therefore its shape—rather than underlining it. From this point of view, his shaped pictures of the mid-1970s are a continuation of things he has been concerned with all along and only represent a change of emphasis.

18. Some critics have objected to the gold stripping that Noland uses to frame his pictures. Aside from its protective function, a frame is intended to cancel the object character of the painting and set it off as a pictorial surface. This is all the more important in regard to recent abstract pictures such as Noland's, which depend on a very tactile, material unity of surface. In this case it is helpful if the frame is noticeably different in its tactile properties from both the painting and the wall. A shiny metallic edge serves this purpose well. The dark margin or shadow lining between the gold facing and the canvas edge permits the surface to float free of the frame and therefore sets it off even more. Abstract painters have used stripping since the mid 1940s. The shadow box came in the late 1950s. Up until then the framing was raw wood. In 1958 or 1959, Noland says, he was tempted to leave the picture unframed. Rothko and others had done this. It gave the painting a "rough look" that was much valued at the time. However, Greenberg convinced Noland that this was only a look and that he should continue to frame his paintings. Eventually he and Louis settled on the use of gold stripping, which has since become standard for many painters. In the mid-1970s Noland began to use aluminum instead of gold stripping.

19. I am somewhat simplifying and telescoping the development. The plaids continued through 1974. (About one hundred or so exist; many others were destroyed.) The period from early 1974 to the end of 1975 was a very experimental one and shows no very clear direction. Noland had several months of unsuccessful experimentation, especially in 1974, and many pictures done during this time were destroyed. In 1974 he began experimenting with a spray gun, and he continued to use it in 1975. In my view Noland had

very little success with it. But it was a further way to use tactile differences to differentiate figure and ground. Some of the 1975 diamonds and large rectangles and a few of the shaped pictures show sprayed areas. Actually, the first artist to make sprayed paintings was David Smith, and Noland had used a spray gun for a concentric circle picture in 1959. Both Olitski and Noland had seen Smith's spray paintings when they were shown at French & Company. Noland has said, "When I begin to make a change from one kind of painting to another I usually go back to a very loose type of painting [of the 1950s] ... in order to put it together, as it were, by hand. As I can get on to a certain size or scale or spatial or tactile thing, then I can begin to set the process." *Archives*, p. 27.

This statement is especially true of the period between the plaids and the shaped paintings. As was true of Louis, Noland is very experimental in his transitional periods. He takes many risks, and the pictures can come out looking almost dilettantish. But this is exactly the point. He wants to break down his own preconceptions about the well-made picture. So there are many failures, often horrendous failures. This is the way abstract painting is now made. The artist turns for revitalization to the direct use of materials, much in the way that older artists turned to nature.

20. To be sure, Noland did use nonparallel ray bands in a few pictures in late 1963 and early 1964 (*Tripex*, 1963, plate 127; *Solar Thrust*, 1963, plate 128; *Cadmium Radiance*, 1963, plate 41; *Number Seven*, 1964, plate 149, and others), but in these pictures he organized the ray bands symmetrically. In the 1975 pictures he set them in opposition and placed them asymmetrically. Jack Bush, the Canadian stain painter who was decisively influenced by Noland in the first place, used wedge or raylike bands in 1967.

21. Another formulation of this would be that, instead of relating the centralized configuration to the centralized support of the diamond, i.e., organizing everything on the basis of centrality, Noland made the inside reflect the diagonality of the edges of the support. But although true as far as it goes, this formulation does not account for the divergence and asymmetry of these diagonal areas. The divergent diagonal

edges of the raylike bands made the leftover areas of ground more active and positive. It seems to me that the will to unite figure and ground was probably a more central consideration in Noland's thinking, something that has been especially true since the beginning of the plaid series.

22. The critic Michael Fried was the first to notice this, and Noland followed his suggestion.

23. It is instructive to think of Noland's shaped canvases in relation to the needle diamonds. There, too, diagonal bands meant diagonal exterior edges, and there, too, when the square diamond had proved to be static or independent, Noland made the outside a less graspable, more responsive shape. But since in the needle diamonds he was working with all regular and parallel bands, his literal edges remained all regular and parallel. With the shaped canvases he was working with divergent, nonparallel edges, so his literal edges followed suit.

24. The rectangles were done in the fall of 1975, and together with three shaped canvases they were shown in November of that year at the André Emmerich Gallery, New York. After the show, Noland cut some of the rectangles into shaped canvases. After that, he has exclusively done shaped pictures.

25. All this reminds one of Louis' Unfurleds, but unlike them in these works it is not only the incident but also the support that possess that openness that the diagonal makes possible.

26. E. A. Carmean, Jr., has made a very interesting and probably related point when he stated that the cutting, diagonal, literal edges of a diamond shape—and this is also true of the recent shaped pictures—seem to interrupt a continuous field while avoiding the feeling of containment. This may be because, as Carmean states, the sides do not equate with the limits, or more simply because the object character of the painting is now more evident. See E. A. Carmean, Jr., "Kenneth Noland and the Compositional Cut," *Arts Magazine*, vol. 50, no. 4 (December 1975), p. 81.

27. All this is the opposite of older art, in which the inside is accommodated to the outside; now the outside is arrived at last and in response to the dictates of the inside. So, too, in older art, one interior area is bal-anced out against another while in much contemporary abstract painting the inside as a whole is balanced out against the outside as a whole.

With the horizontals, Noland was able to paint a large canvas with many stripes and then cut it into several pictures of different sizes and shapes. The structure of the plaids made this even easier to do. Several series of plaid pictures that have the same colors and bands but very different sizes and shapes also exist. Seen in this perspective, the shaped canvases are a further step in Noland's loosening of the relationship between the inside of the picture and the outside, thus freeing the latter—the picture's size, shape, proportions—as an area of choice and invention.

28. Noland painted these pictures flat on the floor as rectangles and viewed them from above, standing on a tall ladder. Edges were masked off with paper or folded back; then the picture was stretched on a stretcher built especially for it.

Very much part of the process whereby Noland creates these shaped canvases is the determination of which way the picture will hang after it is stretched. Conceiving of this choice as part of the creative process is common among abstract painters today, but Noland has now made the range of possibilities here much greater. Cropping and hanging were two areas of choice not open to older painters, but inherent in abstract picture making. With his shaped canvases, Noland has considerably expanded these two areas of choice.

Thus far Noland has kept the picture's center of gravity near the actual center of the canvas. The canvases are not radically eccentric in shape and are usually boxy or roughly circular. He often aligns one of the edges or axes parallel with the vertical but even more often with the horizontal. In general, he ensures that the picture reads primarily as a flat surface and only secondarily as a shape, i.e., he sees to it that the presiding relationship is not between the picture and the wall but between the inside and the outside. But Noland would like to be able to paint pictures that are asymmetrical and unbalanced.

29. The crucial step was making the outside an equal factor in establishing the overall coherence of the painting. Noland did not set out with this in mind but arrived at it as the logical result of the kind of interior incident that he was working with. Innovation often occurs this way, by indirection, as it were. But for this reason the artist has to be very alert and keep everything as open as possible. It is becoming increasingly evident that creativity in abstract painting is more a question of attitude than anything else.

30. All this shows that to really count, innovation has to come with quality. The shaped canvas, like the idea of nonobjective painting, existed long before its fulfillment. In both cases, the fulfillment had to be worked out in its own terms, to become "necessary." It could not be merely an assertion of abstract possibility but a realization of concrete possibility. Noland's shaped pictures represent such an expansion of possibilities both for himself and most probably for other painters as well. In this regard, Noland's work of the mid-1970s seems already to have had an important influence on one of the most strikingly original of our young painters, Darryl Hughto.

31. Donald Judd, "The Shaped Canvas," *Arts*, vol. 39, no. 5 (February 1965), pp. 56–57.

CHAPTER SIX

1. Leider, *op. cit.*, p. 21.

2. Suzanne Langer, *Form and Feeling*, New York, 1953, p. 31.

3. Traditional art, after all, makes the same point. Much of Chinese painting and most of Rembrandt's pictures sacrifice a full range of color and concentrate on light and dark.

W. Darby Bannard has suggested that "color offers such variation of combination *within itself*; it balances all that can be done without color: volume, placement, drawing, shading, and the rest." See his statement in the catalogue *The Structure of Color*, Whitney Museum of American Art, New York, 1971, p. 12.

4. See Clement Greenberg, "Post Scriptum," in the catalogue *Morris Louis 1912–1962*, Museum of Fine Arts, Boston, 1967, p. 84. Greenberg here makes a similar point about the work of Morris Louis.

PLATES

72. *Lunar Episode*. 1959. Oil on canvas, 70½ x 68½".
Collection, Mr. and Mrs. Charles Gilman, Jr., New York, New York

73. *Song*. 1958. Acrylic on canvas, 65 x 65".
Whitney Museum of American Art, New York, New York.
Gift of the Friends of the Whitney Museum of American Art

74. *Rocker*. 1958. Acrylic on canvas, 55 x 55½".
Private collection, New York, New York

75. *Blue Painted Blue*. 1959. Acrylic on canvas, 34 x 34".
Collection, Diane R. Jacobson, New York, New York

76. *A Warm Sound in a Gray Field*. 1961. Oil on canvas, 82½ x 81".
Harry N. Abrams Family Collection, New York, New York

77. *Round*. 1959. Acrylic on canvas, 92 x 92".
Collection, Mr. and Mrs. Algur H. Meadows, Dallas, Texas

78. *Bloom*. 1960. Acrylic on canvas, 67 x 67½".
Kunstsammlung Nordrhein-Westfalen, Düsseldorf, West Germany

79. *Rose*. 1961. Acrylic on canvas, 81½ x 81½".
Collection, Mr. and Mrs. Harry W. Anderson, Atherton, California

80. *Ring*. 1964. Acrylic on canvas, 4 x 4'.
Pat & Charles Sonabend, Ltd., London, England

81. *Turnsole*. 1961. Synthetic polymer paint on canvas, 94¼ x 94¼".
Museum of Modern Art, New York, New York. Blanchette Rockefeller Fund

82. *Spring Cool*. 1962. Acrylic on canvas, 8 x 8'.
Collection, Mr. and Mrs. Frederick R. Weisman, Beverly Hills, California

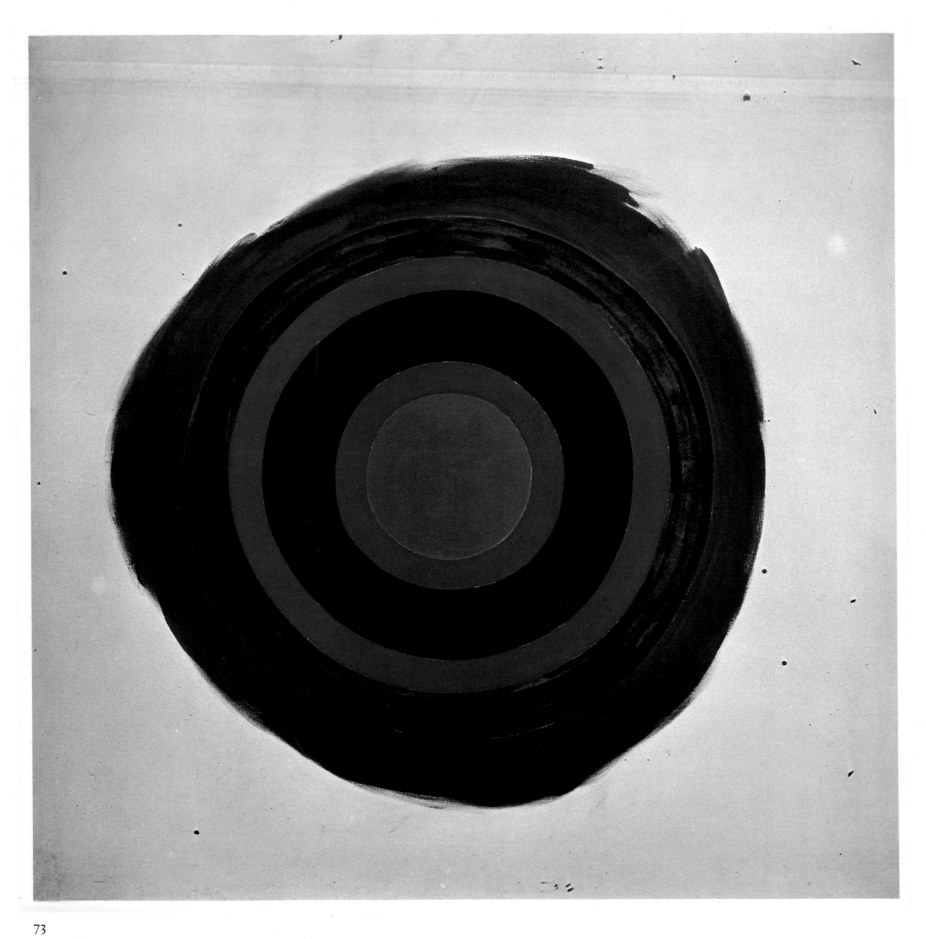

73

74

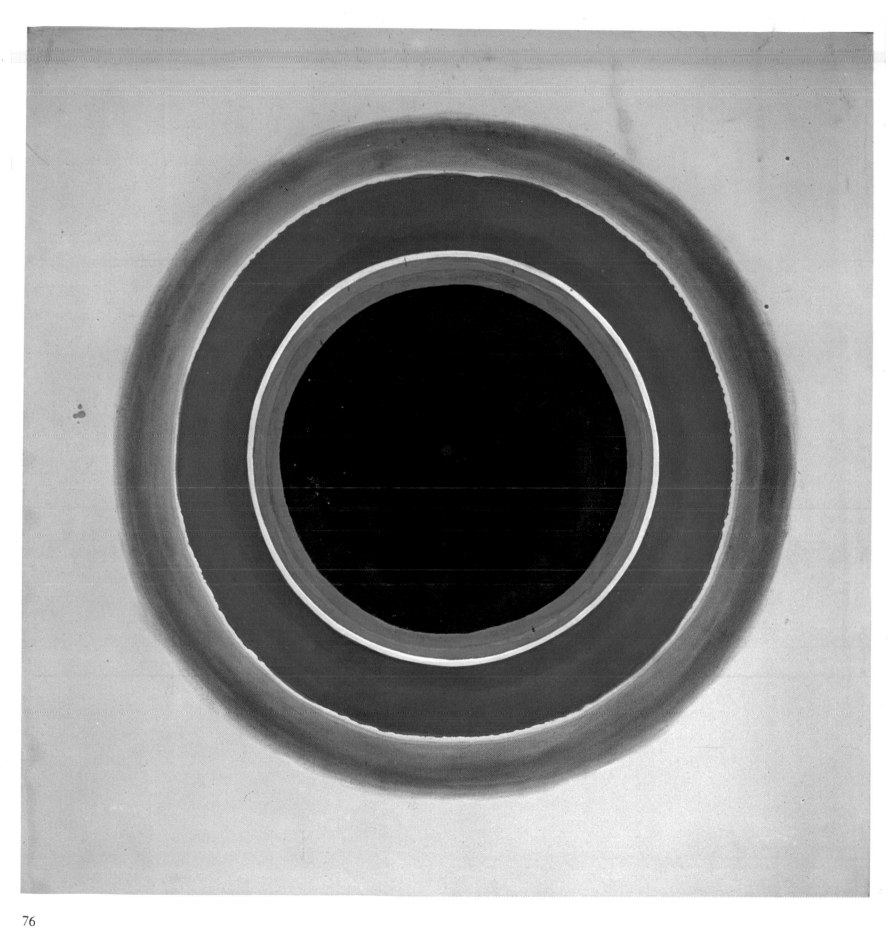

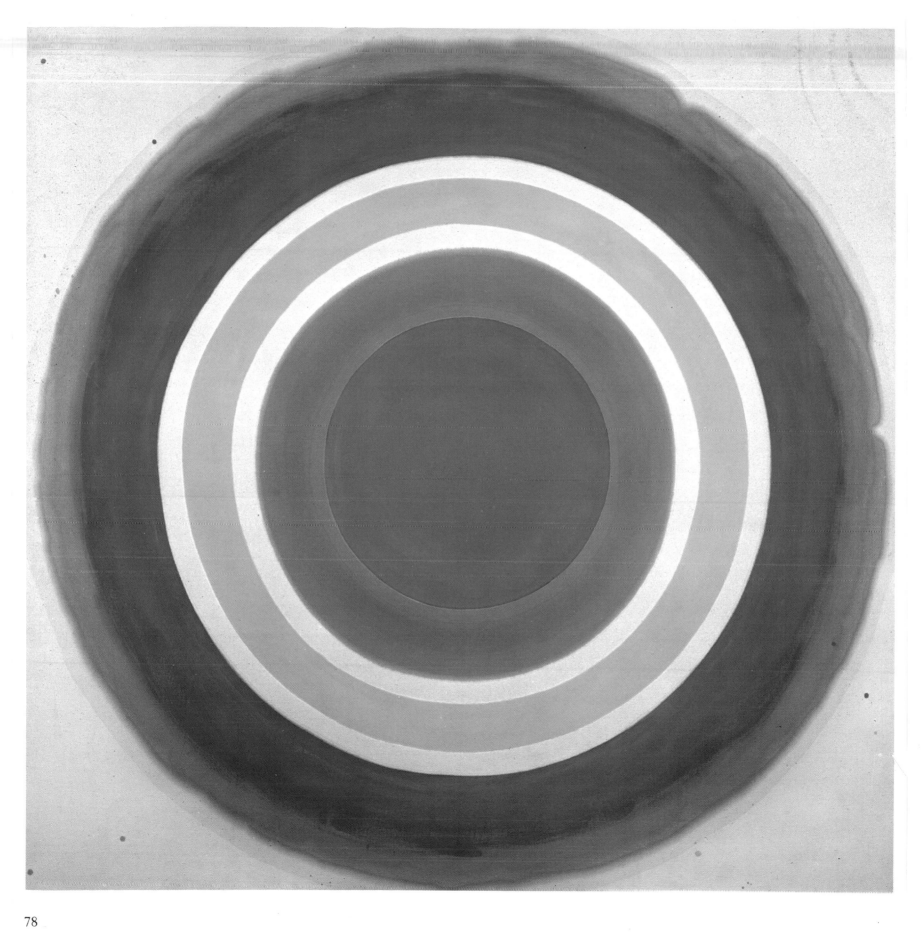

78

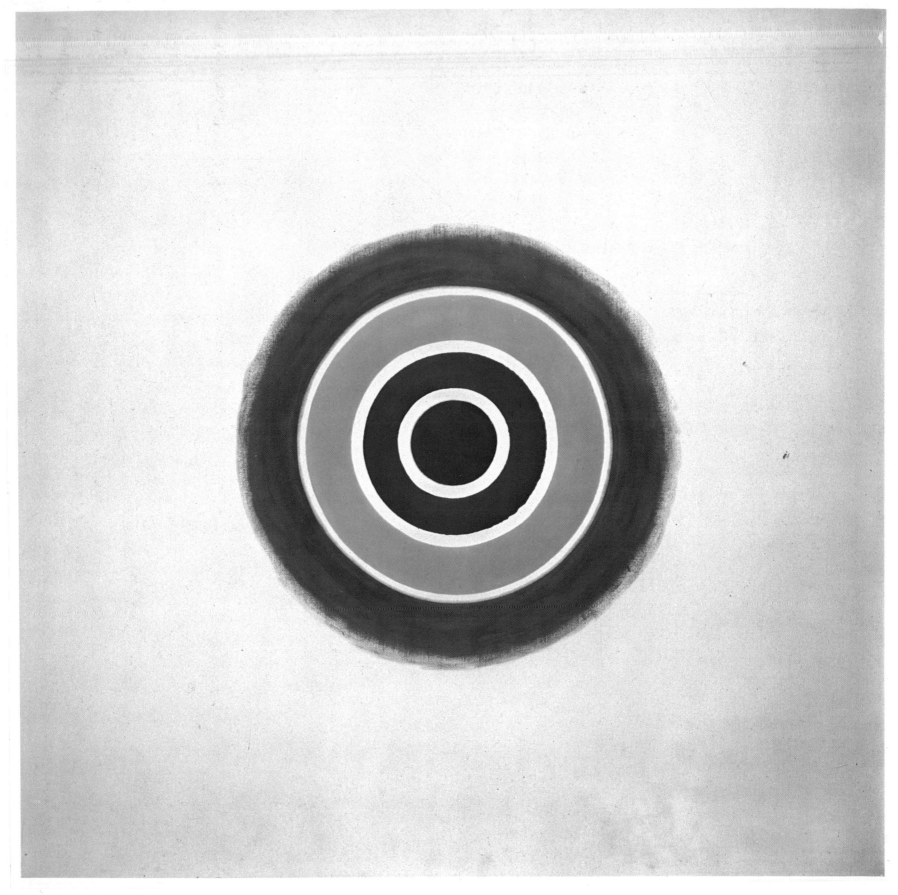

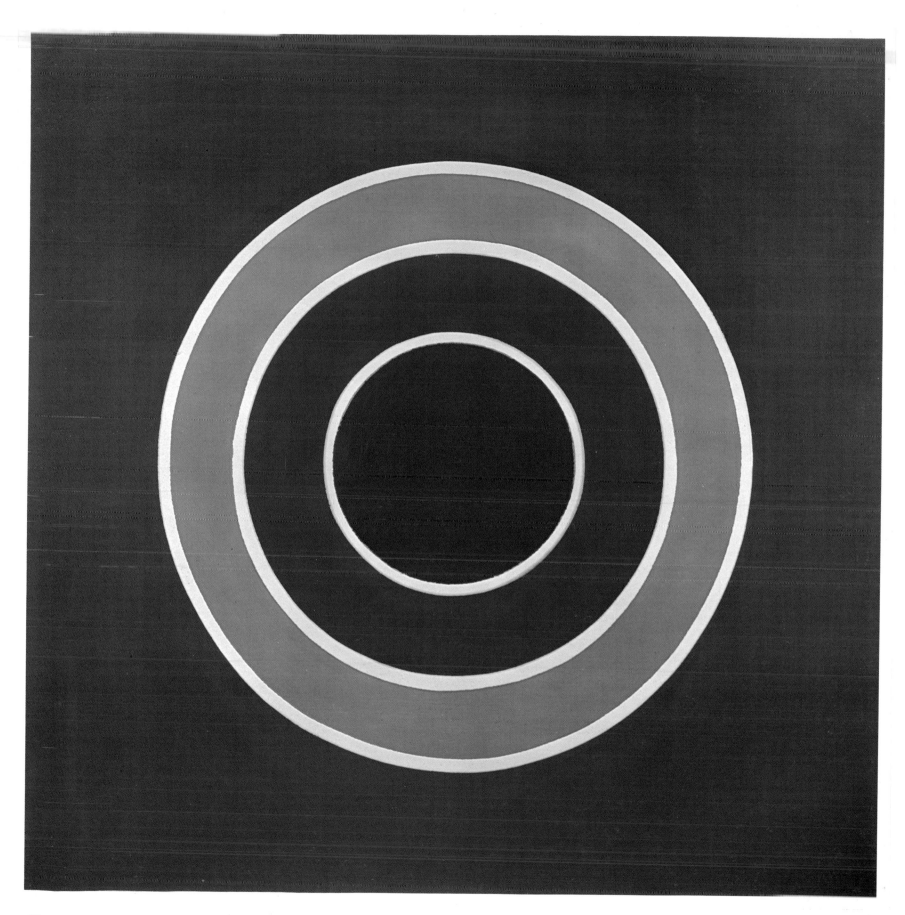

81

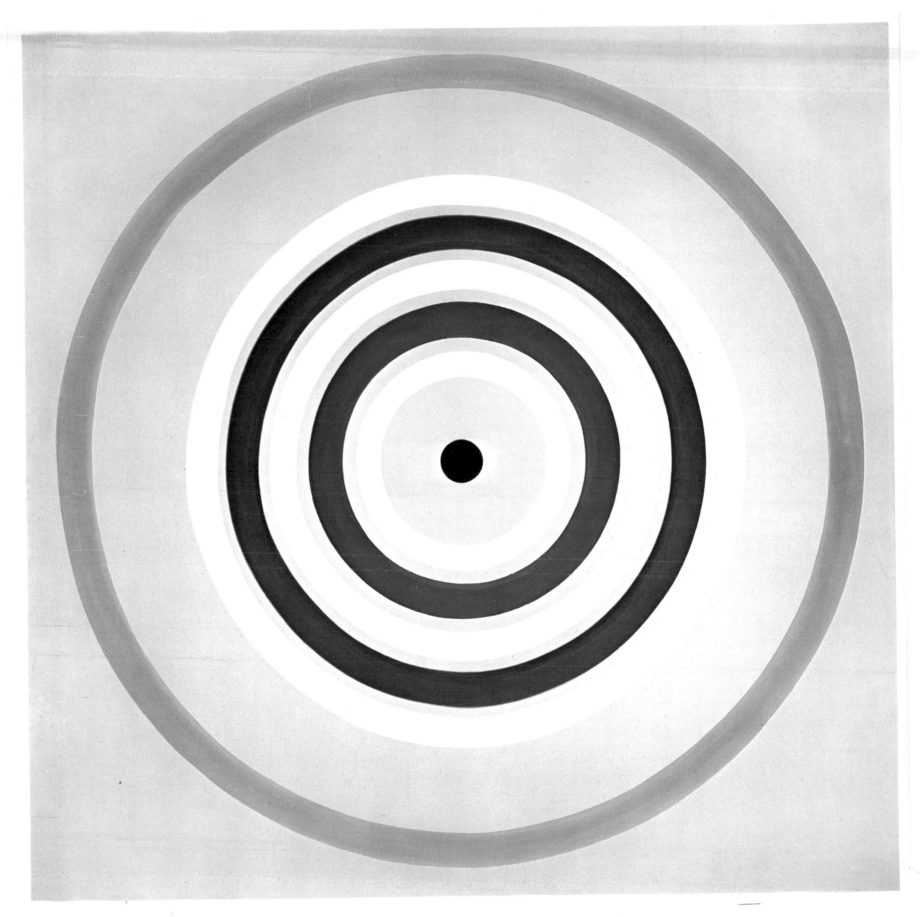

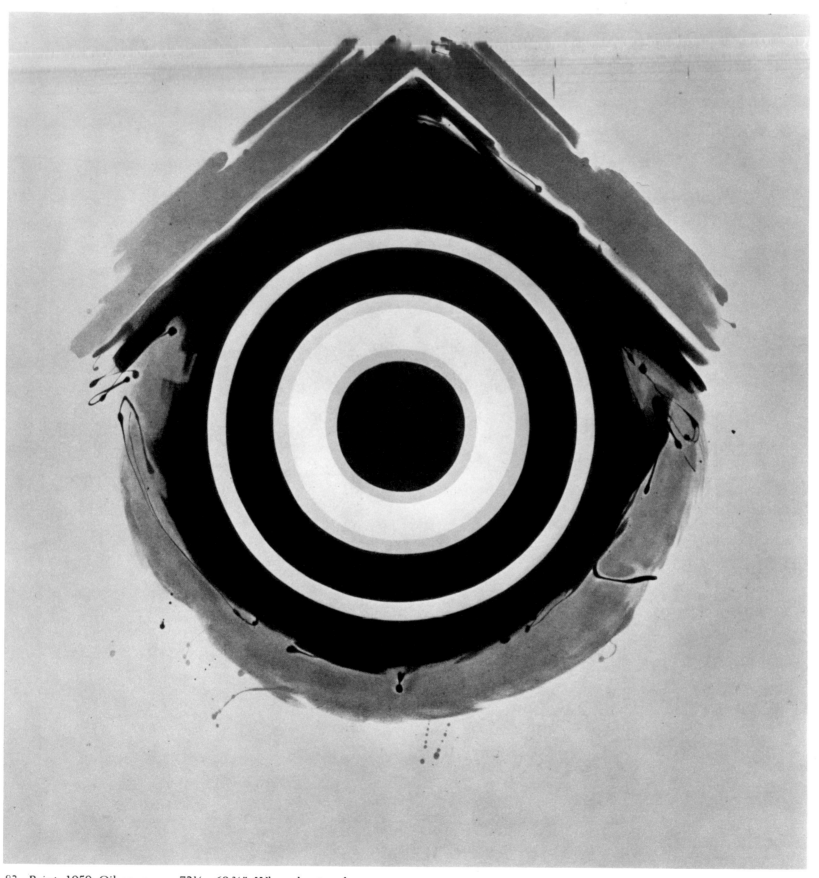

83. *Point*. 1959. Oil on canvas, 72½ x 69 ¾″. Whereabouts unknown

84. *Mesh*. 1959. Oil on canvas, 65 ¾ x 63 ¾". Collection, Alvin and Sheila Ukman, Chicago, Illinois

85. *Alliance*. 1960. Oil on canvas, 69½ x 69½″. The David Mirvish Gallery, Toronto, Ontario

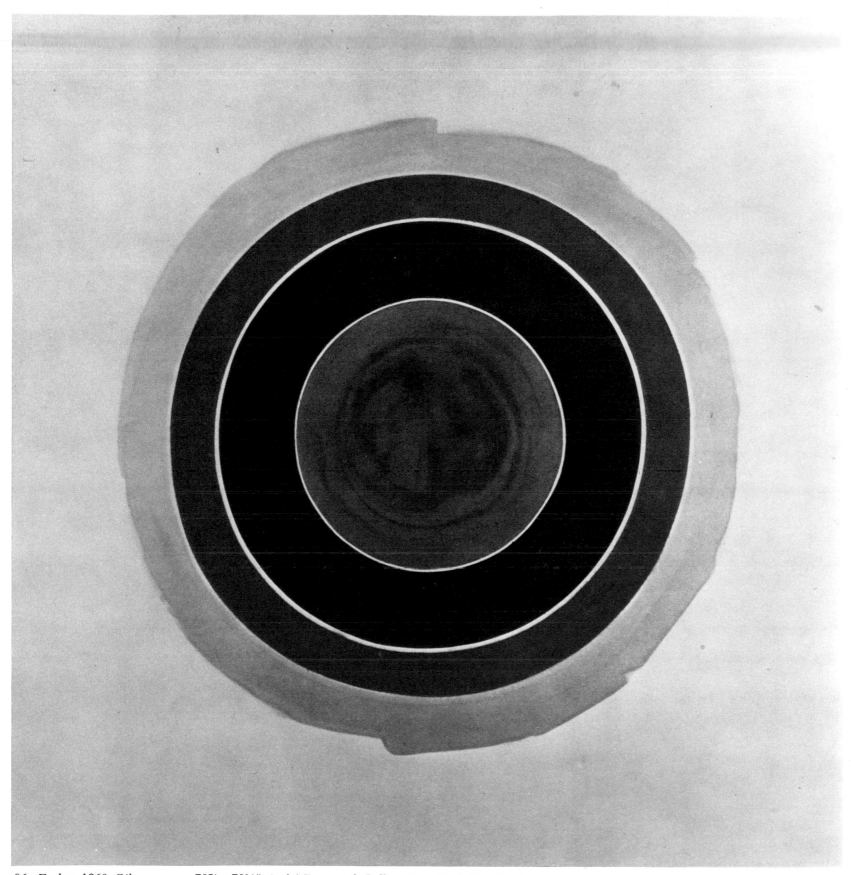

86. *Ember.* 1960. Oil on canvas, 70⅞ x 70⅛". André Emmerich Gallery, New York, New York

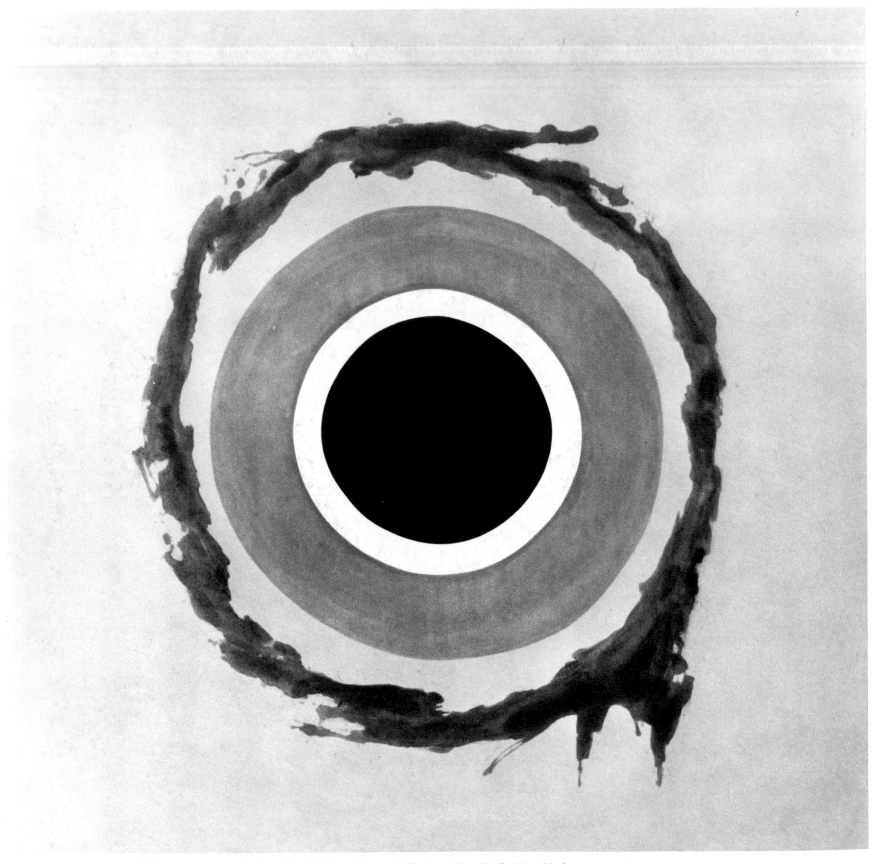

87. *Spread*. 1958. Oil on canvas, 117 x 117". New York University Art Collection, New York, New York

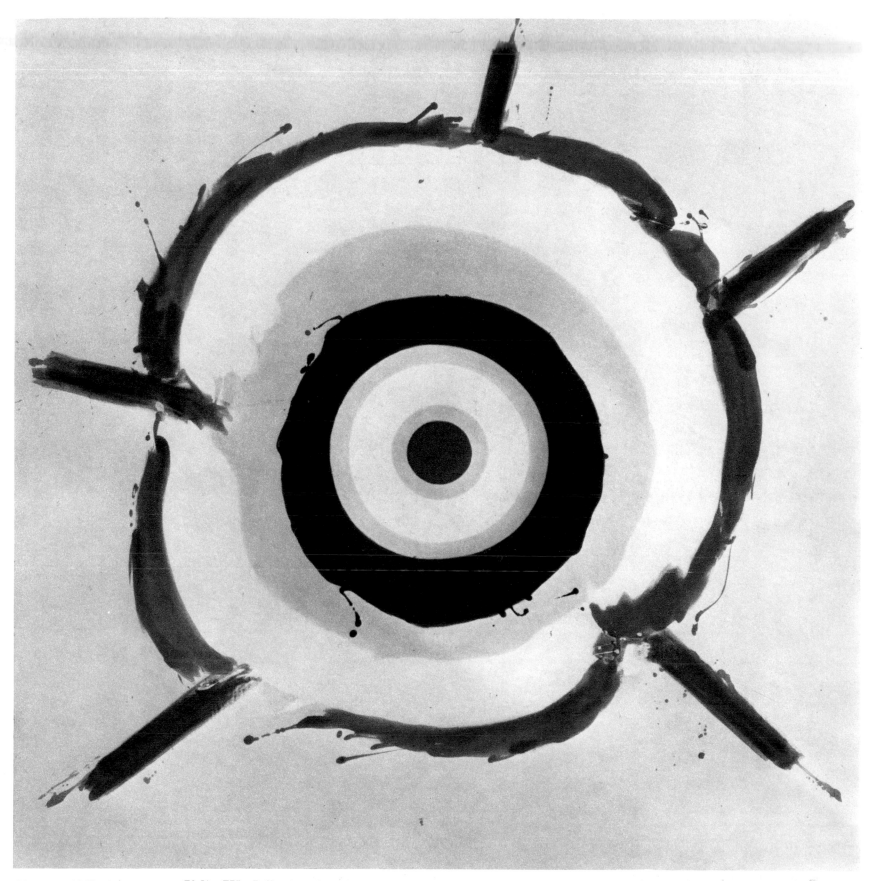

88. *Fete*. 1959. Oil on canvas, 71 ⅝ x 72". Collection, the artist

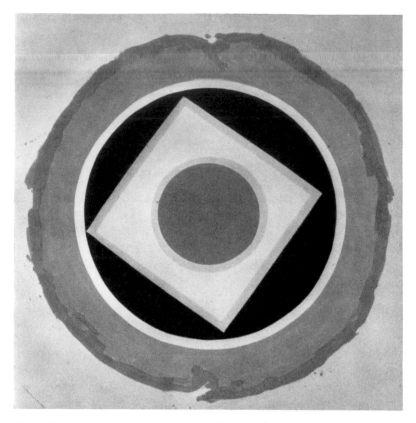

89. *Split*. 1959. Acrylic on canvas, 94 x 94 ¾".
Collection, Vincent Melzac, Washington, D.C.

91. Untitled. 1959–60. Oil on canvas, 18 x 21".
Collection, Christa and Harry Noland, Reston, Virginia

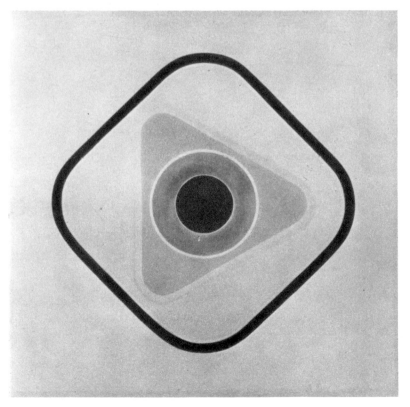

90. *Missus*. 1959. Oil on canvas, 69 x 68¼".
David Mirvish Gallery, Toronto, Ontario

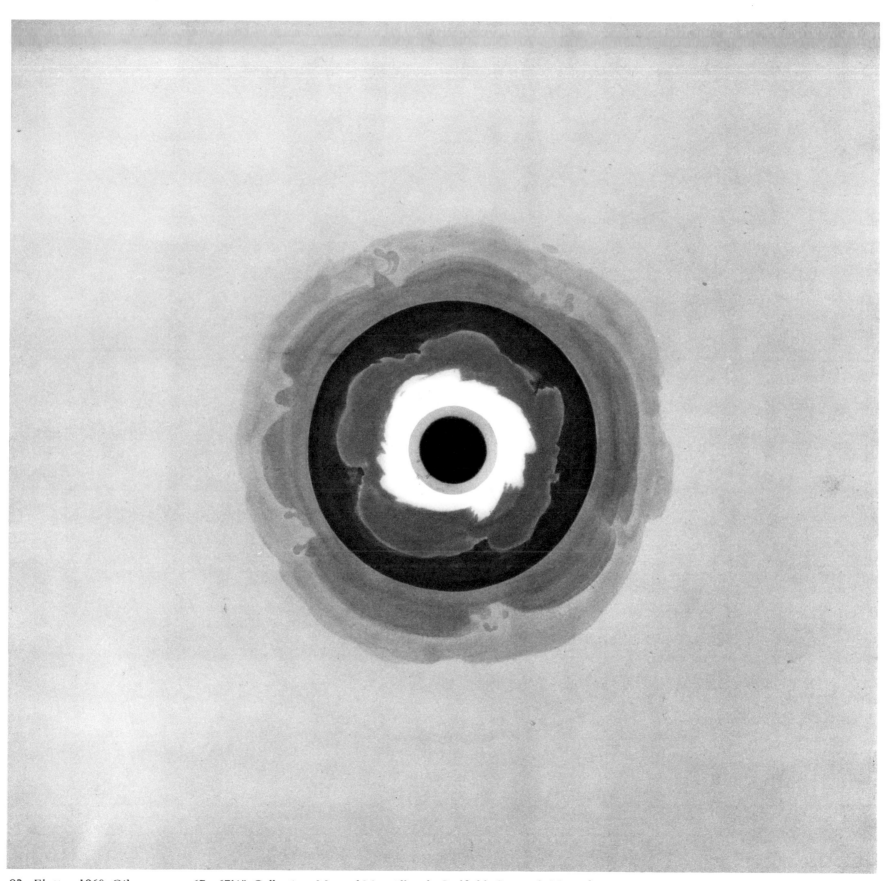

92. *Flutter.* 1960. Oil on canvas, 67 x 67¼". Collection, Mr. and Mrs. Albrecht Saalfield, Concord, Massachusetts

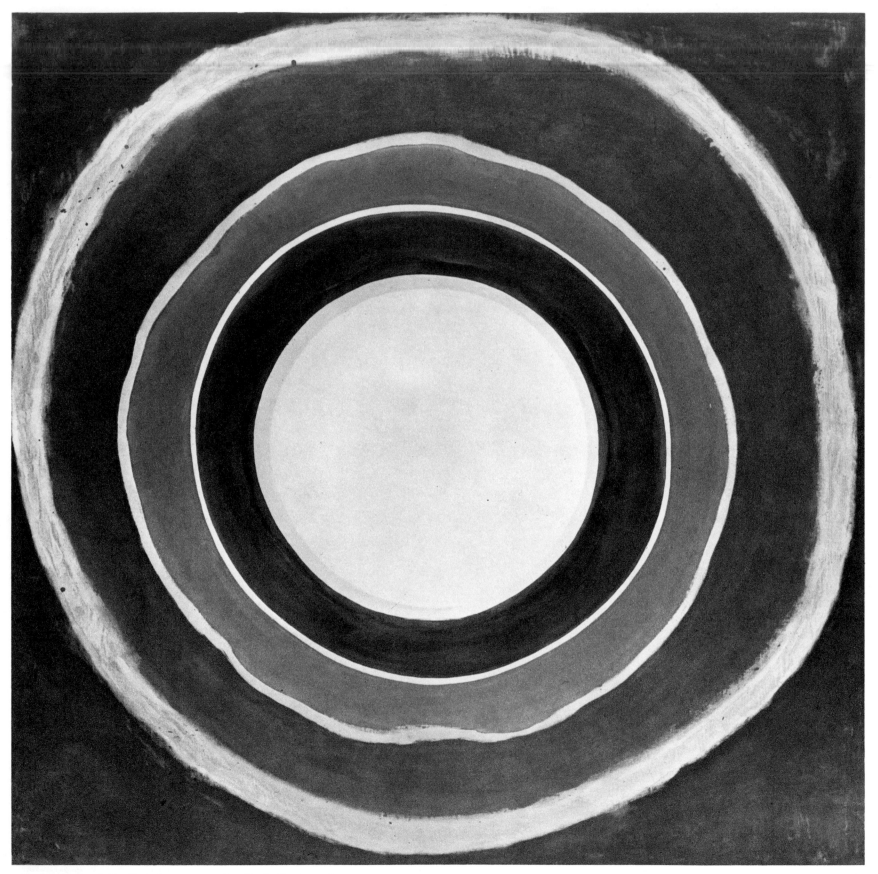

93. Untitled. 1958–59. Oil on canvas, 7 x 7′. Collection, the artist

94. *Breath*. 1959. Oil on canvas, 66 x 66" Collection, Mr. and Mrs. Joseph Pulitzer, Jr., St. Louis, Missouri

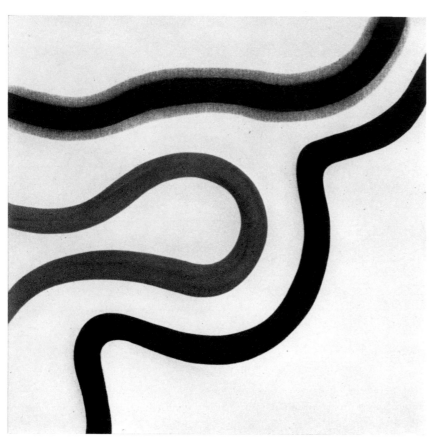

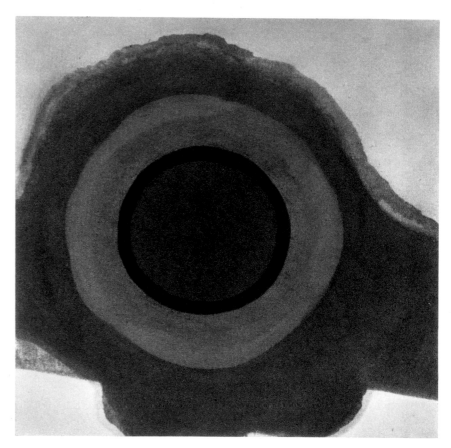

95. *Franklin.* 1960. Acrylic on canvas, 36 x 36".
Collection, Mr. and Mrs. Harry W. Glasgall, New York, New York

96. *Blue Circle.* 1960. Oil on canvas, 13 x 13".
Collection, Mr. and Mrs. Harold Tanner, Scarsdale, New York

97. *Probe*. 1959. Oil on canvas, 69¼ x 68½".
Collection, Mr. and Mrs. Morton Neumann, Chicago, Illinois

98. Untitled. 1959. Oil on canvas, 5 x 5'.
Collection, the artist

99. *Fiord*. 1960. Acrylic on canvas, 80½ x 80½".
The David Mirvish Gallery, Toronto, Ontario

100. *Shallows*. 1961. Acrylic on canvas, 117¾ x 118". Dartmouth College Art Collection, Hanover, New Hampshire

101. *Time's Motion*. 1959. Oil on canvas, 70 x 71".
Collection, Mr. and Mrs. Ronald K. Greenberg, St. Louis, Missouri

102. Untitled. 1959. Oil on canvas, 8 x 8'.
Collection, the artist

103. Untitled. 1959. Oil on canvas, 96 x 94". Collection, the artist

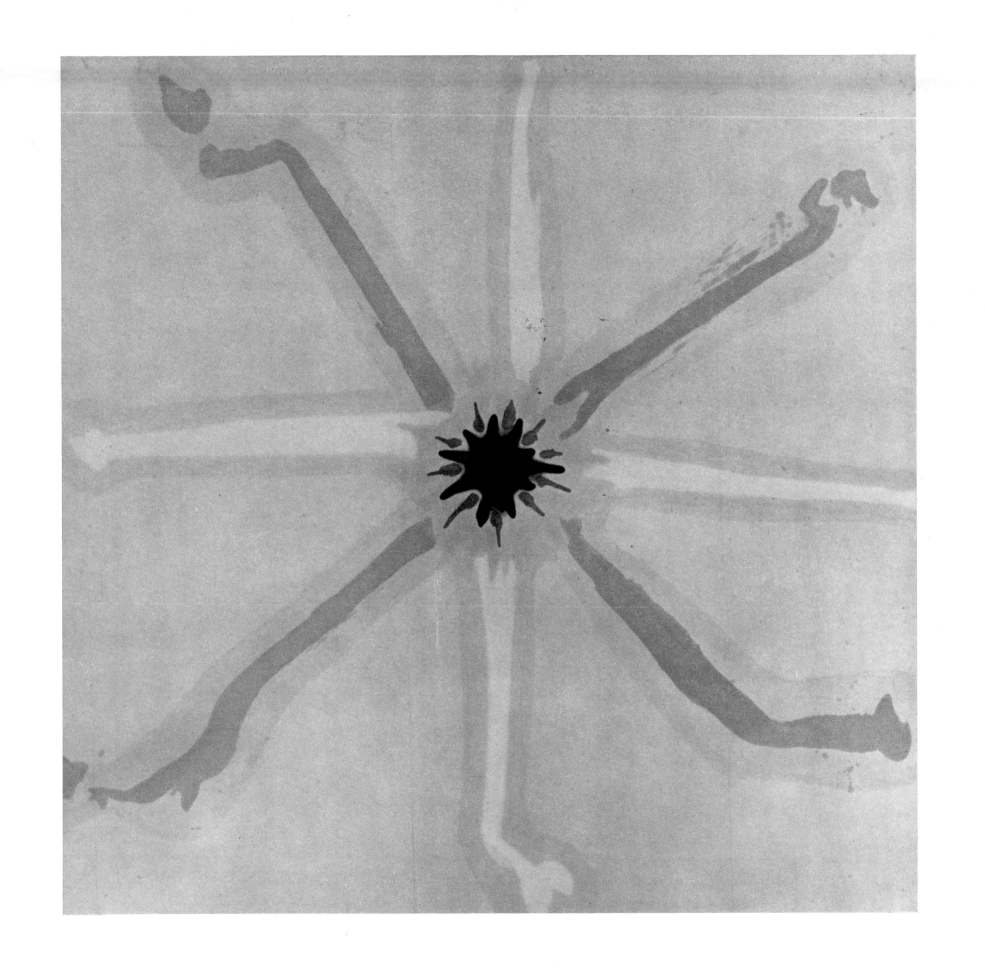

104. *Straight Flush*. 1959. Acrylic on canvas, 5 x 8'.
Private collection, Briarcliff Manor, New York

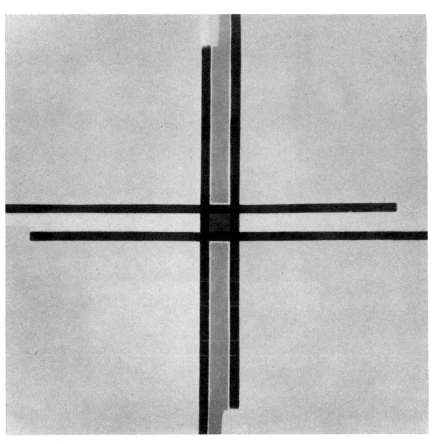

105. *William*. 1960. Oil on canvas, 7 x 7'.
Collection, the artist

106. *Quadrum*. 1961. Oil on canvas, 67 x 69".
The David Mirvish Gallery, Toronto, Ontario

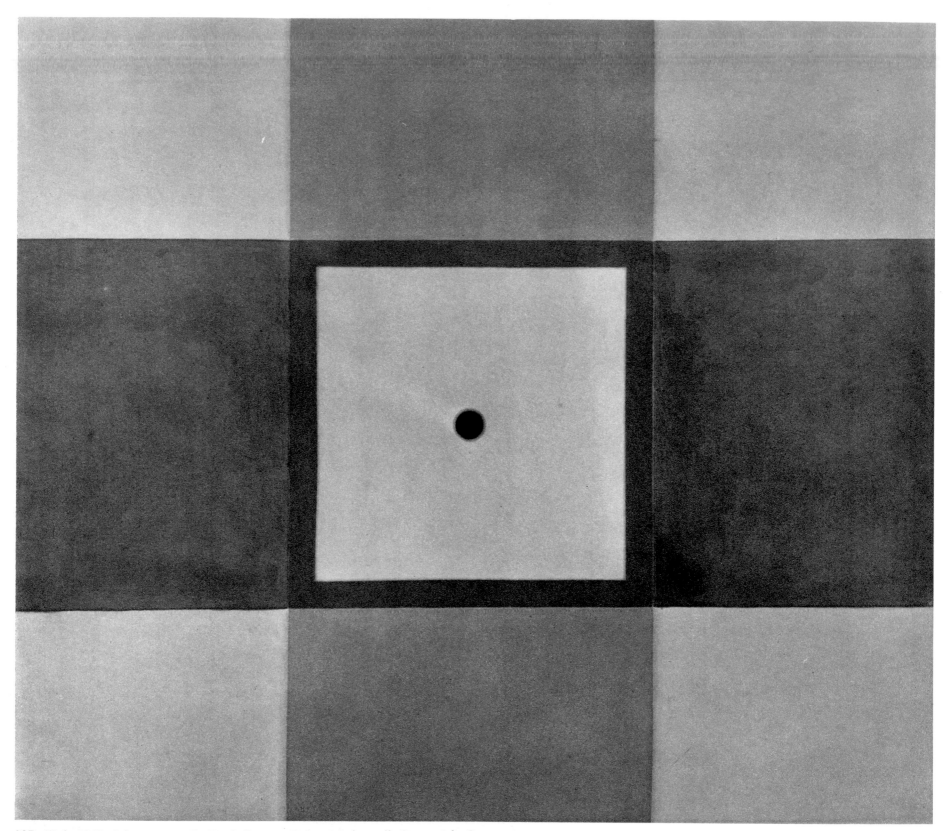

107. *Hub*. 1961. Oil on canvas, 7 x 7'. Collection, Robert Motherwell, Greenwich, Connecticut

108. *Harvest*. 1962. Acrylic on canvas, 8 x 8′. The David Mirvish Gallery, Toronto, Ontario

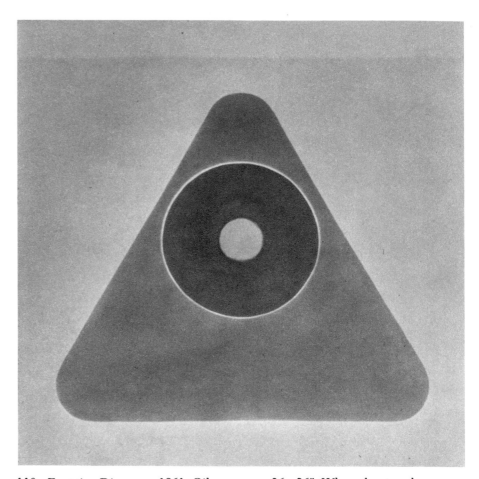

109. *New Green*. 1961. Acrylic on canvas, 34 x 34″.
Collection, Mr. and Mrs. Arthur A. Cohen, New York, New York

110. *Egyptian Discovery*. 1961. Oil on canvas, 36 x 36″. Whereabouts unknown

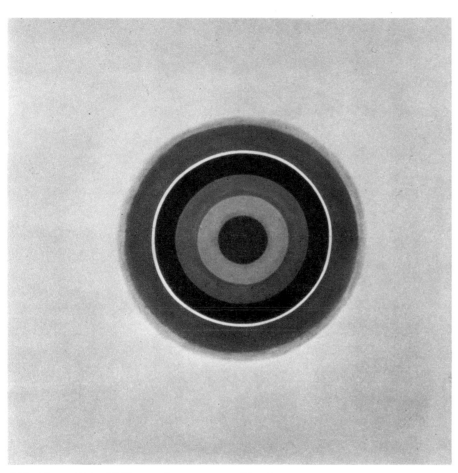

111. *Teton Noir.* 1961. Acrylic on canvas, 81 x 81″.
Collection, Carter Burden, New York, New York

112. *Karen's Gift.* 1961. Magna on canvas mounted on board, 36″ in diameter.
Collection, Mr. and Mrs. Jesse Cook, Jr., Lothian, Maryland

113. *Ex Nihilo*. 1958. Oil on canvas, 64½ x 71½″. Collection, the artist

114. *Reverberation*. 1961. Acrylic on canvas, 8 x 8′.
Collection, Kimiko and John Powers, Aspen, Colorado

115. *Drought*. 1962. Acrylic on canvas,
69½ x 69½″: The Tate Gallery, London, England

116. Installation view of Noland exhibition at Kasmin Limited, London, England, 1963

117. *Noon Afloat*. 1962. Acrylic on canvas, 48 x 48".
Private collection, New York, New York

118. *Shield*. 1962. Acrylic on canvas, 123 x 138".
Dartmouth College Art Collection, Hanover, New Hampshire

119. *Red and Purple Octuple*. 1962. Acrylic on canvas, 22 x 22".
Collection, Lawrence Rubin, New York, New York

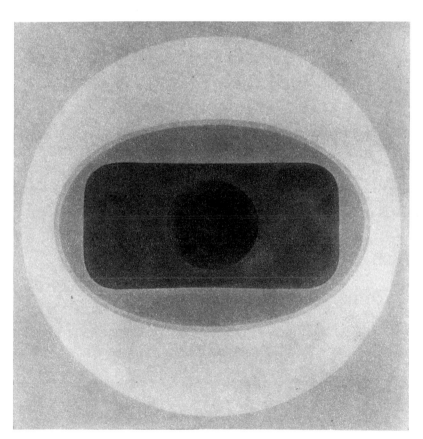

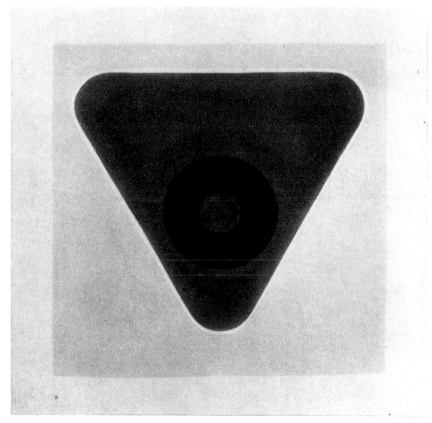

120. *Lebron*. 1962. Acrylic on canvas, 69¾ x 69¾".
Collection, Mr. and Mrs. Harry W. Anderson, Atherton, California

121. *Inner Warmth*. 1961. Acrylic on canvas, 46 x 46".
The David Mirvish Gallery, Toronto, Ontario

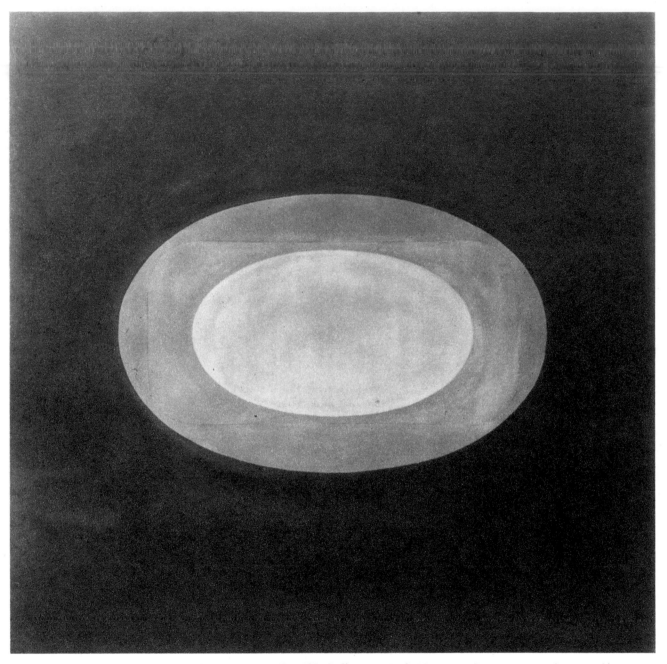

122. *Horizontal Focus*. 1963. Acrylic on canvas, 68 x 68". Collection, Lady Henrietta Guinness, London, England

123. *Fugle*. 1962. Acrylic on canvas, 4 x 4'.
Collection, Mr. and Mrs. Bagley Wright, Seattle, Washington

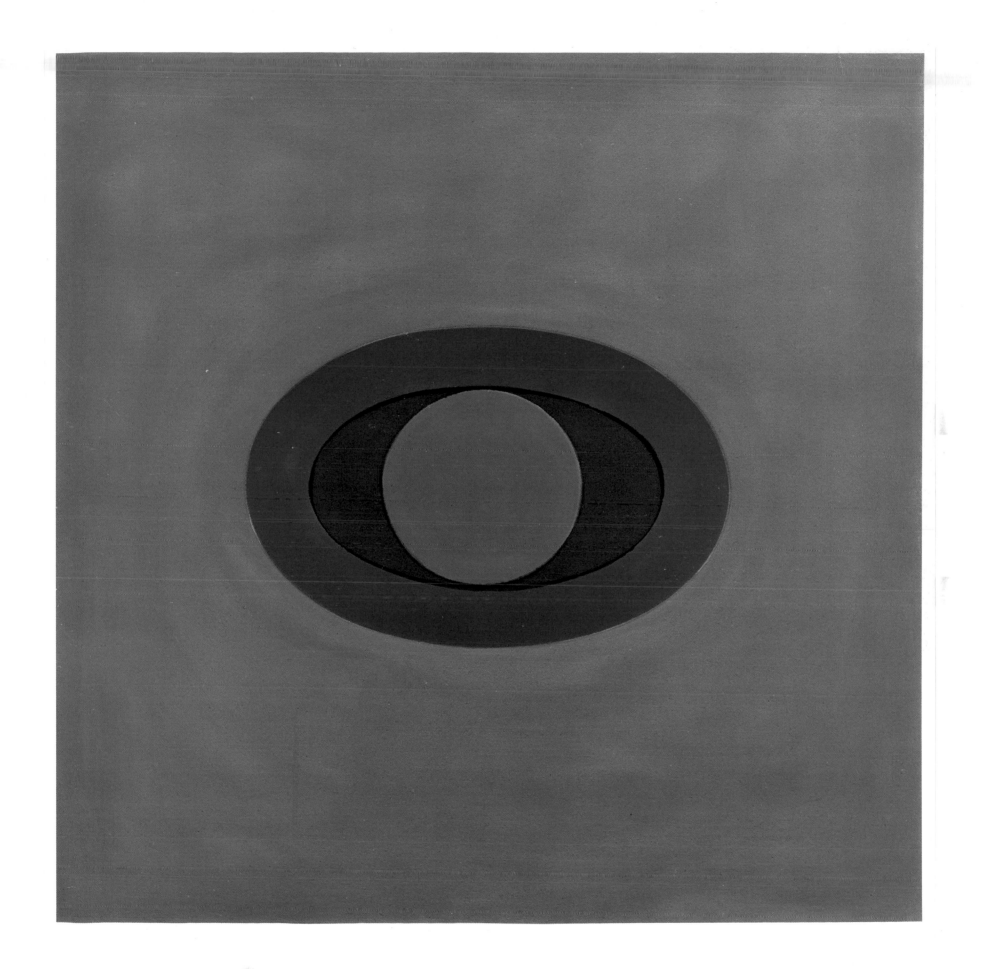

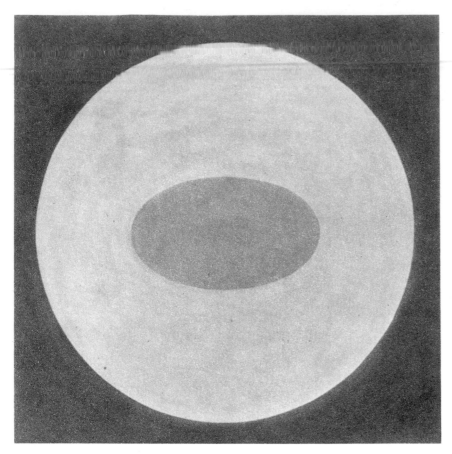

124. *Tinge*. 1963. Acrylic on canvas, 69½ x 69¼".
The David Mirvish Gallery, Toronto, Ontario

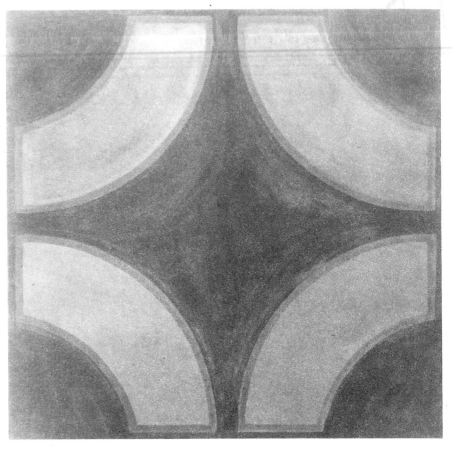

125. *Advert*. 1963. Acrylic on canvas, 47 x 47".
Dartmouth College Art Collection, Hanover, New Hampshire

126. *Rite*. 1963. Acrylic on canvas, 6 x 6'.
The David Mirvish Gallery, Toronto, Ontario

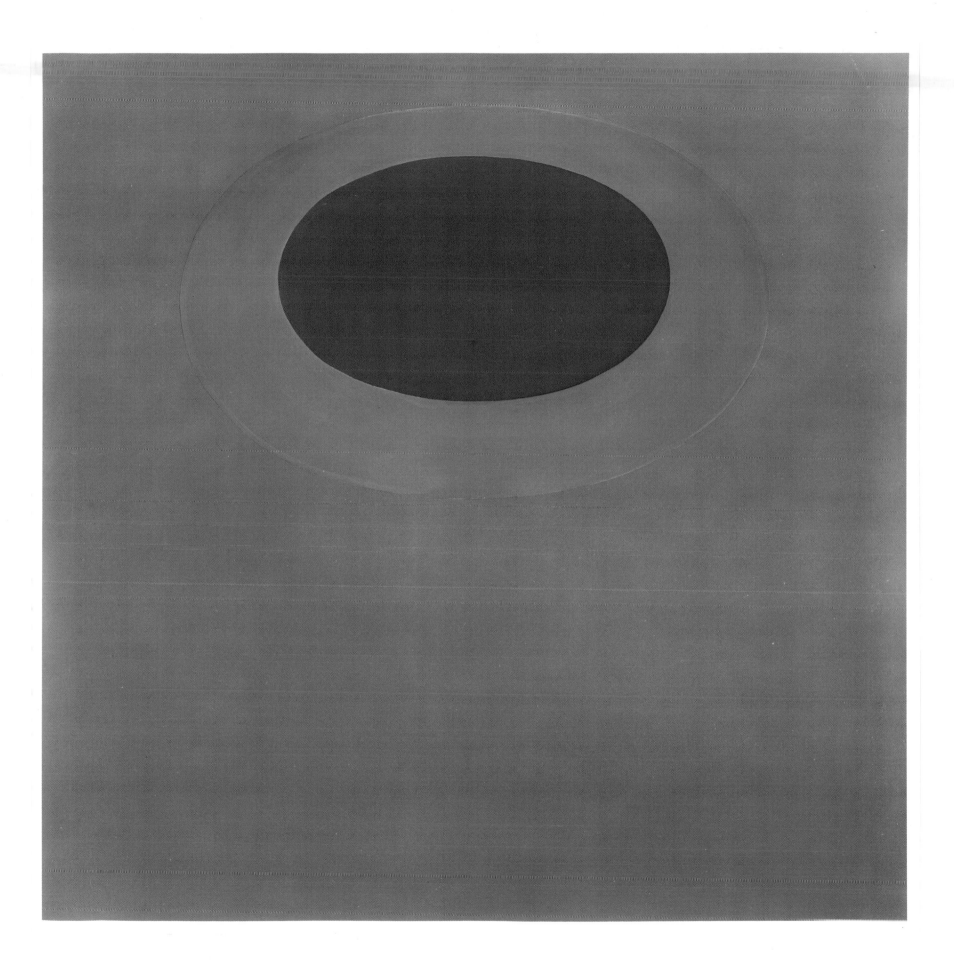

127. *Tripex*. 1963. Acrylic on canvas, 105 x 70″. Whereabouts unknown.

128. *Solar Thrust*. 1963. Acrylic on canvas, 67 x 70″.
Collection, Lillian H. Florsheim, Chicago, Illinois

129. *Dusk*. 1963. Acrylic on canvas, 94 x 76″. Joseph H. Hirshhorn
Museum and Sculpture Garden, Smithsonian Institution, Washington, D.C.

130. *Blue Veil*. 1963. Acrylic on canvas, 6 x 6′.
McCrory Collection, New York, New York

131. *Blue-Green Confluence*. 1963. Acrylic on canvas, 70 x 70″.
Private collection, Europe

132. *Magenta Haze*. 1964. Acrylic on canvas, 70 x 70″.
Collection, Diane R. Jacobson, New York, New York

133. *Sarah's Reach*. 1964. Acrylic on canvas, 94⅛ x 91⅝″.
Collection, Vincent Melzac, Washington, D.C.

134. *Morning Span*. 1963. Acrylic on canvas, 103¾ x 142½″.
Collection, Alaister McAlpine, London, England

135. *Embrown*. 1964. Acrylic on canvas, 101 x 144″.
Collection, Mr. and Mrs. David Mirvish, Toronto, Ontario

136. *17th Stage*. 1964. Acrylic on canvas, 93½ x 80½″.
Collection, Carter Burden, New York, New York

137. *Bridge*. 1964. Acrylic on canvas, 89 x 98″.
Collection, Mrs. Harry Davidson, Toronto, Ontario

138. *No Bid*. 1965. Acrylic on canvas, 46 x 46″.
Collection, Mr. and Mrs. David Mirvish, Toronto, Ontario

131

133

134

135

136.

143. *Into the Hot.* 1964. Acrylic on canvas, 69½ x 164½". Rutgers University Fine Arts Collection, New Brunswick, New Jersey

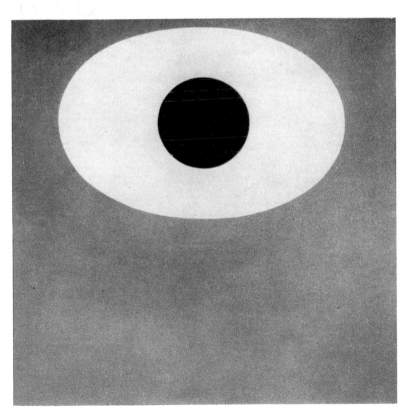

144. *Beam.* 1964. Acrylic on canvas, 69½ x 69½".
Collection, Mr. and Mrs. John D. Murchison, Dallas, Texas

142. *Alongside*. 1967. Acrylic on canvas, 2 x 8′.
Collection, Mr. and Mrs. Julius E. Davis, Minneapolis, Minnesota

140. *Flush.* 1963. Acrylic on canvas, 69½ x 69½".
Dayton's Gallery 12, Minneapolis, Minnesota

141. *Yellow Half.* 1963. Acrylic on canvas, 69 x 69": Albright-Knox Art Gallery,
Buffalo, New York, Gift of Seymour H. Knox

139. *Shoot*. 1964. Acrylic on canvas, 103½ x 126¾".
Collection, Vincent Melzac, Washington, D.C.

145. Untitled. 1963. Oil on canvas, 93 x 120″. Collection, the artist

146. *Absorbing Radiance*. 1964. Acrylic on canvas, 64 x 64″ diagonally.
Collection, Anthony and Sheila Caro, London, England

147. *Eight*. 1964. Acrylic on canvas, 44½ x 44½″.
Collection, Des Moines Register and Tribune Company, Des Moines, Iowa

148. *Sun Dried—Japanese Space*. 1963. Acrylic on canvas, 63½ x 63½"
Collection, Mr. and Mrs. John D. Murchison, Dallas, Texas

149. *Number Seven*. 1964. Acrylic on canvas, 43 x 43".
Department of Art, Brown University, Providence, Rhode Island

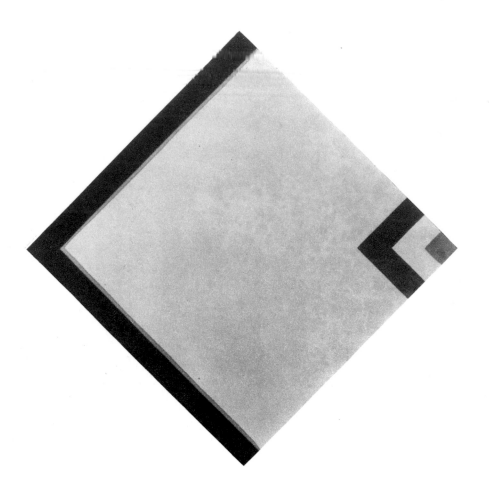

150. *Aim*. 1964. Acrylic on canvas, 4 x 4′.
Collection, Mr. and Mrs. Aubrey H. Ettenheimer, Detroit, Michigan

151. *Diamond Shaped Picture*. 1964. Acrylic on canvas, 68 x 68″.
Collection, Dr. and Mrs. Ernest Kafka, New York, New York

152. *Color Temperature*. 1964. Acrylic on canvas, 101 x 174″.
Norton Simon Museum of Art, Pasadena, California.
Gift of Mr. and Mrs. Jack Lionel Warner, 1972

153. *Drive*. 1964. Acrylic on canvas, 69½ x 69½".
City Art Museum of St. Louis, Missouri

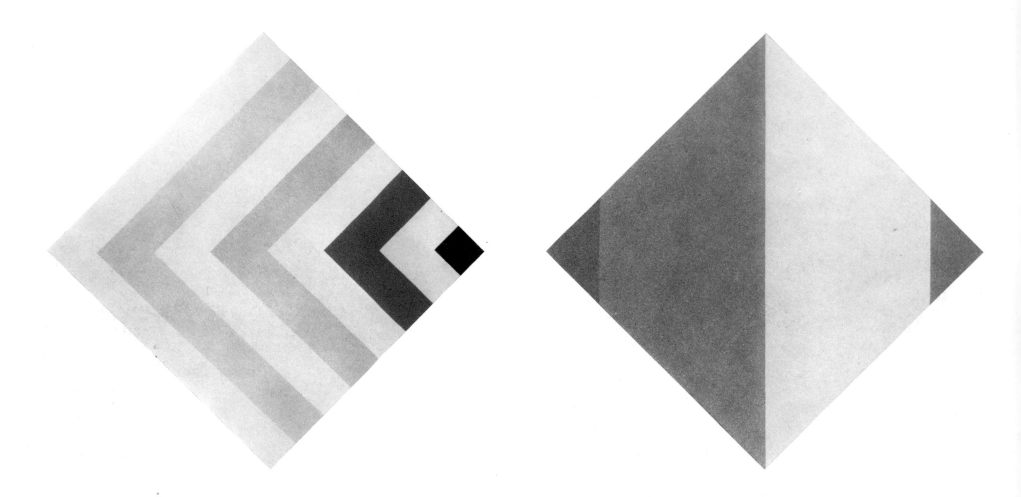

154. *March 22.* 1965. Acrylic on canvas, 61 x 61″.
Collection, Mr. and Mrs. Arnold Ginsburg, Harrison, New York

155. *Tony's Gift.* 1966. Acrylic on canvas, 2 x 2′.
Collection, Anthony and Sheila Caro, London, England

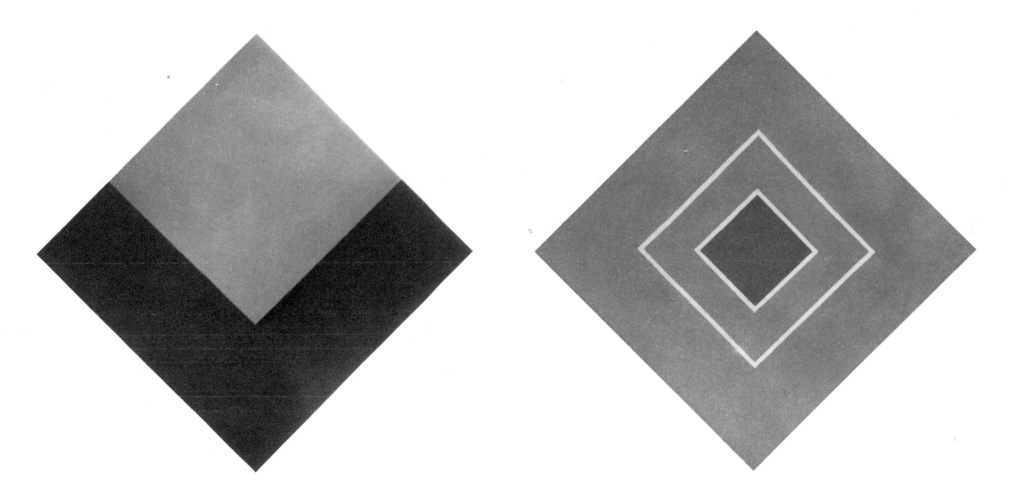

156. *Mr. S.* 1965. Acrylic on canvas, 61 x 61″.
Collection, William Pall, New York, New York

157. *Alkis' Gift.* 1967. Acrylic on canvas, 22½ x 22½″ diagonally.
Collection, Alkis P. Klonaridis, Toronto, Ontario

159. *Trans West.* 1965. Acrylic on canvas, 102⅜ x 205⅝".
Stedelijk Museum, Amsterdam, The Netherlands

160. *Mach II*. 1964. Acrylic on canvas, 98 x 208″. Collection, Kimiko and John Powers, Aspen, Colorado

161. *Grave Light*. 1965. Acrylic on canvas, 102 x 204″. Collection, Robert A. Rowan, Pasadena, California

162. *Dark Sweet Cherry*. 1965. Acrylic on canvas, 71½ x 90".
Collection, Mr. and Mrs. David Mirvish, Toronto, Ontario

163. *Ambsace*. 1966. Acrylic on canvas, 9 x 5′. Collection, Mr. and Mrs. William S. Ehrlich, New York, New York

164. *Call.* 1966. Acrylic on canvas, 99 x 46″.
Collection, Dr. Theodore Zekman, Chicago, Illinois

165. *Saturday Night*. 1965. Acrylic on canvas, 5 x 5'.
Private collection, New York, New York

166. *Daydream*. 1965. Acrylic on canvas, 1 x 1'.
Collection, Lawrence Rubin, New York, New York

167. *Transist*. 1965. Acrylic on canvas, 7 x 7′ diagonally.
André Emmerich Gallery, New York, New York

168. *And Again*. 1964. Acrylic on canvas,
69 x 69″ (100″ in diameter).
Collection, Mr. and Mrs. Bagley Wright,
Seattle, Washington

169. *Return*. 1965. Acrylic on canvas, 5 x 5'.
Collection, Lawrence Rubin, New York, New York

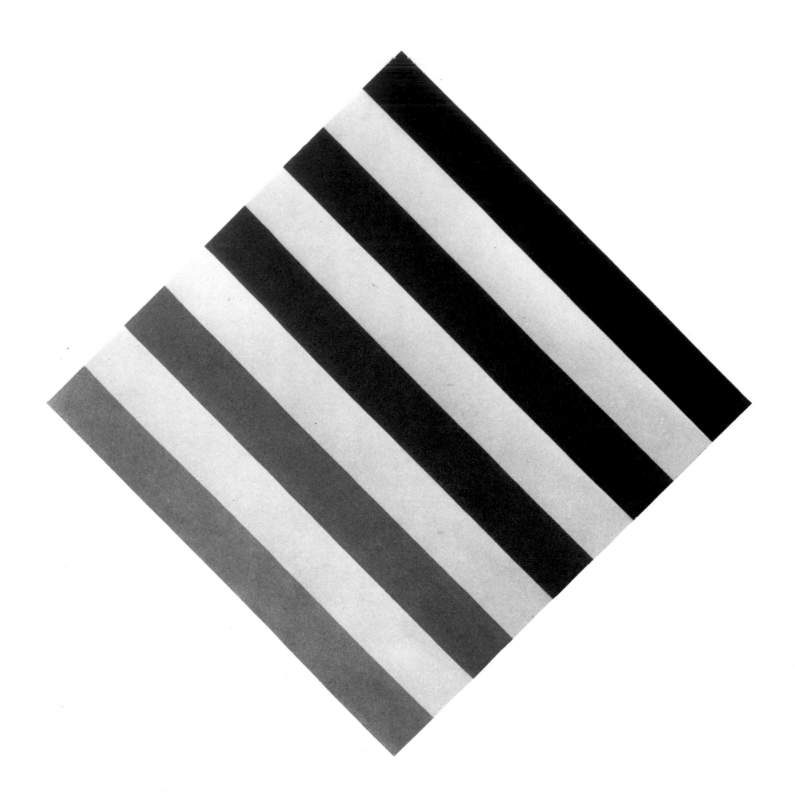

170. *Southline*. 1966. Acrylic on canvas, 4 x 4′. Collection, Katharine Graham, Washington, D.C.

171. *Twist*. 1966. Acrylic on canvas, 60 x 102″. Collection, Philip M. Stern, Washington, D.C.

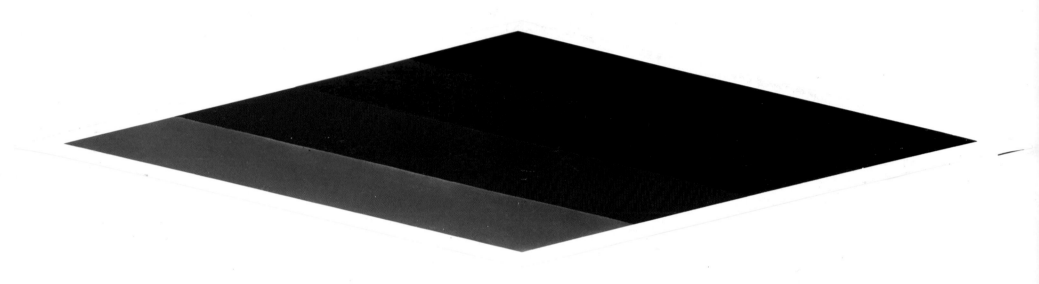

172. *Steps*. 1967. Acrylic on canvas, 23½ x 101″. Graham Gund Collection, Cambridge, Massachusetts

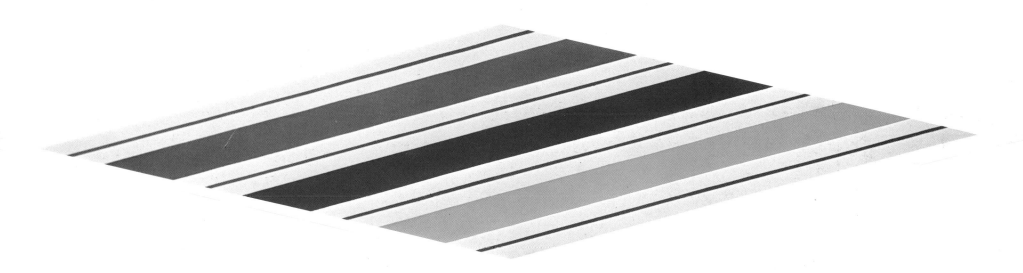

173. *Ado*. 1967. Acrylic on canvas, 2 x 8′. Collection, Mr. and Mrs. Stephen D. Paine, Boston, Massachusetts

174. *Bright Ray*. 1967. Acrylic on canvas, 2 x 8′.
Waddington Gallery, London, England

175. *Shade*. 1966. Acrylic on canvas, 22 x 96″. Private collection, New York, New York

176. Installation view of Noland exhibition at Lawrence Rubin Gallery, New York, New York, 1969.
Left: *Via Flow*. 1968. Acrylic on canvas, 54 x 148″. Right: *Via Token*. 1969. Acrylic on canvas, 100 x 240″

177. *Via Blues*. 1967. Acrylic on canvas, 90⅛ x 264″. Collection, Robert A. Rowan, Pasadena, California

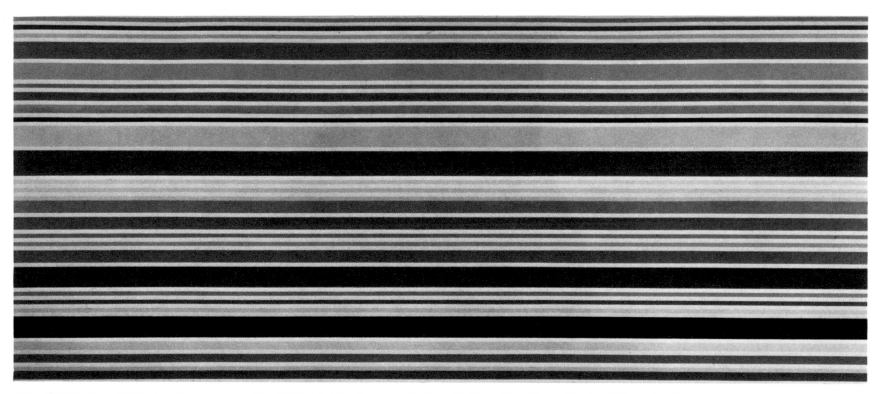

178. *Wild Indigo.* 1967. Acrylic on canvas, 89 x 207″. Albright-Knox Art Gallery, Buffalo, New York. Charles Clifton Fund

179. *Lilium*. 1968. Acrylic on canvas, 58½ x 149″. Graham Gund Collection, Cambridge, Massachusetts

180. *Via Flow*. 1968. Acrylic on canvas, 54 x 148″. Graham Gund Collection, Cambridge, Massachusetts

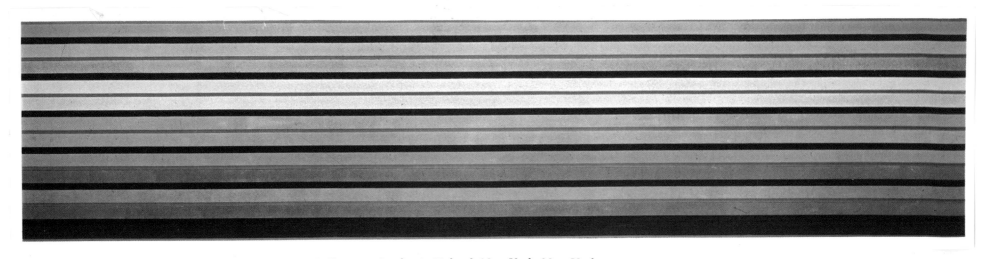

181. *It's Mine*. 1969. Acrylic on canvas, 33½ x 144″. Collection, Stephanie Noland, New York, New York

182. *Via Median*. 1969. Acrylic on canvas, 78¼ x 138″. Metropolitan Museum of Art, New York, New York. Gift of Henry Geldzahler, 1974

183. *Air Beauty*. 1969. Acrylic on canvas, 60 x 104″. Private collection, New York, New York

184. *Lucent*. 1970. Acrylic on canvas, 23¼ x 103⅛″.
Private collection, Brussels, Belgium

185. *Intent*. 1970. Acrylic on canvas, 10 x 144″.
Collection, Mr. and Mrs. William S. Ehrlich, New York, New York

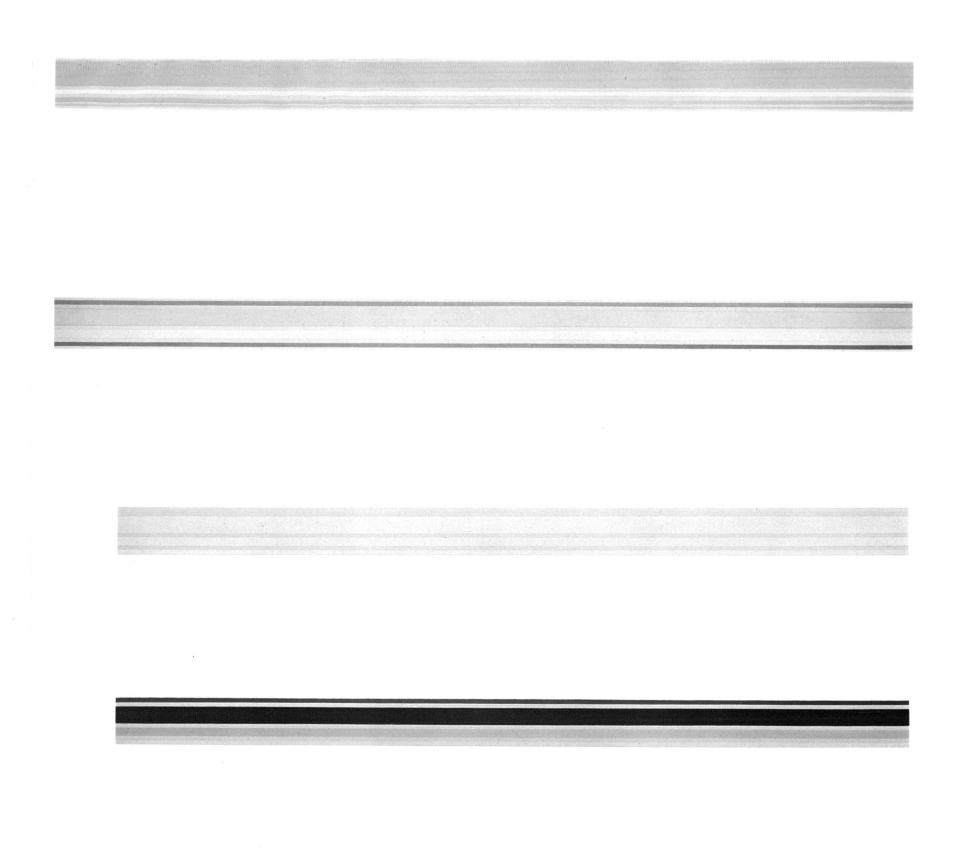

188. *Appearance*. 1970. Acrylic on canvas, 94⅜ x 192". Collection, Theo Hotz, Zürich, Switzerland

186. Top to Bottom. *Untitled D.* 1971. Acrylic on canvas, 6½ x 105".
Untitled A. 1971. Acrylic on canvas, 6½ x 105".
Enisle. 1969. Acrylic on canvas, 6 x 96".
Heptad. 1969. Acrylic on canvas, 6 x 96".
Collection, Mr. and Mrs. David Mirvish, Toronto, Ontario

187. *Little Rouges.* 1969. Acrylic on canvas, 49⅜ x 103". Graham Gund Collection, Cambridge, Massachusetts

189. *Oakum*. 1970. Acrylic on canvas, 89¾ x 240″. Australian National Gallery, Canberra, Australia

190. *April Tune*. 1969. Acrylic on canvas, 65¾ x 104⅛″. Solomon R. Guggenheim Museum, New York, New York

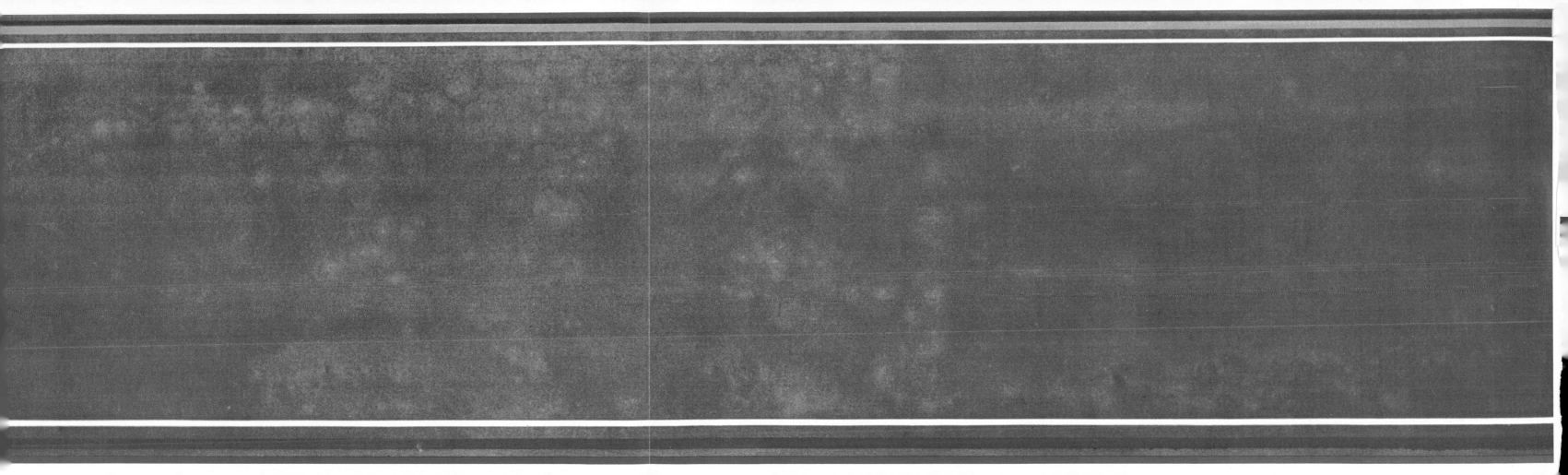

191. *Mexican Camino*. 1970. Acrylic on canvas, 44 x164″. Collection, Mr. and Mrs. Harry W. Anderson, Atherton, California

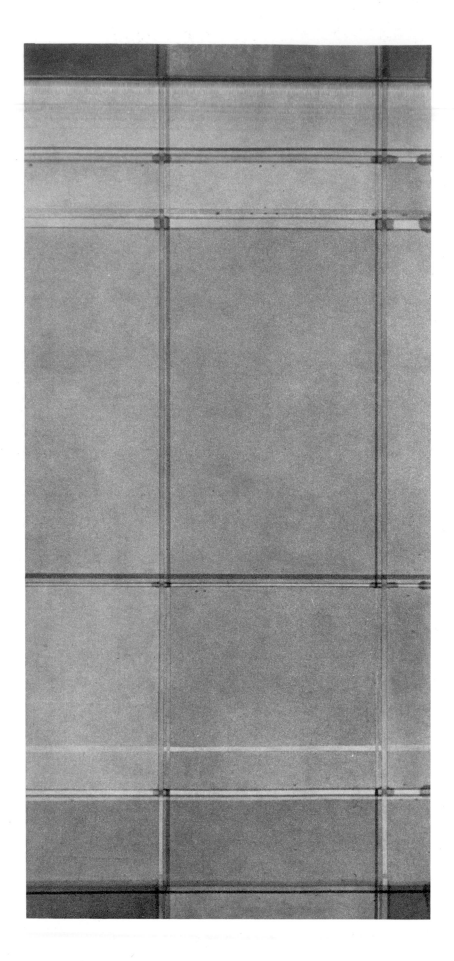

192. *Out of the Red*. 1971. Acrylic on canvas, 91⅜ x 37⅞"
Property of Cecil Blaffer Furstenberg

193. *Until Tomorrow*. 1971. Acrylic on canvas, 93¾ x 86".
Private collection, Philadelphia, Pennsylvania

194 Left: *Blue Intentions*. 1971. Acrylic on canvas, 107 x 39½″.
Right: And *Blues*. 1971. Acrylic on canvas, 107 x 16¼″.
Collection, Joanne du Pont, New York, New York

195. *Aires Solo*. 1971. Acrylic on canvas, 92¾ x 39¼".
Art Gallery of South Australia, Adelaide, Australia

196. *Passion Flower.* 1972. Acrylic on canvas, 85⅝ x 20⅛".
Andre Emmerich Gallery, New York, New York

197. *Merge.* 1972. Acrylic on canvas, 74⅛ x 72".
Collection, the artist

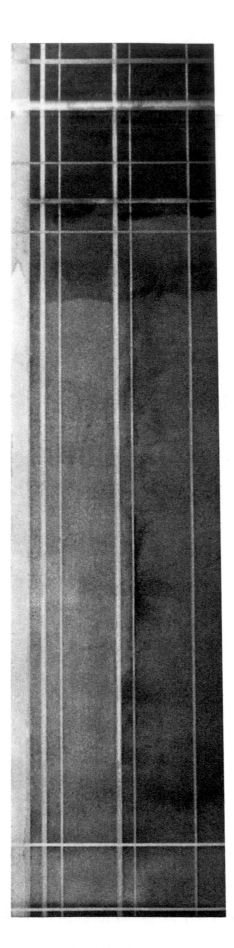

198. *Twice Around*. 1973.
Acrylic on canvas, 93¾ x 58¼".
Collection, Mr. and Mrs.
Henry Shapiro, Chicago, Illinois

199. *Over and Under*. 1972. Acrylic on canvas, 89½ x 163″. Collection, the artist

200. *Added Distance.* 1973. Acrylic on canvas, 63 x 104″. The David Mirvish Gallery, Toronto, Ontario

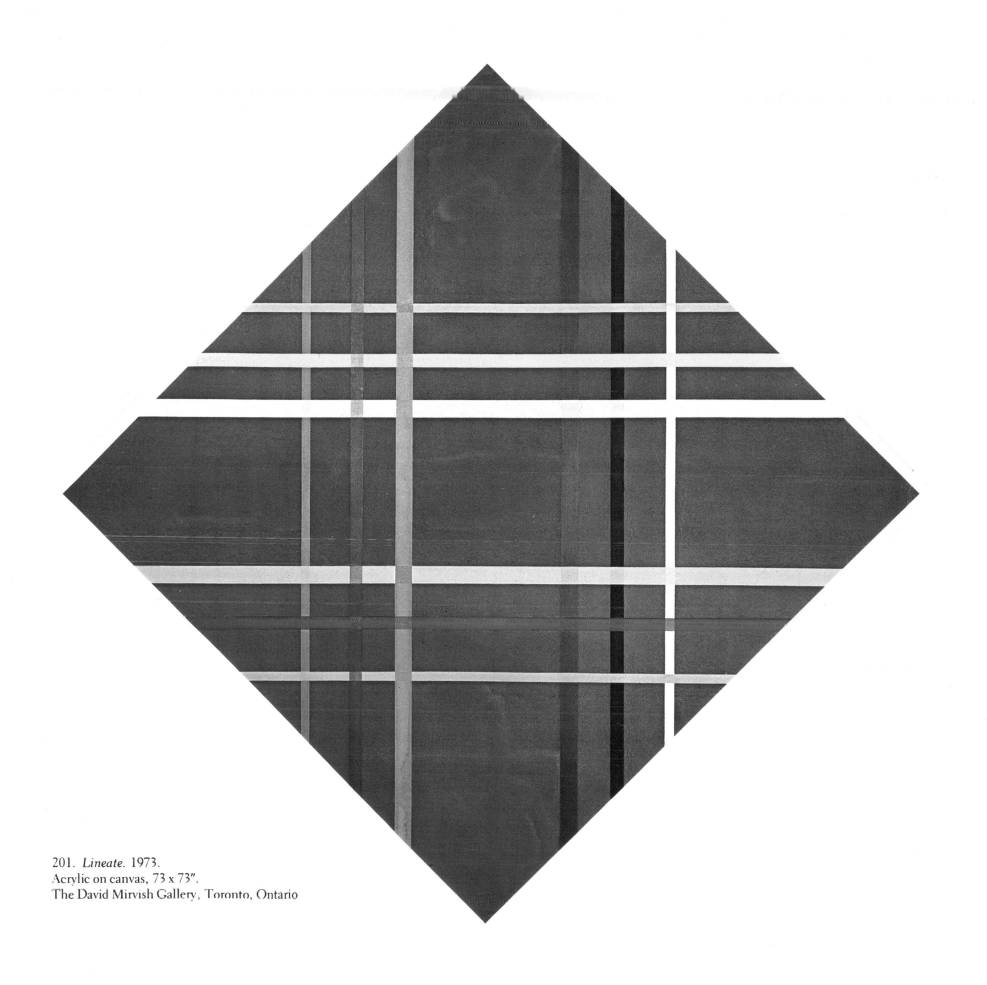

201. *Lineate*. 1973.
Acrylic on canvas, 73 x 73".
The David Mirvish Gallery, Toronto, Ontario

202. Untitled. 1973.
Acrylic on canvas, size unknown.
Collection, the artist

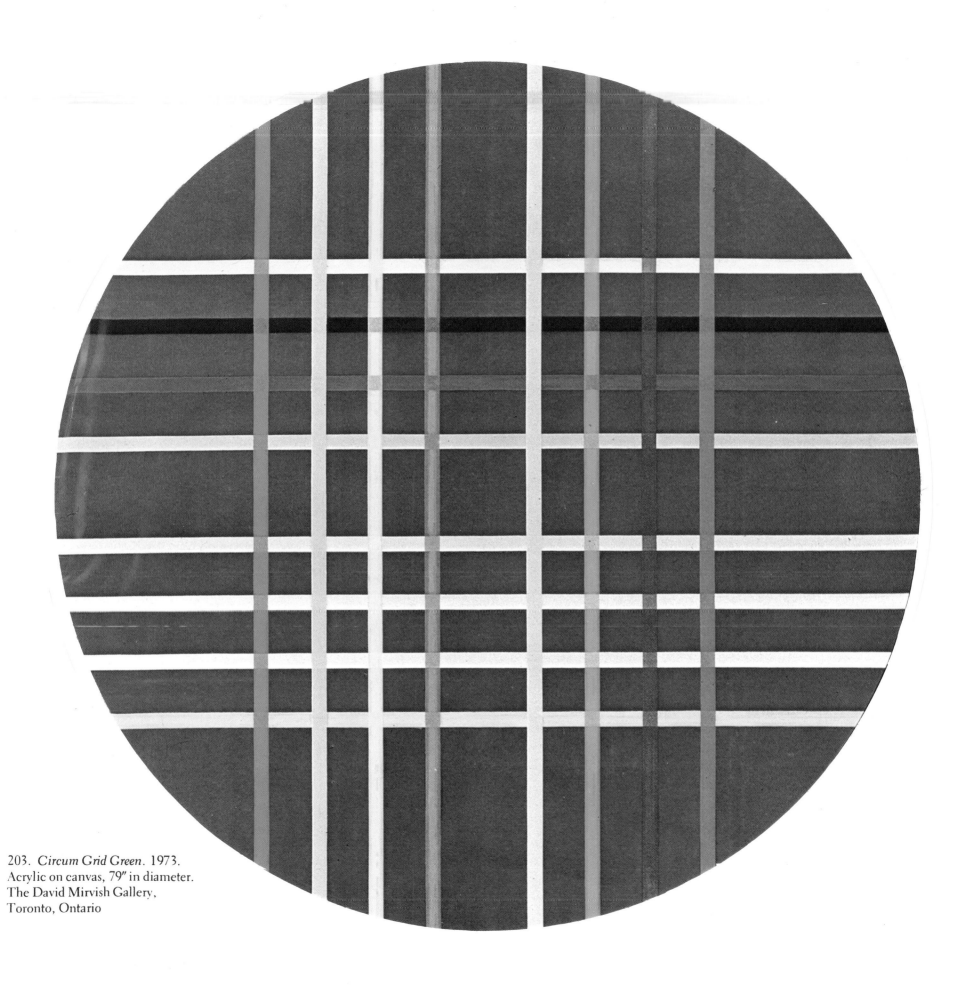

203. *Circum Grid Green*. 1973.
Acrylic on canvas, 79″ in diameter.
The David Mirvish Gallery,
Toronto, Ontario

204. *Following Sea*. 1974. Acrylic on canvas, 98¼ x 98¼".
Collection, Mr. and Mrs. David Mirvish, Toronto, Ontario

205. *Pairs*. 1974. Acrylic on canvas, 69½ x 69½".
Collection, Ethan B. Stroud, Dallas, Texas

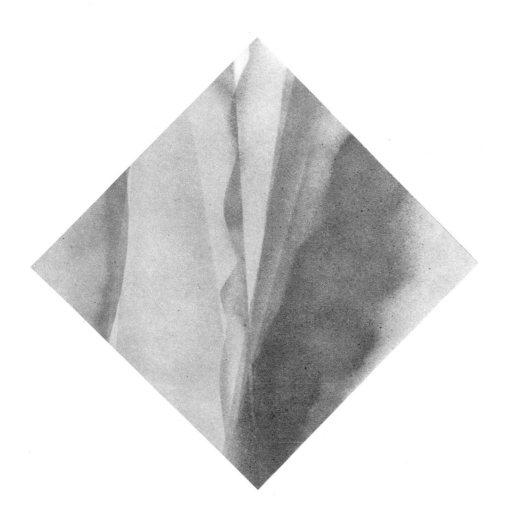

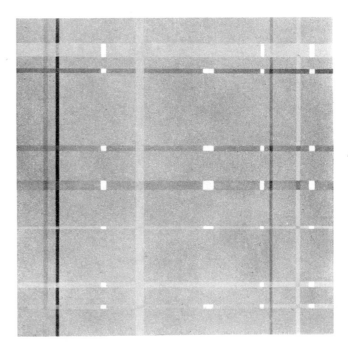

206. Untitled (Diamond). 1974. Acrylic on canvas, 98 x 98″.
Collection, Anthony and Sheila Caro, London, England

207. *Closing Meet*. 1974. Acrylic on canvas, 59¼ x 59¼″.
Collection, Mr. and Mrs. David Mirvish, Toronto, Ontario

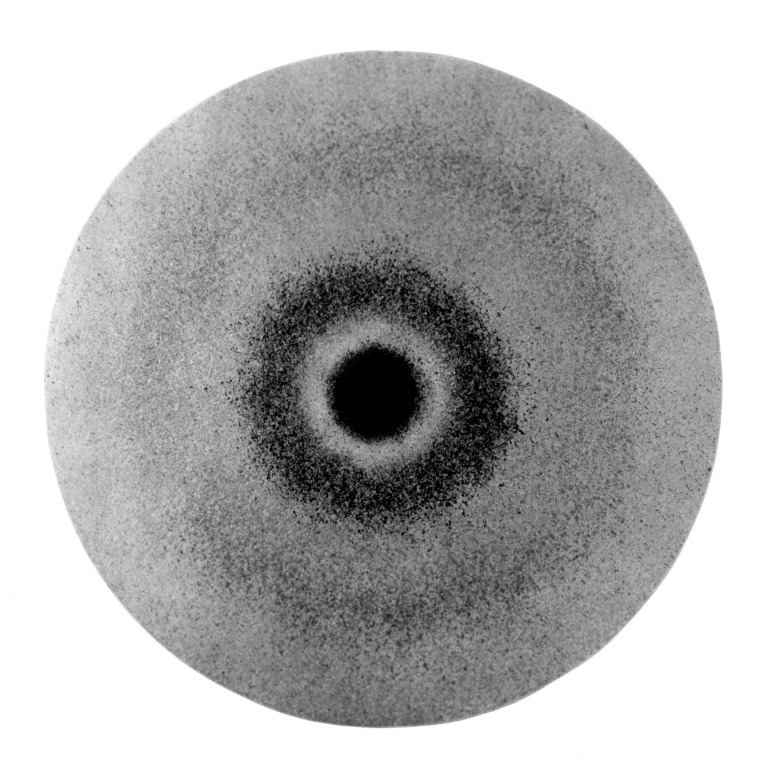

208. Untitled. 1974. Spatter on canvas, 4′ in diameter. Collection, the artist

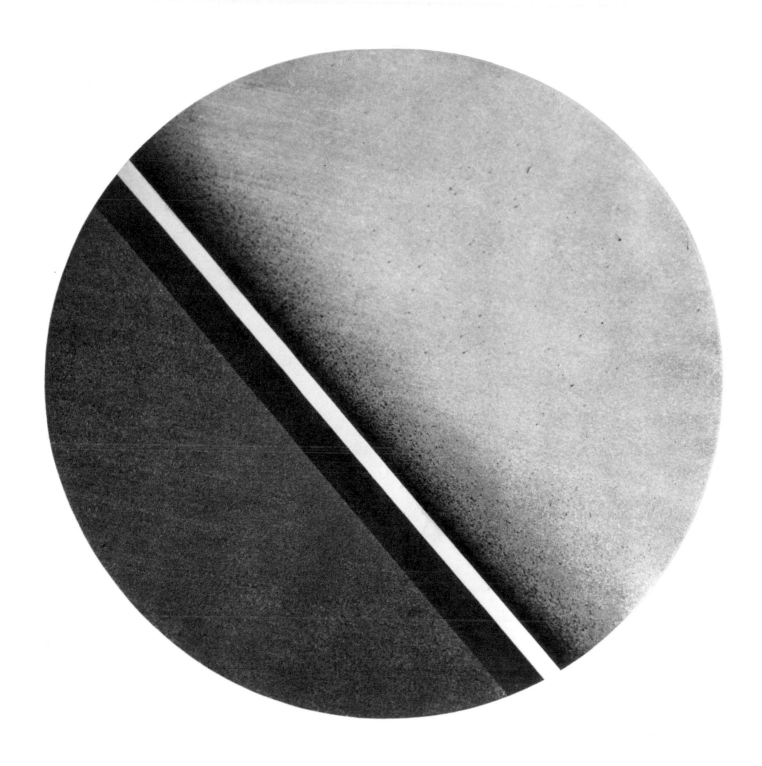

209. Untitled. 1975. Spatter on canvas, 4' in diameter. Collection, the artist

210. Installation view of Noland exhibition at Watson/de Nagy & Company, Houston, Texas, 1975. Left to right: *Curious Course; Voyager; Here-In*

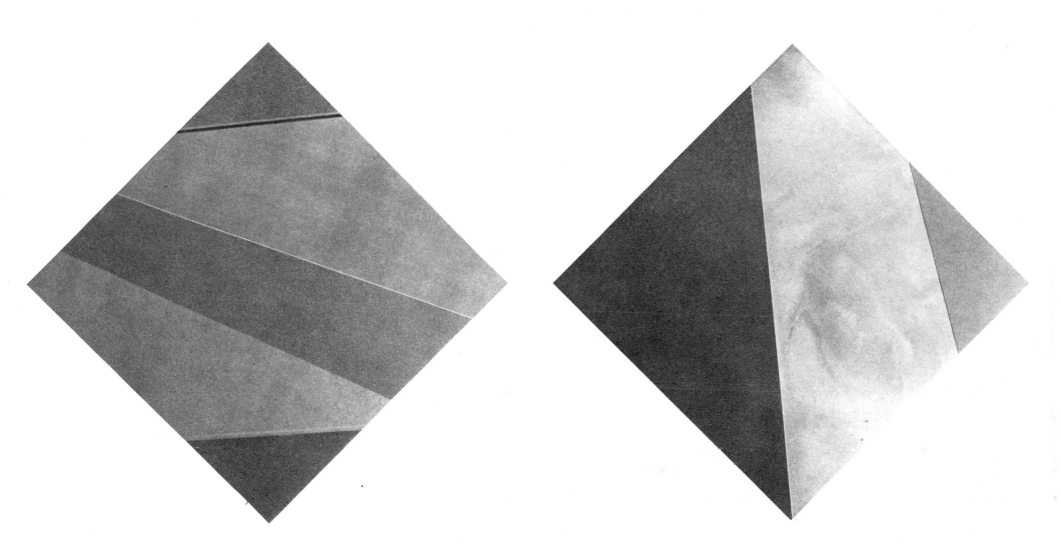

211. *Maker's Mark*. 1975. Acrylic on canvas, 70 x 70″.
Watson/de Nagy & Company, Houston, Texas

212. *Blue Power*. 1975. Acrylic on canvas, 70 x 70″.
Collection, Mr. and Mrs. Bagley Wright, Seattle, Washington

213. *Gradient*. 1975. Acrylic on canvas, 99 x 219″. Collection, the artist

214. *Eagle Yellow* (first version). 1975. Acrylic on canvas, approx. 8½ x 15'. Collection, the artist

215. Installation view of Noland exhibition at André Emmerich Gallery, New York, New York, 1975.
Left: Untitled. 1975. Acrylic on canvas, 98 x 110″. Right: *Beam*. 1975. Acrylic on canvas, 96¾ x 172½″

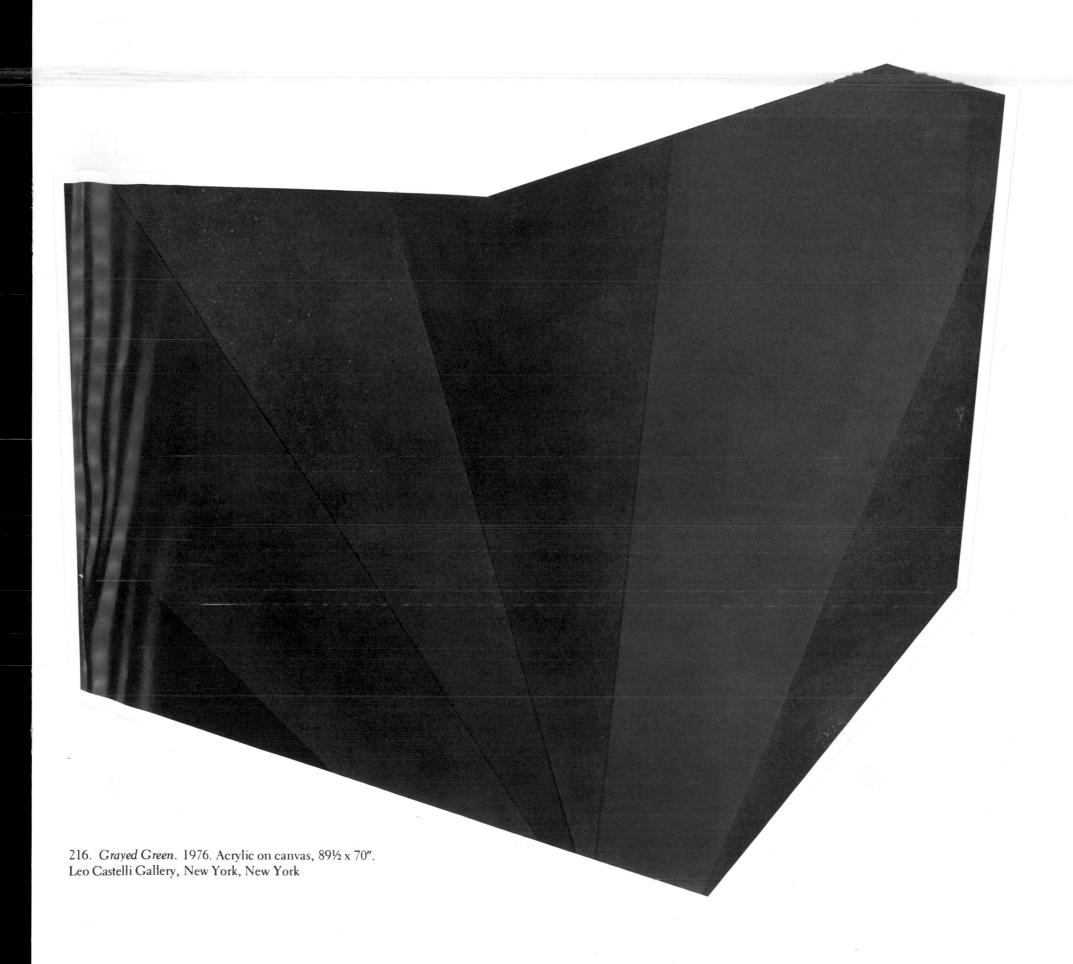

216. *Grayed Green*. 1976. Acrylic on canvas, 89½ x 70″.
Leo Castelli Gallery, New York, New York

217. *Pend*. 1976. Acrylic on canvas, approx. 7½ x 8½'.
Collection, the artist

218. *Ovaray*. 1976. Acrylic on canvas, 85 x 106¾″.
Leo Castelli Gallery, New York, New York

219. *Halflong.* 1976. Acrylic on canvas, 98½ x 148½".
Leo Castelli Gallery, New York, New York

220. *Lapse*. 1976. Acrylic on canvas, 76 x 139½″. Leo Castelli Gallery, New York, New York

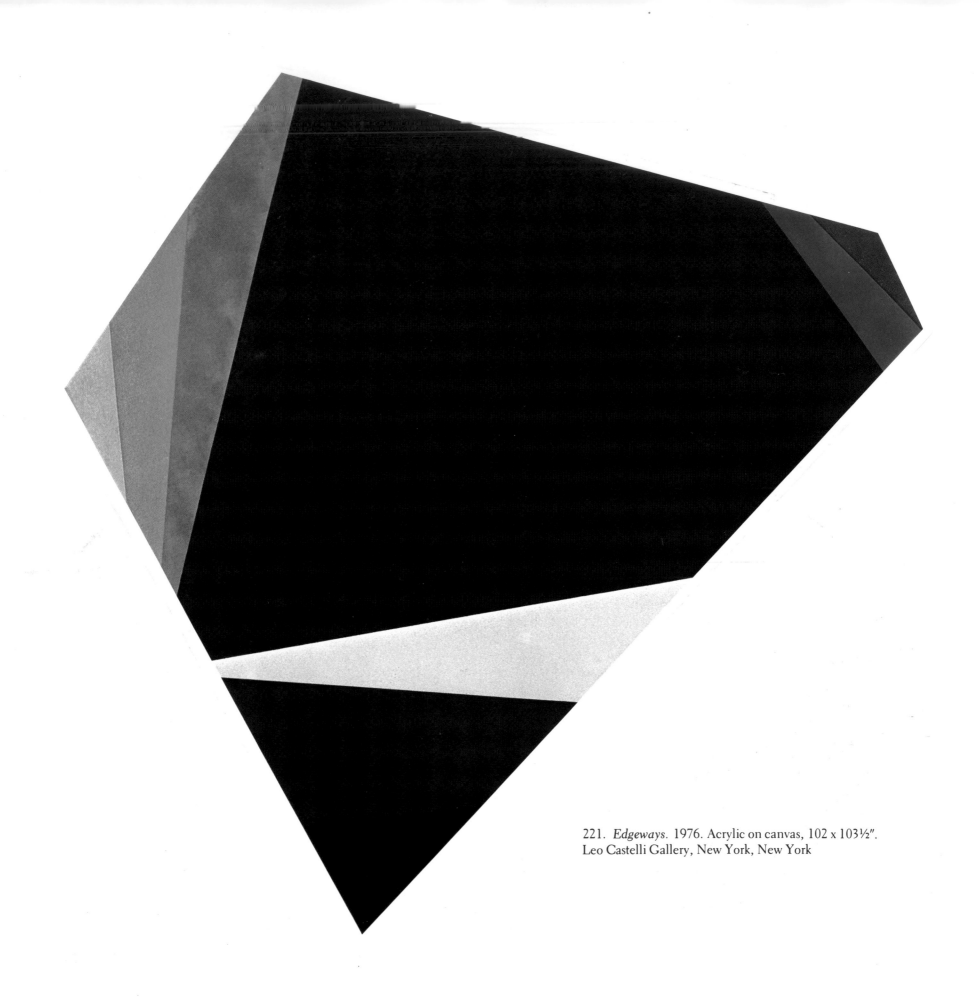

221. *Edgeways.* 1976. Acrylic on canvas, 102 x 103½″.
Leo Castelli Gallery, New York, New York

222. *Determined Course.* 1976.
Acrylic on canvas, 92½ x 101″.
Leo Castelli Gallery, New York, New York

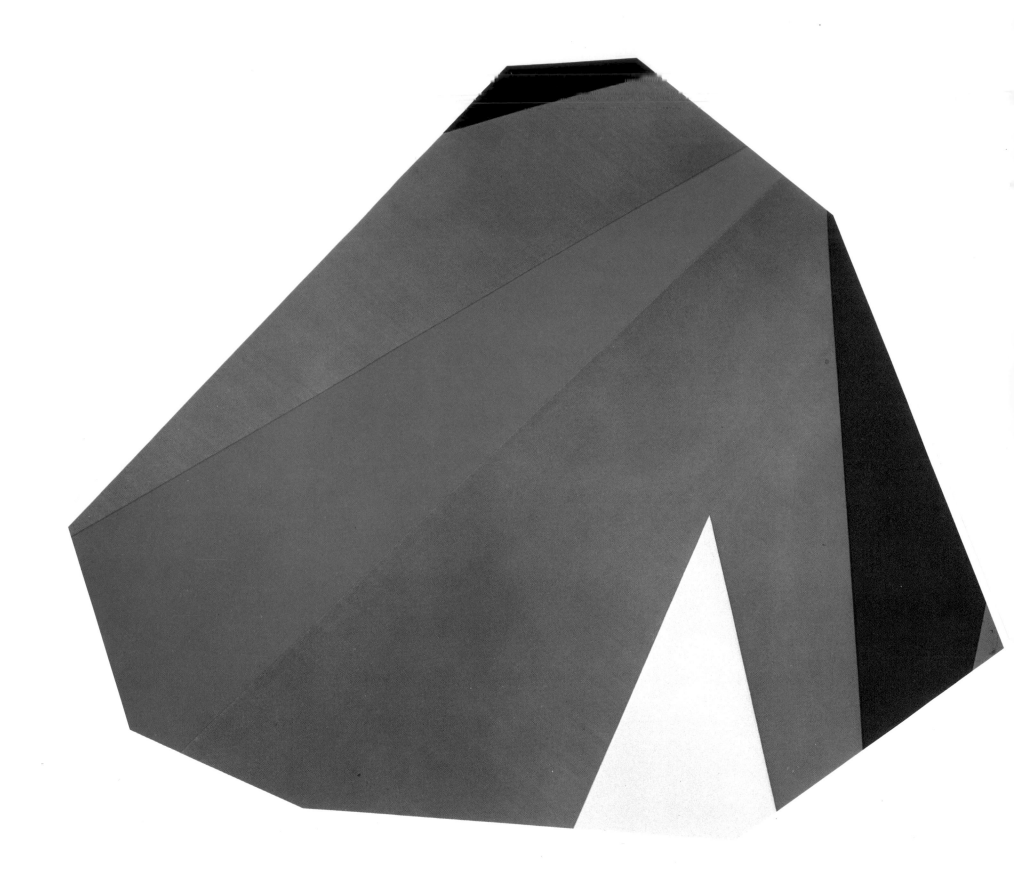

223. *Burnt Beige.* 1976. Acrylic on canvas, 112 x 95½″. Leo Castelli Gallery, New York, New York

LIST OF EXHIBITIONS

ONE-MAN SHOWS

Galerie Creuze, Paris, France: 1949

Tibor de Nagy, New York, New York: 1956,1958

Jefferson Place Gallery, Washington, D.C.: 1958, 1960

French & Company, New York, New York: 1959

André Emmerich Gallery, New York, New York: 1960, 1961, 1962, 1963, 1966, 1967, 1971, 1973, 1975

Galleria dell'Ariete, Milan, Italy: 1960

Galerie Lawrence, Paris, France: 1960, 1963

Bennington College, Bennington, Vermont: 1961

Galerie Neufville, Paris, France: 1961, 1963

Galerie Charles Lienhard, Zürich, Switzerland: 1962

Galerie Schmela, Düsseldorf, West Germany: 1962, 1964

Kasmin Ltd., London, England: 1963,1965, 1968

The Jewish Museum, New York, New York: 1964

The David Mirvish Gallery, Toronto, Ontario, Canada: 1965, 1968, 1974, 1976

Nicholas Wilder Gallery, Los Angeles, California: 1966

Lawrence Rubin Gallery, New York, New York: 1969

Galerie Mikro, Berlin, West Germany: 1972

Jack Glenn Gallery, Corona del Mar: 1974

Janie C. Lee, Houston, Texas: 1974

Rutland Gallery, London, England: 1974

School of the Visual Arts Gallery, New York, New York: 1975

Watson/de Nagy & Company, Houston, Texas: 1975

Leo Castelli Gallery, New York, New York: 1976

1959

"The Biennial Exhibition of Contemporary American Painting," Corcoran Gallery of Art, Washington, D.C.

1963

"Three New American Painters: Louis, Noland, Olitski," Norman MacKenzie Art Gallery, Regina, Saskatchewan, Canada. Catalogue with essay by Clement Greenberg, reprinted in *Canadian Art*, No. 20 (May 1963), pp. 172–75.

"The Biennial Exhibition of Contemporary American Painting," Corcoran Gallery of Art, Washington, D.C.

1964

"Premio Nacional e Internacional," Instituto Torcuato di Tella, Buenos Aires, Argentina. Catalogue with essays by Clement Greenberg, Pierre Restany, and Jorge Romero Brest.

"Post Painterly Abstraction," Los Angeles County Museum of Art, Los Angeles, California; Walker Art Center, Minneapolis, Minnesota; Art Gallery of Toronto, Toronto, Ontario, Canada. Catalogue with introduction by Clement Greenberg, reprinted in *Art International*, vol. 7, nos. 5–6 (Summer 1964), pp, 63–65.

"XXXII Biennale di Venezia: Four Germinal Painters," Venice, Italy. Catalogue with essay by Alan R. Solomon.

"Painting and Sculpture of A Decade: 54–64," organized by the Caluste Gulbenkian Foundation, the Tate Gallery, London, England. Catalogue with unsigned essay.

"Kenneth Noland," The Jewish Museum, New York, New York. Catalogue with foreword by Hans van Weeren-Griek and essay by Michael Fried.

1964–65

"The Pittsburgh International Exhibition of Contemporary Painting and Sculpture," Carnegie Institute, Pittsburgh, Pennsylvania.

1965

"Three American Painters: Noland, Olitski, Stella," Fogg Art Museum, Cambridge, Massachusetts; Pasadena Art Museum, Pasadena, California. Catalogue with essay by Michael Fried.

"The Responsive Eye," Museum of Modern Art, New York, New York; City Art Museum of St. Louis, St. Louis, Missouri; Seattle Art Museum, Seattle, Washington; Pasadena Art Museum, Pasadena, California; Baltimore Museum of Art, Baltimore, Maryland. Catalogue with essay by William Seitz.

1965–66

"The Washington Color Painters," Washington Gallery of Modern Art, Washington, D.C.; University Art Galleries, Austin, Texas; University of California Art Gallery, Santa Barbara, California; Rose Art Museum, Brandeis University, Waltham, Massachusetts; Walker Art Center, Minneapolis, Minnesota. Catalogue with essay by Gerald Nordland.

1966

"Systemic Painting," Solomon R. Guggenheim Museum, New York, New York. Catalogue with essay by Lawrence Alloway.

"Art of the United States: 1670–1966," Whitney Museum of American Art, New York, New York.

"The First Flint Invitational," Flint Institute of Arts, Flint, Michigan.

1966–67

"Vormen van de Kleur" ("Shapes of Color"), Stedelijk Museum, Amsterdam, The Netherlands. Catalogue with essay by W.A.L. Beeren. *Formen der Farbe*, Wuerttembergischer Kunstverein, Stüttgart, Germany. Catalogue with essay by Dieter Honisch. Kunsthalle, Bern, Switzerland. Catalogue with essay by H.S.

1967

"Two Decades of American Painting," circulated by the Museum of Modern Art, New York, New York, to the National Museum of Modern Art, Tokyo, Japan; the National Museum of Modern Art, Kyoto, Japan; Lalit Kala Academy, New Delhi, India; National Gallery of Victoria, Melbourne, Australia; Art Gallery of New South Wales, Sydney, Australia. Catalogue with essays by Irving Sandler, Lucy Lippard, and G. R. Swenson.

"The Biennial Exhibition of Contemporary American Painting," Corcoran Gallery of Art, Washington, D.C.

"International Biennial," Tokyo and other cities in Japan (sponsored by Mainichi Newspapers).

"Form, Color, Image," Detroit Institute of Arts, Detroit, Michigan. Catalogue with essay by Gene Baro.

"The Pittsburgh International Exhibition of Contemporary Painting and Sculpture," Carnegie Institute, Pittsburgh, Pennsylvania.

"A Selection of Paintings and Sculptures from the Collection of Mr. and Mrs. Robert Rowan," University of California, Irvine, California; San Francisco Museum of Art, San Francisco, California.

1967–68

"American Painting Now," U.S. Pavilion, EXPO '67, Montreal, Quebec, Canada, and Institute of Contemporary Art, Boston, Massachusetts.

1968

"Documenta IV," Kassel, Germany.

"Morris Louis, Anthony Caro, Kenneth Noland," Metropolitan Museum of Art, New York, New York, Summer.

"Signals in the Sixties," Honolulu Academy of Arts, Honolulu, Hawaii, October 5-November 10.

L'Art du Réel USA 1948–1968, organized by Museum of Modern Art, New York, New York; Centre National d'Art Contemporain, Paris, France, November 14-December 23.

1968–69

"Serial Imagery," Pasadena Art Museum, Pasadena, California, September 17-October 27, 1968; Henry Art Gallery, University of Washington, Seattle, Washington, November 17-December 22, 1968; Santa Barbara Museum of Art, January 25-February 23, 1969.

1969

"Selections from the Richard Brown Baker Collection," Art Gallery, University of Notre Dame, South Bend, Indiana, January 5-February 23.

"The Development of Modernist Painting: Jackson Pollock to the Present," Steinberg Art Gallery, Washington University, St. Louis, Missouri, April 1–30.

"New York: The Second Breakthrough, 1959–1964," Art Gallery, University of California, Berkeley, California, March 18-April 27.

"Three Centuries of New England Art from New England Museums," Brockton Art Center, Brockton, Massachusetts, January 15-March 2.

"The Direct Image in Contemporary American Painting," Worcester Art Museum, Worcester, Massachusetts, October 16-November 30.

"Stella, Noland, Caro," Dayton's Gallery 12, Minneapolis, Minnesota, November 6-December 6.

"Whitney Annual," Whitney Museum of American Art, New York, New York.

"The Gosman Collection," Pittsburgh, University of

Pittsburgh, Pennsylvania, September 14-October 10.

1969–70

"Contemporary American Painting and Sculpture from the Collection of Mr. and Mrs. Eugene M. Scheartz," Everson Museum, Syracuse, New York, July 13-November 16, 1969; University Art Gallery, Albany, New York, December 3-January 25, 1970.

"New York Painting and Sculpture: 1940–1970," Metropolitan Museum of Art, New York, New York, Fall 1969–Winter 1970.

Galerie Renée Ziegler, Zürich, Switzerland, December 12-January 31, 1970.

1970

"Art in Washington: Twenty Years," Baltimore Museum of Art, Baltimore, Maryland, May 12-June 21.

Waddington Galleries, London, England, Spring-Summer.

"American Artists of the Nineteen Sixties," Boston University, Boston, Massachusetts.

"Selections from the Guggenheim Museum Collection 1900–1970," New York, New York.

"The Opening," The David Mirvish Gallery, Toronto, Ontario.

"Two Generations of Color Painting," Institute of Contemporary Art, University of Pennsylvania, Philadelphia, Pennsylvania.

"Whitney Museum Sculpture Annual," Whitney Museum of American Art, New York, New York.

"New York Painting & Sculpture: 1940–1970," Metropolitan Museum of Art, New York, New York.

"1900–1970: A Tenth Anniversary Selection from the Guggenheim Museum Collection," Solomon R. Guggenheim Museum, New York, New York, May 1-September 13.

"69th American Exhibition," Art Institute of Chicago, Chicago, Illinois, January 17-February 22.

UCLA Art Council Annual Exhibition, University of California at Los Angeles, Los Angeles, California, February 16-March 22.

1970–71

"Pittsburgh International," Museum of Art, Carnegie Institute, Pittsburgh, Pennsylvania, October 30, 1970-January 10, 1971.

"Color and Field 1890–1970," Albright-Knox Gallery, Buffalo, New York, September 15-November 1, 1970; Dayton Art Institute, Dayton, Ohio, November 20, 1970-January 10, 1971; Cleveland Museum, Cleveland, Ohio, February 4-March 28, 1971.

1971

André Emmerich Gallery, New York, New York, October 9-November 4.

"The Structure of Color," Whitney Museum of American Art, New York, New York.

Group Show, Noah Goldowsky, New York, New York.

"The De Lux Show," Museum of Fine Arts, Houston, Texas, August 15-September 12.

1972

"Color Painting," Amherst College, Amherst, Massachusetts, February.

"Whitney Annual," Whitney Museum of American Art, New York, New York, January 25-March 19.

"Kenneth Noland," Jack Glenn Gallery, Orange County, California, October 9-November 13.

"Abstract Painting in the 70's," Museum of Fine Arts, Boston, Massachusetts, April 14-May 21.

1972–73

"New Abstraction," Galerie und Edition Merian, Germany, December 1972-February 1973.

1973

"Whitney Annual," Whitney Museum of American Art, New York, New York.

"Mixed Bags," University of Maryland, College Park, Maryland, January 18-March 9.

"Kenneth Noland: New Paintings," Waddington Galleries II, Montreal, Quebec, Canada, July 10-August 4.

"Ten Years Ago...An Exhibition of Paintings from 1964," The David Mirvish Gallery, Toronto, Ontario, Canada, Fall.

Daniel Templon, Paris, France, November-December.

1974

"The Great Decade of American Abstraction Modernist Art: 1960 to 1970," Museum of Fine Arts, Houston, Texas, January 15-March 10.

"The Basel Art Fair," Basel, Switzerland, June 19-June 24.

"L'Art au Present," Palais Galliera (organized by Daniel Templon), Paris, France.

"Group Show," The David Mirvish Gallery, Toronto, Ontario, Canada, November.

1975

"Large-Scale Painting," André Emmerich Gallery, New York, New York.

"American Abstract Painting," La Bertesca, Genoa, Italy.

"El Lenguaje del Color," Museo de Bellas Artes, Caracas, Venezuela, August.

"34th Biennial of Contemporary American Painting," Corcoran Gallery of Art, Washington, D.C., February 22-April 6.

Waddington Galleries, London, England, April 19-May 10.

1976

"72nd American Exhibition," The Art Institute of Chicago, Chicago, Illinois, March 13-May 9.

"American Color: 1961–1964," Visual Arts Museum, New York, New York, March 29-April 21.

Galerie Ulysses, Hamburg, Germany.

"Painting and Sculpture Today 1976," Indianapolis Museum of Art, Indianapolis, Indiana, June 9-July 18.

SELECTED BIBLIOGRAPHY

Alloway, Lawrence, "Easel Painting at the Guggenheim," *Art International*, vol. 5, no. 10 (December 1961), pp. 26–34.

———, Introduction to the catalogue *Systematic Painting*, Solomon R. Guggenheim Museum, New York, 1966.

Ashbery, John, "Paris Notes," *Art International*, vol. 5, nos. 5–6 (June-August 1961), pp. 42, 92.

Ashton, Dore, "Visual Pleasure from Austerity," *Studio International*, vol. 169, no. 862 (February 1965), pp. 92–93.

———, "New York Commentary: Conditioned Historic Reactions," *Studio International*, vol. 171, no. 877 (May 1966), p. 206.

———, A *Reading of Modern Art*, Cleveland and London, 1969, Part V, pp. 141–200.

Bannard, Walter Darby, "Notes on American Painting of the Sixties," *Artforum*, vol. 8, no. 5 (January 1970), pp. 40–45.

———, "Noland's New Paintings," *Artforum*, vol. 10, no. 3 (November 1971), pp. 50–53.

Baro, Gene, "London Letter," *Art International*, vol. 9, no. 5 (June 1965), pp. 67–70.

Carmean, E. A., Jr., "Kenneth Noland and the Compositional Cut," *Arts Magazine*, vol. 50, no. 4 (December 1975), pp. 80–85.

Carpenter, Ken, "To re-examine the work of Kenneth Noland," *Studio International*, vol. 188, no. 968 (July-August 1974), pp. 21–26.

Cone, Jane Harrison, "On Color in Kenneth Noland's Paintings," *Art International*, vol. 9, no. 5 (June 1965), pp. 36–38.

———, "Kenneth Noland: New Paintings," *Artforum*, vol. 6, no. 3 (November 1967), pp. 36–41.

Coplans, John, "Serial Imagery," *Artforum*, vol. 7, no. 2 (October 1968), pp. 34–43.

Corcoran Gallery of Art, The, *Catalogue of the Vincent Melzac Collection*, Washington, D.C., 1971.

Duberman, Martin, *Black Mountain: An Exploration in Community*, New York, Dutton, 1972, pp. 70, 71, 244, 245, 302, 428, 470.

Elderfield, John, "Mondrian, Newman, Noland: Two Notes on Changing Style," *Artforum*, vol. 10, no. 4 (December 1971), pp. 48–53.

Findley, Gerald, "Louis, Noland, Olitski," *Artforum*, vol. 1, no. 9 (March 1963), pp. 34, 35.

Fried, Michael, "New York Letter," *Art International*, vol. 7, no. 5 (May 1963), pp. 69–71.

———, "Anthony Caro and Kenneth Noland: Some notes on not composing," *Lugano Review*, vol. 1, nos. 3–4 (Summer 1965), pp. 198–206.

———, Introduction to the catalogue *Three American Painters*, Fogg Art Museum, Harvard University, Cambridge, 1965.

———, Introduction to the catalogue *Kenneth Noland*, Jewish Museum, New York, 1965.

———, "Shape as Form: Frank Stella," *Artforum*, vol. 5, no. 3 (November 1966), pp. 39–40.

———, Introduction to the catalogue *Morris Louis, 1912–1962* (Los Angeles County Museum of Art; Museum of Fine Arts, Boston; City Art Museum of St. Louis), Museum of Fine Arts, Boston, 1967.

———, "Recent Work by Kenneth Noland," *Artforum*, vol. 8, no. 10 (Summer 1969), pp. 36–37.

Ginsberg, Sue and Levin, Andrea, Essay in the

catalogue *Color*, UCLA Art Galleries, Los Angeles, 1969.

Goosen, E. C., Introduction to the catalogue *Kenneth Noland*, Galerie Charles Lienhard AG., Zurich, 1962.

Gouk, Alan, "An Essay on Painting," *Studio International* (October 1970), p. 146.

Greenberg, Clement, "Louis and Noland," *Art International*, vol. 4, no. 5 (May 1960), pp. 26–29.

———, "After Abstract Expressionism," *Art International*, vol. 6, no. 8 (October 1962), pp. 24–29.

———, Introduction to the catalogue *The New American Painters: Louis, Noland, Olitski*, Norman Mackenzie Art Gallery, Regina, Saskatchewan, 1963.

———, "Poetry of Vision," *Artforum*, vol. 6, no. 8 (April 1968), pp. 18–21.

Harrison, Charles, "Recent Works by Kenneth Noland at Kasmin," *Studio*, vol. 176 (July 1968), pp. 35–38.

Hudson, Andrew, "Letter From Washington," *Art International*, vol. 9, nos. 9–10 (December 1965), p. 56.

———, "Kenneth Noland: Sarah's Reach—A Mixture of Stillness and Movement," *The Potomac, The Washington Post*, May 8, 1966.

———, "Washington: An American Salon of 1967," *Art International*, vol. 11, no. 4 (April 1967), pp. 73–79.

———, Introduction to the catalogue *Ten Washington Artists: 1950–1970*, Edmonton Art Gallery, Edmonton, Alberta, 1970.

Hunter, Sam, *American Art of the Twentieth Century*, New York, 1973, pp. 106, 191, 211, 246, 269, 316, 317, 321–23, 353, 374.

Judd, Donald, "Exhibition at Emmerich Gallery," *Arts Magazine*, vol. 36, no. 10 (September 1962), p. 49.

———, "In the Galleries," *Arts Magazine*, vol. 37, no. 10 (September 1963), pp. 53–54.

———, "Exhibition at the Jewish Museum," *Arts Magazine*, vol. 39, no. 6 (March 1965), pp. 54–55.

———, "Kenneth Noland at Emma Lake, 1963," in *Ten Washington Artists: 1950–1970*, Edmonton Art Gallery, Edmonton, Alberta, 1970.

Kozloff, Max, "Abstract Attrition," *Arts Magazine*, vol. 39, no. 4 (January 1965), pp. 46–50.

Krauss, Rosalind, "On Frontality," *Artforum*, vol. 6, no. 9 (May 1968), pp. 40–46.

Leider, Philip, "The Thing in Painting is Color," *The New York Times*, August 25, 1968, pp. 21–22.

Lippard, Lucy, "New York Letter," *Art International*, vol. 9, no. 1 (February 1965), pp. 34–35.

———, "New York Letter: Off Color," *Art International*, vol. 10, no. 4 (April 1966), pp. 73–75.

———, "Constellation by Harsh Daylight: The Whitney Annual," *The Hudson Review*, vol. 21, no. 1 (Spring 1968), pp. 172–82.

McCaughey, Patrick, "Pictorialism and Some Recent Sculpture," *Arts Magazine* (Summer 1971), pp. 21–22.

McConogha, Al, "Noland Wants His Painting to Exist as Sensation," *Minneapolis Tribune*, March 13, 1966, p. 4.

Moffett, Kenworth, "Noland Vertical," *Art News*, vol. 70, no. 6 (October 1971), pp. 48–49, 76–78.

———, "Noland," *Art International*, vol. 17, no. 6 (Summer 1973), pp. 22–33, 91–93, 100.

———, "Kenneth Noland's New Paintings and the Issue of the Shaped Canvas," *Art International*, vol. 20, nos. 4–5 (April–May 1976), pp. 8–15, 28–30.

Nodelman, Sheldon, "Sixties Art, Some Philosophical Perspectives," *The Yale Architectural Journal-Perspecta II*, 1967, pp. 73–89.

Noland, Kenneth, "Letter to the Editor," *Art News*, vol. 61 (November 1962), p. 6.

Nordland, Gerald, Introduction to the catalogue *The Washington Color Painters*, Washington Gallery of Modern Art, 1965.

Rose, Barbara, "Kenneth Noland," *Art International*, vol. 8, nos. 5–6 (Summer 1964), pp. 58–61.

Rubin, William, "Younger American Painters," *Art International*, vol. 4, no. 1 (January 1960), pp. 28–29.

Sandler, Irving, "Reviews and Previews," *Art News*, vol. 60, no. 3 (May 1961), p. 15.

———, "Reviews and Previews," *Art News*, vol. 62, no. 3 (May 1963), p. 11.

Siegel, Jeanne, Introduction to the catalogue *Kenneth Noland, Early Circle Paintings*, Visual Arts Gallery, School of Visual Arts, New York, 1975.

Solomon, Alan, Introduction to the catalogue *New American Art: Four Germinal Painters*, XXXII Biennale di Venezia, New York, 1964.

Tillem, Sidney, "Scale and the Future of Modernism," *Artforum*, vol. 6, no. 2 (October 1967), pp. 14–18.

———, "Evaluations and Re-evaluations: A Season's Miscellany . . . ," *Artforum*, vol. 6, no. 10 (Summer 1968), pp. 20–23.

Truitt, James McC., "Art-Arid D.C. Harbors Touted New Painters," *The Washington Post*, December 21, 1961, p. A20.

Wilkin, Karen, Introduction to the catalogue *Kenneth Noland*, Edmonton Art Gallery, Edmonton, Alberta, Canada, 1975.

INDEX

Numerals in roman type refer to pages.
Numerals in ( ) signify footnotes to be found on the page preceding the parentheses.
Numerals in *italic* type indicate plates.
Numerals preceded by an * designate colorplates.

Absorbing Radiance, 100(27); *146*
Abstract Expressionism, Abstract Expressionists, 18, 19, 21, 22, 24, 33, 36, 39, 40, 42, 43, 46, 47, 52, 87
Abstract Impressionism, 96(54)
abstraction: geometrical, 19, 31, 97(12); painterly, 31, 33; *see also* Abstract Expressionism
action painting, 21, 22, 40, 42, 46; *see also* Abstract Expressionism
Added Distance, 200
Ado, *173
Advert, 125
Aim, 150
Air, 61
Air Beauty, *183
Aires Solo, *195
Albers, Josef, 13, 15, 16–17, 18, 19, 27, 37, 38, 39, 54, 94(5–6)(12)(18), 95(19–20)(27), 97(14), 99(2); *Homage to the Square: Apparition*, *10*
Alkis' Gift, 157
Alliance, 100(19)(30); *85
alloverness, 32–34, 36, 37, 38, 60, 76, 97(5)
Alongside, 142
Ambsace, 62, 100(27); *163
American Abstract Artists, 18
Amino, Leo, 20
And Again, *168
And Blues, *194
Appearance, 188
April Tune, *190
Around, 59

automatism, 40, 42
Avery, Milton, 31

Bauhaus, 13, 15, 16, 17, 18, 19, 20
Beam, 55, 144, 215
Bend Sinister, 62
Berkowitz, Ida, 20
Berkowitz, Leon, 20
Black Mountain College, 13, 15, 17, 18, 19, 20, 21, 94(3)(5)(18)
Bloom, *78
Blue Circle, 96
Blue-Green Confluence, 100(23); *131
Blue Intentions, *194
Blue Painted Blue, *75
Blue Plus Eight, 61
Blue Power, 212
Blue Veil, *130
Bolotowsky, Ilya, 13, 15–17, 18, 19, 27, 37, 94(5–6)(12–14), 95(19–20); *Arctic Diamond*, *11*
Bond, Robin, 20, 95(34)
Bonnard, Pierre, 30
Braque, Georges, 30, 31, 54
Breath, 94
Bridge, 61; *137
Bright Ray, *174
Burnt Beige, *223

Cadmium Radiance, 58, 103(20); *41
Cage, John, 94(18)
Call, *164
Caro, Anthony, 77, 89; photograph of, 62; *Shaftsbury*, *61*
Catherine, 28
Cézanne, Paul, 30, 31, 36, 86
Cherry, Herman, 27
Circum Grid Green, *203
Closing Meet, 102(7); *207
color, as subject matter, 39–43; development toward primacy of, 29–38
Color Temperature, 152
cubism, 17, 18, 19, 22, 30, 31, 32, 33, 34, 40, 51, 54, 57, 73, 75
Curious Course, 210

Dada, 17, 94(18)
Dark Sweet Cherry, 62; *162
Davis, Gene, 27, 95(35)
Davis, Ronald, 77–78, 82, 102(15); *Two-Thirds Yellow*, *53*
Day, 62, 100(27)
Daydream, *166
de Kooning, Elaine, 20
de Kooning, Willem, 20, 21, 22, 27, 31, 33, 39, 43
Delaunay, Robert, 31, 54, 65; *Disc*, 38
De Stijl, 15, 17, 18, 87

Determined Course, *222
Diamond Shaped Picture, 151
Downing, Thomas, 27, 96(49)
Drive, 153
Drought, 115
Duberman, Martin, 15, 94(3)
Dusk, 129
Dzubas, Friedel, 39, 40, 43, 98(1)

Eagle Yellow (first version), 214
Edgeways, *221
Egyptian Discovery, 110
Eight, 100(27); *147
Ember, 86
Embrown, *135
Enisle, *186
Ex Nihilo, 113

Fauve color, Fauves, Fauvism, 30, 31, 36, 37, 68, 73, 76, 87, 96(2); abstract equivalent/version, 38, 87, 98(15)
Fete, 88
field painting, 68
Fiord, *99
Flush, 100(23); *140
Flutter, 92
Following Sea, 204
Francis, Sam, 43

Frankenthaler, Helen, 20, 22, 24, 27, 34, 36, 38, 39, 40, 42, 43, 49, 96(52), 101(3); *Mountains and Sea*, 22; 20
Franklin, 95
Fugle, *123
Fuller, Buckminster, 20

Gauguin, Paul, 30, 36
Gianpetro, Alex, 20
Globe, 49; *34
Go, 61, 62, 100(27)
Goodman, Paul, 20
Gorky, Arshile, 78
Gottlieb, Adolph, 39, 42, 46, 98(9)
Gradient, *213
Grave Light, *161
Grayed Green, *216
Greenberg, Clement, 20, 21, 22, 24, 27, 34, 39, 51, 95(46), 96(47–48), 98(2), 103(18); photograph of, 24
Grippe, Peter, 20

Halflong, *219
Halfway, 62
Happenings, 17
Harvest, 108
Heptad, *186
Here-In, 210
Hofmann, Hans, 31, 98(9)
Homage: David Smith, 89; 69
Horizontal Focus, 122
Hover, 58
Hub, 107

Impressionism, Impressionist color, Impressionists, 29, 30, 31, 32, 36, 37, 73, 76, 96(2); abstract equivalent/version, 38, 98(15)
In the Garden, 21
Inner Warmth, 121
Inner Way, 52
Inside, 15
Intent, *185
Into the Hot, 143
Inverted Mordent, 55
It's Mine, *181

jam painting, 22, 24, 40
Jenny, 89; 60
Johns, Jasper, 99(2)
Judd, Donald, 82

Kahnweiler, Daniel-Henry, 30
Kandinsky, Wassily, 17, 97(12)
Karen's Gift, 112
Karma, 62
Kelly, Ed, 27
Kelly, Ellsworth, 77, 82
Klee, Paul, 18, 19, 20, 22, 27, 51, 87, 95(27)(30); *Arab Song*, 14
Kline, Franz, 21, 22, 31
Krasner, Lee, 27

Langer, Suzanne, 86
Lapse, *220
Lebron, 120
Lilium, *179
Lineate, *201
Lippold, Richard, 20
Little Rouge, *187
Loom, 89; 65, 66
Louis, Morris, 20, 22, 24, 27, 36, 37, 38, 39, 40, 42, 43, 46, 58, 61, 70–71, 77, 87, 101(42)(3), 103(18); *Horizontal VII*, 49; *Ksi*, 48
Lucent, *184
Lunar Episode, *72

Mach II, *160
Magenta Haze, *132
Maker's Mark, 211
Malevich, Kasimir, 17, 97(12)
Manet, Édouard, 57
March 22, 154
Matisse, Henri, 18, 19, 20, 27, 30, 31, 36, 37, 49, 54, 68, 70, 73, 87
Matter of Midnight, 58
Mehring, Howard, 27
Merge, 197
Mesh, 84
Mexican Camino, *191
Miller, Dorothy, 27
Miró, Joan, 18
Missus, 90
Mr. S., 156
Mondrian, Piet, 15, 16, 17, 18, 19, 31, 32–33, 34, 38, 42, 57, 61, 65, 66, 75, 76, 87, 94(13), 97(5–6)(12), 102(7)(10); *Composition with Red, Yellow, Blue, Black*, 13; *Lozenge in Red, Yellow, and Blue*, 42; *New York City No. 2*, 51
Monet, Claude, 29–30, 31, 86
Morning Span, *134
Motherwell, Robert, 21, 22, 40

Neo-Impressionism, 96(2)

Neoplasticism, 15, 16
New Green, 109
New York painting, 21, 24, 27
New York School, 16
Newman, Barnett, 27, 42, 46, 65–66, 96(49), 98(9), 99(2); *Onement #3*, 45
No Bid, *138
Noland, Bill, photograph of, 8
Noland, Cady, photograph of, 8
Noland, Cornelia, 96(48), 99(2)
Noland, Harry, 13, 18
Noland, Harry, Sr., 13; *Still Life*, 4
Noland, Kenneth: as student in Paris, 17–19, 20, 95(26); as teacher, 15, 20, 27; at Black Mountain, 13–18, 19, 20, 94(5), 100(24); background, 13; Cat's Eyes, 57–58, 60, 62, 100(17–20); chevrons, 27, 38, 46, 47, 58, 60–61, 62, 64, 73, 100(20)(23); comments on his own attitudes and work, 17–19, 22, 39, 40, 45–46, 47, 49, 50, 51, 54, 56, 57, 65, 73, 86, 95(45), 99(10)(13), 101(38), 102(4), 103(19); comments on: Albers, 15, 17; Bolotowsky, 17, 95(19); Caro, 89; Frankenthaler, 22; Greenberg, 95(46); Klee, 19; Louis, 20–21, 22; Olitski, 102(9); Pollock, 19; Zadkine, 17–18; concentric circles, 20, 27, 38, 50, 51, 52, 54, 58, 61, 62, 96(53), 99(2)(10), 100(19); content in the work of, 85–87; development: early, 13–27; later, 49–71, 72–82, 98(25), 103(19); diamonds, 38, 46, 47, 56, 61–65, 73, 79, 80, 100(24)(26)(28)(31), 104(23)(26); exhibitions: 20, 27, 76, 96(51–53)(55); 100(27), 104(24); installation views of, 2, 46, 52, 55, 116, 158, 176, 210, 215; horizontal-bands (stripes), 38, 46, 47, 61, 62, 64, 65–69, 72, 73, 76, 77, 79, 100(27), 101(33)(38), 102(3)(5)(6), 104(27); photographs of, 3, 5, 9, 19, 24, 57, 62; plaids, 47, 73–76, 89, 102(5–6), 104(27); relationship with Morris Louis, 20–21, 22, 24, 27, 37, 39, 40, 43, 71, 96(47), 101(12), sculpture, 17, 89; 58–69, 71; series paintings, 27, 38, 51, 56, 74–75, 98(15); shaped canvases, 77, 79–82, 102(6), 103(17), 104(23–24)(26–28)(30); subject matter of the work of, 39–43, 47, 85; targets, 46, 47, 52, 56, 57, 64, 71, 73, 80, 99(3); tondos, 52, 54, 56, 58, 61, 79, 99(12); Washington, D.C., years in, 20–22, 24, 27; working procedures, 20, 27, 40, 43, 45–46, 98(20), 99(10), 100(16), 101(40)(42)(3), 102(6), 103(18–19), 104(28)
Noland, Lyndon, photograph of, 8
Noland, Neil, 13
Noon Afloat, *117
Number Seven, 103(20); 149
Nursery, 50

Oakum, *189
Olitski, Jules, 27, 36, 37, 38, 43, 68, 70, 76, 77, 82,

87, 98(15), 102(9), 103(19); *Seventh Loosha*, *47
One Way, 61, 62
Out of the Red, 192
Ovaray, *218
Over and Under, *199

Pairs, 205
Paris: Grande Chaumière, 17; School of, 18, 19
Passion Flower, 196
Pend, *217
Picasso, Pablo, 18, 30, 31, 33, 54, 86
Plunge, 36
Point, 83
Pollock, Jackson, 16, 17, 18, 21, 22, 24, 27, 31, 33–34, 36, 37, 38, 39, 40, 42, 43, 46, 49, 65, 76, 77, 85, 87, 99(3), 101(36); *One*, *30
Poons, Larry, 43, 77
Pop Art, 17
Probe, 97

Quadrum, 106

Rauschenberg, Robert, 17
Red and Purple Octuple, 100(19); 119
Return, *169
Reverberation, 52; 114
Ridge, 89; 71
Ring, *80
Rite, *126
Rocker, *74
Rose, *79
Rothko, Mark, 27, 42, 46, 78, 98(9)
Round, *77
Rubens, Peter Paul, 29

Sarah's Reach, 61; *133
Saturday Night, *165
17th Stage, 61; *136
Shade, 101(33); *44
Shade, *175
Shadow, 67, 68
Shallows, 100
Shield, 118
Shoot, 139
Smith, David, 17, 27, 43, 89, 96(48), 103(19); *Voltri V*, 70
Solar Thrust, 103(20); 128
Song, *73
Southline, 170
Splay, 56
Split, 89
Spread, 87
Spring Cool, *82
stain painting, 34, 97(10)(12), 98(15)(8)

Stamos, Theodoros, 20
Stella, Frank, 54, 56, 77, 78–79, 80, 81, 103(16–17);
  Irregular Polygons, installation view of, 54; *Sinjerli
  II*, 54, 56; *40*
Steps, *172
Still, Clyfford, 27, 42, 43, 46, 98(9)
Straight Flush, 104
Strand, 62, 100(27)
Sun Dried—Japanese Space, 100(27); *148*
Sunshine, 52; *37
Surrealism, 17, 40, 42, 51, 94(18)

Teton Noir, 111
That, 100(19); *29
Time's Motion, 101
Tinge, 124
Tip, 50; *35*
Tondo, *39
Tony's Gift, 155
Trans West, 159

Transit, *167
Tripex, 58, 103(20); *127*
Tropical Zone, 62, 100(30); *43
Truitt, Anne, 27
Turnsole, 52; *81
Twice Around, 198
Twist, 171

Until Tomorrow, *193
Untitled, 1947, *12*
Untitled, 1950, *16*
Untitled, 1951–52, oil, *17*
Untitled, 1951–52, watercolor, *18*
Untitled, 1952, *22*
Untitled, 1953, *23*
Untitled, 1955, *31*
Untitled, c. 1955, *32*
Untitled, 1956, *33*
Untitled, c. 1956, 99(3); *25*
Untitled, 1957, *26*

Untitled, c. 1957, *27*
Untitled, 1958–59, 93
Untitled, 1959, 5 x 5', 98
Untitled, 1959, 8 x 8', *102*
Untitled, 1959, 96 x 94", *103*
Untitled, 1959–60, 91
Untitled, 1963, *145*
Untitled A, 1971, *186
Untitled B, 1971, *186
Untitled, 1973, *202
Untitled (Diamond), 1974, *206*
Untitled, 1974, 208
Untitled, 1975, acrylic, *215*
Untitled, 1975, spatter, 209

Van Gogh, Vincent, 30, 36
Venetian painters, 29
Vermont, 89; 63, 64
Via Blues, 68; *177
Via Flow, 176; *180
Via Median, *182

Via Token, 176
Virginia Site, *1
Voyager, 210

Warm Sound in a Gray Field, *76
Washington, D.C.: artists in, 20, 27; Catholic Univer-
  sity, 15, 20, 27; Institute of Contemporary Art, 20,
  95(33); Phillips Collection, 20, 95(35); Workshop of
  the Arts, 20; *see also* Noland, Kenneth
Whistler, James Abbott McNeill, 57
Wild Indigo, 178
William, 105
World War II, 31

Yellow Half, 100(23); *141*

Zadkine, Ossip, 17, 18, 20, 89

PHOTOCREDITS

The author and the publisher wish to thank museums and private collectors for permitting the reproduction of works of art in their collections and for supplying the necessary photographs. Photographs from the following sources are gratefully acknowledged.

Baker, Oliver, New York, 13; Beville, Henry, Washington, D.C., 112, 133, 170, 171; Burstein, Barney, Boston, 173; Leo Castelli Gallery, New York, 56, 217; Clements, Geoffrey, New York, 43, 74, 88, 103, 104, 129, 130, 136, 145, 175, 183; The Cleve-land Museum of Art, Cleveland, 160; Cunning Wright-Watson Associates, Ltd., London, 109; Davis, Ronald, Los Angeles, 53; Dovydenas, Jonas, Chicago, 97; Dudley, Hardin, and Yang, Seattle, 123, 168; André Emmerich Gallery, New York, 20, 48, 49, 50, 82, 85, 90, 99, 101, 110, 114, 120, 134, 139, 140, 142, 143, 144, 148, 152, 154, 156, 165, 177, 188, 189, 192, 195, 198, 199, 205, 206; French & Co., Inc., New York, 36; de Gery, X., Menlo Park, California, 191; The Solomon R. Guggenheim Museum, New York, 38, 117, 138, 174, 181, 184, 185, 186, 193, 194, 201, 203; Hayward Gallery, New York, 61; Hublitz, Fred M., Alexandria, Virginia, 89; Kasmin Limited, London, 94, 122; Klima, Joseph Jr., Detroit, 40, 150; Knoedler, M. and Co., New York, 47; Mates, Robert E., New York, 11; The Metropol-itan Museum of Art, New York, 111; The David Mirvish Gallery, Toronto, 157; Nickel, Richard, Chicago, 128; Noland, Harry, 5; Noland, William, 9; Pollitzer, Eric, New York, 35, 39, 41, 72, 75, 76, 95, 96, 132, 137, 151, 163; Pulsifer, C. R., 127; Roos, George, New York, 34; Lawrence Rubin Gallery, New York, 80, 105, 106, 107, 119, 121, 166; Scribner, David, Bennington, Vermont, 57, 58, 59, 62, 63, 64, 65, 66, 67, 68, 69, 71; Strehorn, Bill Jr., Dallas, 44; Thomson, John F., Los Angeles, 37, 126, 161; Uht, Charles, New York, 92; Ward, Cora, New York, 8, 9; Watson, de Nagy, and Co., Houston, 212; Wellesley College, Department of Art, Wellesley, Massachu-setts, 172; Galerie Renée Ziegler, Zurich, 147.